# LINGUISTIC THEORY AND THE ROMANCE LANGUAGES

# AMSTERDAM STUDIES IN THE THEORY AND HISTORY OF LINGUISTIC SCIENCE

General Editor

E. F. KONRAD KOERNER

(University of Ottawa)

Series IV - CURRENT ISSUES IN LINGUISTIC THEORY

*Advisory Editorial Board*

Volume 122

John Charles Smith and Martin Maiden (eds)

*Linguistic Theory and the Romance Languages*

# LINGUISTIC THEORY
# AND THE
# ROMANCE LANGUAGES

Edited by

## JOHN CHARLES SMITH
*University of Manchester*

## MARTIN MAIDEN
*University of Cambridge*

JOHN BENJAMINS PUBLISHING COMPANY
AMSTERDAM/PHILADELPHIA

∞TM  The paper used in this publication meets the minimum requirements of American National Standard for Information Sciences — Permanence of Paper for Printed Library Materials, ANSI Z39.48-1984.

**Library of Congress Cataloging-in-Publication Data**

Linguistic theory and the Romance languages / edited by John Charles Smith, Martin Maiden.
    p.    cm. -- (Amsterdam studies in the theory and history of linguistic science. Series IV, Current issues in linguistic theory, ISSN 0304-0763 ; v. 122)
    Chiefly updated versions of papers presented at a conference on Romance linguistics held at the Manoir de Brion in Dragey, Manche, May 1989
    Includes index.
    1. Romance languages--Congresses. I. Smith, John Charles, 1950- . II. Maiden, Martin, 1957- . III. Series.
PC11.L54      1995
440--dc20                                                                          95-280
ISBN 90 272 3625 9 (Eur.) / 1-55619-576-1 (US) (alk. paper)                        CIP

John Benjamins Publishing Co. • P.O.Box 75577 • 1070 AN Amsterdam • The Netherlands
John Benjamins North America • P.O.Box 27519 • Philadelphia PA 19118-0519 • USA

*In memoriam*
*Adrian C. Battye*

# Contents

# Contributors' Addresses:

Michael Allan Jones
Department of Language and Linguistics
University of Essex
Wivenhoe Park
COLCHESTER  CO4 3SQ
U.K.

Christopher Lyons
Department of Modern Languages
University of Salford
SALFORD  M5 4WT
U.K.

Martin Maiden
Downing College
CAMBRIDGE  CB2 1DQ
U.K.

M. Mair Parry
Department of European Languages
University of Wales Aberystwyth
Hugh Owen Building
ABERYSTWYTH  SY23 3DY
U.K.

John Charles Smith
Department of Linguistics
University of Manchester
Oxford Road
MANCHESTER  M13 9PL
U.K.

Jean-Philippe Watbled
Département d'Études du monde anglophone
Université de Provence (Aix-Marseille I)
Centre d'Aix
29 avenue Robert Schuman
13621 AIX-EN-PROVENCE CEDEX
FRANCE

Max W Wheeler
School of Cognitive & Computing Sciences
University of Sussex
Falmer
BRIGHTON  BN1 9QH
U.K.

# Introduction

The Manoir de Brion, situated in the commune of Dragey, *département* of the Manche, in the Basse-Normandie region of France, began life in 1066 as a Benedictine priory founded by the abbot of the nearby Mont-Saint-Michel. Over the years, it came to serve as a summer residence for the abbots, and as a guest house, where distinguished visitors to the abbey were received. It was greatly extended in the early sixteenth century, assuming something like its present appearance. This period also saw one of the most significant events in the Manoir's history, when Jacques Cartier, the discoverer of Canada, came for an audience with the French king François I$^{er}$ before one of his voyages. The Manoir is now owned by Vincent and Chantal Cronin, who generously made it available to us for a three-day conference on Romance Linguistics in May 1989. We thank them for allowing us to invade their home.

The participants, with one exception, held appointments at universities in Great Britain. Their enthusiastic participation in the conference reflects the vigour of the discipline in the United Kingdom. In a period of decline in state support, both moral and financial, for British universities, Romance linguistics has achieved survival and success, notably by the nurturing of a generation of young scholars, and is now a discipline with a strong sense of identity. But the strong sense of community amongst British Romance linguists has not made them inward-looking or isolationist. The health and internationalism of our subject are perhaps best manifest at the annual Romance Linguistics Seminar, held every January at Trinity Hall, Cambridge, which brings together some fifty Romanists from Britain and abroad. That the field should be flourishing to this extent is due largely to the efforts of two British scholars who were, alas, unable to attend the Brion conference — Joe Cremona and Martin Harris.

This book brings together updated versions of most of the papers given at the conference, and also includes two papers by colleagues who could not attend the meeting (Parry and Wheeler). All the papers have been revised in the light of comments by referees, whose anonymity we are pledged to respect, but to whom we owe a debt of gratitude, which we are pleased to record here. In addition to the studies which appear in this collection, papers were also presented by Rebecca Posner on Romance plural formation and Nigel Vincent on the personal infinitive in Neapolitan. Unfortunately, the authors of these contributions were unable to submit them for publication in this volume.

A characteristic of British approaches to Romance Linguistics, however diverse, is the combination of two virtues which are too often felt to be mutually exclusive — respect for primary data and concern for theory. Its practitioners do not regard observation as an end in itself, but use the facts they have gleaned as a stepping-stone to accurate description and, where possible, explanation, whilst recognizing, conversely, that no coherent generalization is possible unless it is founded in empirical observation. In this view, Romance Linguistics is not narrowly philological, but is rather General Linguistics practised with reference to particular data. The point has been made many times, but is worth reiterating, that Latin and the Romance languages offer an unrivalled wealth of synchronic and historical documentation, and provide both a stimulus and a test-bed for ideas about language structure, language change, and language variation.

It is not surprising, then, that the papers in this volume can be interpreted as using Romance data to throw light on general problems in linguistic theory, or on the structure of languages beyond Romance. Battye's examination of data on quantification from several contemporary varieties and historical stages of French leads him to consider the long-standing question 'Do Quantifiers and Quantifier Phrases exist as independent syntactic categories?', concluding that they do not. Jones undertakes an exhaustive discussion of a uncharted area of Sardinian syntax, and in so doing raises the issue of the theoretical status of pronouns in the wake of recent controversy about the structure of the noun-phrase. Lyons looks at the variety of values associated with the pronoun *se* in Spanish and French and assesses their implications for argument structure. Maiden surveys evidence from a range of Italian dialects, on the basis of which he proposes putatively universal characteristics of the internal structure of phonological prosodic constituents. Parry offers a meticulous account of clitic syntax in the north-western Italian dialect of Cairo Montenotte which she conceives as demonstrating 'the importance of the study of non-standard varieties for testing the predictions and for the development of contemporary linguistic theory'. Smith adduces implicational hierarchies based on data concerning past participle agreement in a large number of Romance varieties; these hierarchies are then presented as supporting the view that considerations of sentence-processing may constitute an important superordinate tier of explanation in syntax. Watbled investigates features of southern French pronunciation which have implications for the criteria we use to establish the validity of a phonological representation. Wheeler's detailed scrutiny of Catalan serves as the basis for a discussion of the role underspecification may play in the description of lexical specifiers.

But theory and data can be viewed from a complementary perspective, in which the analytical tools of linguistic theory are brought to bear on structural problems in Romance. In this light, Battye is making a further contribution to a long-running debate on the status of quantifiers, exemplified from French and other varieties of Gallo-Romance. Jones is testing a hypothesis about Case theory in claiming that the distribution of the prepositional accusative in Sardinian is determined by syntactic, rather than semantic, factors. Lyons shows how Case theory and theta-theory yield a unified analysis of constructions which have previously been treated as disparate. Maiden offers a refinement of the theory of prosodic constituents in phonology, which he uses to illuminate Italo-Romance data. Parry balances the competing claims of syntactic, semantic, and pragmatic theory in her discussion of the syntax of clitics in Piedmontese. Smith maintains that recoverability can be a crucial factor in constraining language change, and that failure to recognize this fact has vitiated previous accounts of past participle agreement in Romance. Watbled argues for a non-linear theory of phonological represention involving n-ary branching and applies it to French; and Wheeler's paper constitutes an extension of underspecification theory to account for the distribution of Catalan quantifiers. The point we wish to stress is that the symbiosis of theory and data is here complete; to ponder which comes first is as fruitful as asking the same question about the chicken and the egg.

Several contributions make illuminating comparisons with Romance languages beyond those with which they are immediately concerned: Smith takes a pan-Romance perspective; Lyons draws parallels with structures in Romance tongues beyond French and Spanish; Parry makes frequent allusion to Italo-Romance varieties other than the dialect with which she is primarily dealing, as well as French, Spanish, Portuguese, and Catalan; Wheeler, in his discussion of Catalan lexical specifiers, also refers to French, Spanish, and Italian. The reader will find that every study, implicitly or explicitly, suggests comparisons with other Romance varieties. For instance, the phenomenon of the prepositional accusative is widespread in Romance, but Jones's revealing dissection of the phenomenon in Sardinian surely invites a reconsideration of the phenomenon as it is manifested elsewhere. Indeed, there is a discernible tendency in these studies to reveal unexpected, new, facets of problems which are relatively familiar in general descriptions of Romance varieties (for example, Battye on quantifiers, Smith on participial agreement), or even to discuss phenomena which have not hitherto been widely known and have still to be considered in the theoretical literature (for instance, Maiden on the prosodic phonology of Italo-Romance dialects).

The collection is, we believe, a coherent one, and many of the papers can fruitfully be read in conjunction with others in the volume. For instance, Parry's detailed discussion of *se* constructions in Piedmontese both complements and is complemented by Lyons's survey of similar phenomena in French and Spanish; Battye and Wheeler each illuminate the other's comments on quantifiers; and both Jones and Lyons, in their treatments of quite different phenomena, are concerned to assess the role that factors such as human reference and definiteness may play in syntax.

In addition to Vincent and Chantal Cronin, we should like to thank the following sponsors for their ready generosity, without which the conference could not have taken place: Monsieur le Président du Conseil Régional de Basse-Normandie; Monsieur le Président du Conseil Général de la Manche; Mr and Mrs Alan Rousell; Mr and Mrs Paul Tozer; Barclays Bank, plc, Bath Branch; Cross Manufacturing Company (1938), Ltd., Bath; Hiram Walker-Allied Vintners, Ltd., Shepton Mallet; Shell U.K., Ltd.; Sun Life Assurance Society, plc; Tesco Stores, Ltd. The conference was organized under the ægis of the School of Modern Languages and International Studies of the University of Bath, to which both the editors were attached at the time, and we should record our thanks to friends and colleagues there. Thanks, too, to Martin Barry, Kersti Börjars, Thomas D. Cravens, Alan Cruttenden, Suzanne Fleischman, and John E. Joseph, all of whom assisted us in various ways. We are particularly grateful to Konrad Koerner and Yola de Lusenet for their encouragement to publish this volume and for their forbearance during its gestation.

One of the contributors, Adrian Battye, a good friend and a valued colleague, died as we were preparing this collection for the press. We dedicate this book to his memory.


John Charles Smith
Martin Maiden
Manchester — Cambridge
December 1994

# Aspects of Quantification in French in its Regional and Diachronic Varieties

## †Adrian C. Battye

## 0. Theoretical background: the status of Quantifier Phrase (QP)

The use of the label QP (= Quantifier Phrase) is widespread in the generative literature (see, for instance, Longobardi & Giorgi's seminal study of
NP structure (Longobardi & Giorgi 1991), Obenauer (1983; 1984), and
Wheeler (this volume) for recent uses). However, even in the early 1970s,
Joan Bresnan was sounding a note of caution with respect to this label
when she went so far as to suggest that it was 'merely a temporary convenience' (1973:277).[1] Whether the label QP need be included within a universal set of categories is a real theoretical issue — and one where the
Romance languages (and French in particular) yield interesting insights.

X-bar theory (see Chomsky 1970; 1981 and Jackendoff 1977) provides
the basic rule schema that applies to the projection of all syntactic categories: $X^n \rightarrow \ldots X^{n-1}\ldots$ To put this insight in another fashion, one might
say that syntactic heads project maximal (i.e., phrasal) categories; thus N
projects NP; A, AP; P, PP, etc. Stowell (1981) and Chomsky (1986) have
proposed syntactic analyses which involve two types of projections which
are reminiscent of the division found in traditional syntax between content
and form words (for further work on this division see Radford 1988). To
be specific, the generally accepted X-bar framework is composed of four
lexical projections (NP, AP, PP, VP) and a variable array of what might be
termed functional or grammatical projections. The set of formatives to be
found under this second heading is much less well established, but candidates for inclusion would certainly be IP (= Inflectional Phrase or the
maximal projection of INFL) and CP (= Complementizer Phrase or the
maximal projection of COMP). This class of projection would also probably include DP (= Determiner Phrase) (see Abney 1987).

The question which now presents itself is: to which (if either) of these two types of projections does QP belong? On the one hand it might be argued that the quantifiers which head QPs are content words (i.e., they are meaningful); but this is not a sufficient condition for QP's inclusion among what we are calling the lexical projections, because, within very restricted limits, the so-called grammatical or functional formatives do have some inherent meaning.

Indeed, one good reason for perhaps excluding QP from the class of lexical projections (i.e., NP, AP, PP, VP) is that QP does not fit easily into this class, which, according to Chomsky (1974), can be exhaustively described in terms of the primitive features [±N] and [±V] (that is to say that A is [+N, +V]; N, [+N, –V]; V, [–N, +V], and P [–N, –V]). In order to include QP within this class, one would have to propose a revision or complication of the primitive features which describe it.[2] However, before undertaking such a radical revision of an analysis which has produced much insightful work in the tradition of the lexicalist hypothesis in generative grammar, an alternative analysis might be examined. It is precisely such an alternative approach (i.e., that QP, as such, does not exist) that will be pursued here.

Before turning to this alternative approach, let us briefly consider whether QP should be included in the class of functional or grammatical formatives. What typifies the items which can head projections such as CP, DP, etc. is that they form a closed set in which little (if any) lexical creativity is possible. The set of complementizers in French would probably run to no more than five[3] (i.e., *que* (and *qui*) = [+finite, +declarative]; *à*, *de* = [–finite, +declarative]; *si* = [±finite, +interrogative], and perhaps *ce que* = [+finite, +declarative] in structures such as *je m'attendais à ce qu'il vienne* 'I was expecting him to come'). Similarly the class of determiners in French, while being more extensive than the class of complementizers, is still to be considered a closed set of items. Consider, in the light of these considerations, the lexical items which are generally included under the heading of so-called quantifiers (i.e., *beaucoup* 'a lot; much/many', *peu* 'a little', *quelques* 'some', *pas mal* 'quite a lot', *vachement* 'tons/bags', etc.). These items show a good deal more variety and creativity (on this point see §3.1) than is normally associated with the class of grammatical/functional formatives.

Therefore it would appear that QP does not fit comfortably into either of the classes of lexical or functional/grammatical items reviewed so far. An alternative approach to this question might be to consider QP not as a homogeneous syntactic class but rather as a homogeneous semantic class of lexical items (i.e., they all share a common semantic feature [+quantification]) which is realized heterogeneously in syntax; a case of what Barbara Hall Partee refers to as 'multi-form variation', where 'several syntactic structures may be given the same semantic interpretation' (1975:201).

## 1. On the syntactic status of quantifiers in French

### 1.1. Adjectival quantifiers

If the distribution in syntax of the quantifiers of French is now considered, it can be easily established that there are at least two and possibily three types of quantifier. First, consider agreement phenomena; we find that in the orthography there are quantifiers such as *quelques* 'some', and *plusieurs* 'several' which, by virtue of the their final *s*, appear to agree in number with the head noun they are related with;[4] and, indeed, in liaison contexts, this final orthographic *s* (as would be expected for the marker of plurality (see Tranel 1987:171)) does have a phonetic reflex:

(1)   a.   *Quelques étudiants*   /kɛlkə zetydjã/
              'Some students'
       b.   *Plusieurs histoires*   /plyzjœʀ zistwaːʀ/
              'Several stories'

In the light of this observation, it is interesting to note that numerals such as *deux* 'two' and *trois* 'three', which are unquestionably quantificational in their semantics, behave in the same way as *quelques* and *plusieurs*:

(2)   a.   *Deux histoires*   /dø zistwaːʀ/
              'Two stories'
       b.   *Trois étudiants*   /tʀwa zetydjã/
              'Three students'

The agreement behaviour seen here is typical of that of the adjective in French, and so, as a working hypothesis, let us assume that *quelques, plusieurs, deux,* and *trois* are adjectives. Besides agreement with its head noun, another feature of the category Adjective in French is its ability to co-occur with determiners such as definite articles (e.g., *les grands hommes* 'the great men'). With respect to this characteristic, we find that *quelques, deux,* and *trois* behave exactly as expected:

(3)  a.  *Les quelques étudiants que je connais ...*
         'The some students that I know ...'
     b.  *Ces deux histoires que j' ai lues ...*
         'Those two stories that I've read ...'
     c.  *Les trois hommes qui sont venus ...*
         'The three men who have come ...'

However, the case of *plusieurs* appears to be more problematical, since it is excluded from contexts like (3), as is shown in (4):

(4)  *\*Les plusieurs histoires que j' ai apprises par coeur ...*
     'The several stories that I've learnt by heart ...'

On the surface, the behaviour of *plusieurs* may appear difficult to reconcile with the analysis being proposed for the other (related) quantifiers, but reference to Italian may help to clarify the situation. In Italian, where nominal morphology is much richer than in French, the proposal that there be a class of quantifiers which are syntactically adjectives would appear to be in no way contentious (similar remarks can also be made for Spanish, of course); hence a typical quantifier like *molto* 'much/many' agrees in number and gender with the head noun with which it is related and can also appear in an NP introduced by a determiner:

(5)  a.  *Molti libri che ho letto ...*
         'Many books that I have read ...'
     b.  *I molti libri che ho letto ...*
         'The many books that I have read ...'
     c.  *Molte cartoline che si sono perse ...*
         'Many cards that SI are lost ...'
     d.  *Le molte cartoline che si sono perse ...*
         'The many cards that SI are lost ...'

Thus cross-linguistic Romance data seem to justify the postulation of a class of adjectives with quantificational semantics. However, there is one so-called quantifier in Italian which does not fit neatly into this class namely *ogni* 'each' (compare also Spanish *cada* and indeed French *chaque*); it cannot agree morphologically with the nominal head it modifies (since it does not have suffixal morphology), nor does it appear grammatically in NPs which are introduced by determiners:

(6)  a.  *Ogni libro che ho comprato ...*
         'Each book that I have bought ...'
     b.  **L' ogni libro che ho comprato ...*
         'The each book that I have bought ...'
     c.  *Ogni cartolina che ho mandato ...*
         'Each card that I have sent ...'
     d.  **L' ogni cartolina che ho mandato ...*
         'The each card that I have sent ...'

One approach to the problem in Italian could be to analyse *ogni* as a determiner. Although its lack of agreement is still somewhat problematic for such an approach, the failure of *ogni* to co-occur with other determiners would follow as a direct consequence of the impossibility of determiners co-occurring within one NP structure in Italian:

(7)  a.  **I questi problemi*
         'The these problems'
     b.  **Quali le cartoline?*
         'Which the cards?'

Now the very same categorial analysis proposed here for the Italian quantifier *ogni* could be applied to *plusieurs* in French. Indeed *plusieurs* might be considered a possible candidate for inclusion in the class of determiner in French precisely because, if *plusieurs* were analysed as a determiner with quantificational semantics, then the ungrammaticality of the string in (4) is accounted for in the same way as the ungrammatical strings in Italian shown in (7). That is to say that French is just like Italian in not allowing two determiners to co-occur (outside of co-ordination structures) in a single NP:[5]

(8)  a.  **Les ces problèmes*
         'The these problems'
     b.  **Quelles mes cartes postales?*
         'Which my postcards?'

## 1.2. A further type of quantifier?

The question which now begs an answer is that of the categorial status of
such items traditionally labelled quantifiers in French as *beaucoup* 'a lot;
much/many', *trop* 'too much/too many', *assez* 'enough', etc. Even in the
most superficial aspects of their behaviour, these so-called quantifiers behave very differently from the adjectival/determiner class just examined.
In the orthography they have no suffixal morphology; also, because of the
following prepositional marker *de* (see §2.2.2 for a proposal about the
status of this item), they are never to be found in a phonological context
where plural liaison might be expected, and so absence of liaison cannot be
offered as a serious argument against their being adjectival or determiner-
like.

A further argument against their being adjectives can be found in data
such as those in (9), where clearly *beaucoup, trop, assez,* etc., are not able
to co-occur with determiners, in contradistinction to the behaviour of the
adjectival quantifier *quelques* and the numerals:

    (9)   a.   *Les beaucoup de livres que j'ai lus ...*
             'The many of books that I have read ...'
        b.   *Mes trop de gâteaux que nous avons mangés ...*
             'My too-many of cakes that we have eaten ...'
        c.   *Ces assez de bêtises qu'il a faites ...*
             'These enough of antics that he has done ...'

There are two other facets of NP structures containing *beaucoup, trop,
assez,* etc., which distinguish them from NPs containing the adjecti-
val/determiner quantifiers. First (as has already been alluded to above),
these quantifier items are obligatorily followed by the prepositional marker
*de*:

    (10) a.  *Beaucoup *(de) livres*
          'Many of books'
       b.  *Trop *(de) gâteaux*
          'Too-many of cakes'
       c.  *Assez *(de) bêtises*
          'Enough of antics'

whereas the presence of such a marker after *quelques, plusieurs,* or numerals produces ungrammaticality:

(11) a. *Quelques d'étudiants*
'Some of students'
b. *Plusieurs de livres*
'Several of books'
c. *Deux de problèmes*
'Two of problems'.

A second particularity of the quantifiers like *beaucoup, trop,* and *assez* is that they can appear in configurations in which they are separated from their head noun (the so-called *quantification à distance* (= QAD) configuration treated in, for instance, Obenauer (1983; 1984)):

(12) a. *J'ai lu beaucoup de romans.*
'I have read many of novels.'
a'. *J'ai beaucoup lu de romans.*
'I've many read of novels'.
b. *J'ai mangé assez de gâteaux.*
'I've eaten enough of cakes.'
b'. *J'ai assez mangé de gâteaux.*
'I've enough eaten of cakes.'
c. *J'ai fait trop de gaffes.*
'I've made too-many of gaffes.'
c'. *J'ai trop fait de gaffes.*
'I've too-many made of gaffes.'

Again, this possibility is totally excluded with the other class of quantifiers identfied in §1.1:

(13) a. *J'ai rencontré deux hommes.*
'I've met two men.'
a'. *J'ai deux rencontré hommes.*
'I've two met men.'
a''. *J'ai deux rencontré d'hommes.*
'I've two met of men.'
b. *J'ai caressé plusieurs chats.*
'I've stroked several cats.'
b'. *J'ai plusieurs caressé chats.*
'I've several stroked cats.'

b". *_J'ai plusieurs caressé de chats._
'I've several stroked of cats.'

c.  _J'ai eu quelques problèmes._
'I've had some problems.'

c'. *_J'ai quelques eu problèmes._
'I've some had problems.'

c". *_J'ai quelques eu de problèmes._
'I've some had of problems.'

It must be emphasized at this juncture that the pairs of sentences in (12) have a similar, but not identical interpretation. In both pairs of sentences, the direct object has a quantified interpretation, but the scope of the quantifier is somewhat different in the two versions. On an intuitive level, it could be proposed that in (12a), (12b), and (12c) the quantifiers act upon the direct object alone, whereas in (12a'), (12b'), and (12c') the quantifiers' scope bears not only on the direct object, but also on the whole predicate.[6] Considering the different surface positions occupied by the quantifier in these pairs of strings, it is not at all surprising that such differences in interpretation should arise.

A necessary corollary of the QAD construction is that the quantifier item which appears (on the surface, at least) to be detached from its NP must also be able to function independently as an adverbial constituent. The following examples, where these quantifier items act on intransitive predicates, illustrate this independent usage:

(14)  _J'ai beaucoup/trop/assez voyagé._
'I've much/too-much/enough travelled.'

The question of QAD will be returned to in §2.3 below.

This subsection has reviewed sufficient differences between the adjectival/determiner class of quantifiers and the class of French quantifiers consisting of _beaucoup, trop,_ and _assez_ for it to be clear that they are not analysable as adjectives, nor as determiners (in the sense that they behave like articles or demonstratives[7]). Thus it would appear that _beaucoup, trop,_ and _assez_ are members of another lexical class marked [+quantification], and it is precisely to the proposal that they are nouns heading NP projections that the next section of this study will address itself.

## 2. Nominal quantifiers in French

What are the consequences of adopting the approach that structures such as *beaucoup de livres, assez de romans* are NPs containing NPs which are [+quantification] in their semantic interpretation? The first part of this section will briefly review some arguments in favour of analysing these structures as simplex NPs (i.e., as pseudo-partitives). The second part will then consider the consequences of this position and will argue that, by making reference to such subcomponents of the Government-Binding theory as Case theory (see Chomsky 1981:48-55) and by invoking Borer's inflectional rules (see Borer 1984), an illuminating analysis of these quantified NP structures can be arrived at. A preliminary version of some of the basic ideas contained in this section appeared in Battye (1987).

### 2.1. Partitive or pseudo-partitive structures?

Superficially it would appear that strings such as those in (10) could be analysed either as shown in (15) or as shown in (16):

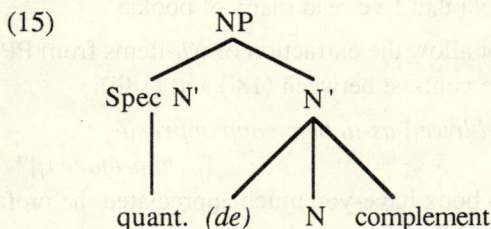

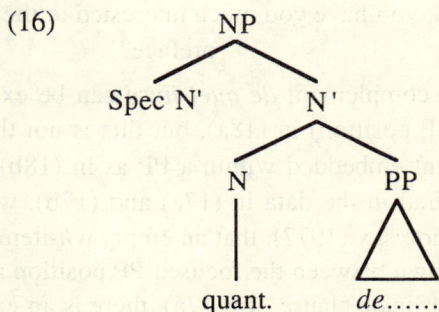

(15)

NP

Spec N'    N'

quant. *(de)*    N    complement

(16)

NP

Spec N'    N'

N    PP

quant.    *de......*

The structural configuration in (15) is that usually associated with the pseudo-partitive (see Selkirk 1977), while that in (16) is a pure partitive configuration. Following Milner (1978) (see also Battye (1991)), it will be argued that a principled choice can be made between (15) and (16) to find which one provides the most insightful analysis of structures such as *beaucoup de livres*, etc.

A first argument in favour of the pseudo-partitive structure (i.e., (15)) is based on the paradigm in (17), taken from Milner:

(17) a.  *C'est* [$_{PP}$ *de Zola$_i$*] *que j'ai lu* [$_{NP}$ *le livre* [$_{PP}$ t$_i$]].
     'It is of Zola that I've read the book.'

   b.  *\*C'est* [$_{PP}$ *de Zola$_i$*] *que j'ai lu le livre* [$_{PP}$ *du frère* [$_{PP}$ t$_i$]].
     'It is of Zola that I've read the book of the brother.'

   c.  *C'est* [$_{PP}$ *de Zola$_i$*] *que j'ai lu* [$_{NP}$ *deux livres* [$_{PP}$ t$_i$]].
     'It is of Zola that I've read two books.'

   d.  *C'est* [$_{PP}$ *de Zola$_i$*] *que j'ai lu* [$_{NP}$ *beaucoup de livres* [$_{PP}$ t$_i$]].
     'It is of Zola that I've read many of books.'

   e.  *C'est* [$_{PP}$ *de Zola$_i$*] *que j'ai lu*
                                  [$_{NP}$ *beaucoup* [$_{PP}$ *de livres* [$_{PP}$ t$_i$]]].
     'It is of Zola that I've read many of books.'

Generally French does not allow the extraction of *wh*-items from PPs. This constraint accounts for the contrast between (18i) and (18ii):

(18) a.  [$_{PP}$ *De quel livre$_i$*] *as-tu beaucoup apprécié*
                               [$_{NP}$ *la préface* t$_i$]?
     'Of which book have-you much appreciated the preface?'

   b.  *\*[$_{PP}$ *De quel livre$_i$*] *t'es-tu beaucoup intéressé*
                               [$_{PP}$ *à la préface* t$_i$]?
     'Of which book you-have you much interested to the
                                 preface?'

Thus it is that the adnominal complement *de quel livre* can be extracted from the direct object (i.e., NP position) in (18a), but this is not the case with an adnominal complement embedded within a PP as in (18b). This very same contrast can be found in the data in (17a) and (17b), where it might be argued, following Chomsky (1977), that an empty *wh*-item establishes the indexing relation shown between the focused PP position and the empty PP position in the subordinate clause. In (17a), there is an example of extraction from an NP direct object position, while in (17b) the empty *wh*-PP would be extracted from within a PP, hence the ungrammaticality.

With this background in mind, attention can now turn to the signifi-
cance of the data in (17c) and (17d). In (17c), it can be seen that extraction
of the adnominal PP from a simplex quantified NP is perfectly grammatical; the quantifier adjective *deux* would be generated under the Spec N' position of the NP and the head of the whole NP would be *livres* in this case.
Now if the same logic is applied to the grammatical structure in (17d), it
must be concluded that here, too, the quantified NP *beaucoup de livres* is a
simplex NP structure, and, in particular, that the sequence *de livres* is not a
PP, but an N' preceded by *de*. In fact, if the quantifier item *beaucoup* was
followed by a PP introduced by *de* (as shown in the structure in (17e)), the
grammaticality of the output would be problematical for the generalization
that PP is an island in French. Thus we have here a first argument which
favours the pseudo-partitive structure (15) for strings such as *beaucoup de
romans, trop de livres*, etc.

Many studies of the pronoun *en* in French have concluded that there are
indeed two distinct sources for this pronominal form; a true PP source
which gives rise to what has been called the *en-génitif* and an N' source
which gives rise to what is referred to as *en-partitif* (see Ruwet 1972, Hark
1982, and Pollock 1986[8]). A whole series of differences which distinguish
*en-partitif* from *en-génitif* are discussed in Pinkham (1982:10-13). Only
one of these differences will be considered here, in so far as it again allows
a principled choice to be made between the structures given in (15) and
(16). If structures such as *beaucoup de livres* are analysed as full partitives
(i.e., as in (16)), then these structures should give rise to *en-génitif* items.
If, on the other hand, the structures in question are to be analysed as
pseudo-partitives (as in (15)), then *en-partitif* should result.

It was Ruwet (1972) who was first in the generative tradition to note
that, while *en-génitif* can give rise to configurations where the pronominal
form *en* has, as its antecedent, an adnominal PP complement, the same does
not apply to *en-partitif* — hence the contrast between (19a') and (19b'):

(19) a. [NP *La cheminée* [PP *de l'usine*]] *est penchée.* ⇒
        'The chimney of the factory is leaning.'
    a'. [NP *La cheminée* t$_i$] *en*$_i$ *est penchée.*
        'The chimney of-it is leaning.'
    b. [NP *Deux cheminées*] *sont penchées.* ⇒
        'Two chimneys are leaning.'

b'.  *[$_{NP}$ *Deux* t$_i$] *en$_i$ sont penchées.*
'Two of-it are leaning.'

The contrast in grammaticality here can be accounted for by referring to the different sources of *en* in these sentences. In (19a') there is an example of *en-génitif*, since its antecedent is an adnominal PP, but in (19b'), there is an example of *en-partitif* which arises from the pronominalization of the N' of the simple NP structure: [$_{NP}$ *deux* [$_{N'}$ *cheminées*]]. Consider now the behaviour of strings such as *beaucoup de cheminées* with respect to this type of *en* pronominalization:

(20)  a.  *Beaucoup de cheminées sont penchées.* fi
'Many of chimneys are leaning.'
      b.  **Beaucoup en sont penchées.*
'Many of-it are leaning.'

The ungrammaticality of (20b) is highly suggestive in the light of the conclusions drawn from the data in (19). The failure of the sequence *de cheminées* to give rise to a grammatical *en* pronominalization leads one to conclude that the type of *en* encountered here is *en-partitif*. This, in turn, suggests that the *de cheminées* sequence is not a PP adnominal complement, but rather an N', and that *beaucoup de cheminées* and similar structures are simplex NP configurations or pseudo-partitives, as in (15).[9]

If we accept an analysis of structures such as *beaucoup de livres* as being pseudo-partitives, we may further suggest that the lexical items *beaucoup, trop, assez*, etc., will occupy the same structural position (i.e., Spec N') as do the quantifier adjective *quelque*, the numerals *deux*, etc., and the quantifier determiner *plusieurs*. Notionally, this seems a highly satisfactory result, as all these items share a common semantic relation with the head of the NP they appear in. In the following sub-section, a more sophisticated theoretical analysis will seek to give this initial conclusion some stronger motivation. This analysis will seek to motivate the basic idea that *beaucoup*, etc., are NPs generated in the Spec N' position, a proposal that is by no means controversial, as even the most cursory reading of Selkirk (1977) will show.

## 2.2. On the presence of *de*

Now that a pseudo-partitive analysis for NP structures such as *beaucoup de livres* has been motivated, it is opportune to put forward some proposals about the internal structure of these strings. The best way to begin an exposition of our analysis of the French pseudo-partitive is to consider the syntactic status of the lexical item *de* in these structures. The first and most evident characteristic of this item is its obligatory presence; its absence produces ungrammaticality:

(21) *J'ai lu beaucoup livres/trop journaux/peu articles.*
'I've read many books/too-many newspapers/few articles.'

Another consequence of the absence of *de* is the impossibility of the QAD configurations which are usually possible with these quantifier items:

(22) a. *J'ai beaucoup lu livres.*
'I've many read books.'
b. *J'ai trop lu journaux.*
'I've too-many read newspapers.'
c. *J'ai peu lu articles.*
'I've few read articles.'

In order to account for the obligatory presence of this formative in these configurations, reference will be made to Case theory. In particular, it will proposed that *de* appears in the pseudo-partitive structures of French because it is a special Case marker.

It is by no means novel to suggest that in a syntactic analysis of certain constructions, the presence of special Case markers has to be recognized. Such an idea has already been developed by Vergnaud (1974) with respect to the formative *à* in the structures in (23):

(23) a. *Il a compté sur l'homme et sur la femme qui se sont rencontrés hier.*
'He has depended on the man and on the woman who each have met yesterday.'
b. *Il a parlé à l'homme et à la femme qui se sont rencontrés hier.*
'He has spoken to the man and to the woman who each have met yesterday.'
c. *Ils se sont assis sur la table et les chaises.*
'They each have sat on the table and the chair.'

    d.  *Ils ont acheté cette maison à Marie et le directeur.*

       'They have bought this house from Mary and the
       headmaster.'

What it is crucial to recognize here is that *à* (a Case marker) and true
prepositions behave differently with respect to certain syntactic processes.
For instance, in (23a) it is seen that a co-ordination of two PPs cannot serve
as the head of a relative clause. Now if the strings *à l'homme* and *à la
femme* in (23b) were to be analysed as PPs, then similar ungrammaticality
would be expected. However this is not so; and the fact that a grammatical
output is obtained in (23b) suggests very strongly that *à l'homme* and *à la
femme* are NPs introduced not by a preposition but by a dative Case marker
(i.e., *à*).

    (23c) and (23d) show a different phenomenon, but one which indicates
that similar conclusions are in order. Two NPs can be co-ordinated under
one governing preposition; this is shown with respect to the preposition *sur*
in (23c). In (23d), on the other hand, *à* does not behave as would be expected, if it were to be analysed along similar lines to *sur*. It does not
permit co-ordination of a governed NP, a feature which, once more, suggests that *à* here is better analysed not as a preposition but as a Case
marker.

    But what is the theoretical motivation for the presence of Case mark-
ers? Their *raison d'être* can be explained as a way of saving NPs from the
effects of the so-called Case filter (see Rouveret & Vergnaud 1980). The
form of the filter that will be invoked here is that proposed by Chomsky in
*On Binding*: '*N, where N has no Case' (Chomsky 1980:25).[10] The choice
of this version of the filter is important for the argumentation which is to
follow, where it is crucial that this filter apply to the head of NP (the whole
NP, it will be assumed, will get Case by percolation).

    Consider now the following contrast:

    (24)  a.  *J'ai donné le livre Paul.*

            'I've given the book Paul.'

      b.  *J'ai donné le livre à Paul.*

            'I've given the book to Paul.'

It can be explained in terms of the above mentioned filter. In (24a), *Paul*
receives no Case from the V (*donner*) and no other Case feature is indicated as being present in the sentence; the structure therefore falls foul of

the Case filter. (24b), on the other hand, shows the presence of the Case marker *à*; *Paul* is therefore Case marked and no longer filtered out as ungrammatical by the Case filter.

It is, then, precisely this sort of mechanism which accounts for the ungrammaticality of the strings in (21) and (22) above, where *de* is absent. Essentially, it is being proposed that *de* is a Case marker which is supplying a Case feature to the head of the indirect object NP here; if this Case feature is not supplied, then the head of the Ns in question falls foul of the Case filter.

Yet why is it that the head of the NP in structures such as *beaucoup de livres* requires a supplementary Case feature? In order to account for this state of affairs, it is necessary to return to the suggestion, already made at the end of §2.0, that, in a structure such as *beaucoup de livrès*, we are faced not with a single NP, but rather with two. Both the head of the structure *livres* and the quantifier are nominal elements which head a maximal projection. (In pseudo-partitives such as *un kilo de...* or *une livre de...*, the nominal nature of the quantifier item is much more self-evident.) Now the consequence of this proposal is that the two Ns which appear in structures of this kind are both subject to the Case filter.

In this way, in a structure such as (25):

(25)

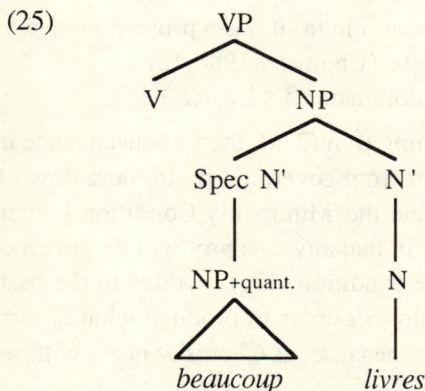

where the verb assigns oblique Case to its direct object, there are two possible heads to which the Case can be assigned; it could be assigned to the NP whose head N is *livres* or, alternatively, to the quantifier NP headed by

*beaucoup*. But in both of these scenarios one nominal head is left without
Case, and therefore ungrammaticality will be the inevitable consequence.

Before we turn to a consideration of the mechanisms which allow these
configurations to be 'saved', it is necessary first to describe briefly how in
the context of the Government and Binding framework it is possible for the
quantifier *beaucoup* in Spec N' to 'absorb' the Case assigned by the V to its
direct object.

### 2.2.1.  Case assignment to Spec N'

How is the absorption of Case by the nominal quantifier in the Spec N'
position to be justified?  To explain this proposal we will make use of an
observation of Chomsky (1986).  The assignment of Case usually takes
place under government, defined in the following way:

> (26)  $\alpha$ governs $\beta$ iff $\alpha$ m-commands $\beta$ and there is no $\gamma$, $\gamma$ a barrier
> for $\beta$, such that $\gamma$ excludes $\alpha$ (Chomsky 1986:9).

From this definition it is clear that what counts as a barrier is crucial.  In
order to establish which nodes count as barriers, Chomsky has proposed the
Minimality Condition, which, in its narrow form, can be characterized as
follows:

> (27)  a.   ... $\alpha$ ... [$\gamma$ ... $\delta$ ... $\beta$ ...] ...
> b.   $\alpha$ does not govern $\beta$ in (a) if $\gamma$ is a projection of $\delta$
> excluding $\alpha$ (Chomsky 1986:42)
> c.   $\gamma$ immediately dominates $\beta$ (*loc. cit.*.).

If $\alpha$ is a lexical category governing $\beta$ in (27a), then a consequence of this is
that the presence of $\delta$ prevents $\alpha$ from governing $\beta$.  In more down-to-earth
terminology, it could be said that the Minimality Condition prevents possible ambiguity of government, in that any category will be governed by its
nearest potential governor.  The condition (27c) is added to the basic statement of the Minimality Condition in order to produce what is termed the
narrow version of this condition, because, as Chomsky notes with reference
to the following structure,

> (28)  They saw [$_{NP}$ Bill's [$_{N'}$ picture of Tom]]

the narrow definition of the Minimality Condition guarantees only in part
the non-ambiguity of government (*ibid.*:43).  In (28), for instance, with a
narrow definition of Minimality, the verb *saw* governs not only the head of

the complement NP (i.e., *picture*) but also the Spec N', namely *Bill*, because this constituent is outside N'. A broader definition of Minimality,
which allowed all maximal projections to be barriers, would not allow for
this kind of ambiguity of government.

Now in this context it will be noted that, with the narrow definition of
Minimality, the same ambiguity of government found in (28) is also present in the French structure exemplified in (24) — that is to say, the verb
*lire* could assign Case to its object NP, whose head is *livres*, or alternatively to the NP *beaucoup* in Spec N'. The consequence of this ambiguity
of government is the double possibility of Case assignment which has already been signalled.

### 2.2.2. On the syntactic status of *de*

The question that now has to be tackled is: what are the means by which
the structure \**J'ai lu beaucoup livres* can be 'saved'? The same question
can be posed with respect to the string \**They saw Bill picture of Tom* in
English, where the rule assigning genitive Case to a specifier NP in the
Spec N' position of NP guarantees a grammatical realization for this NP.
What we wish to suggest here is that a similar rule exists in French, which
allows for the insertion of the Case marker *de*; such a rule would be considered to be an inflectional rule in the sense of Borer (1984):

(29) A.  a.   Let **f** stand for an inflectionally specified grammatical
              feature
         b.   Let **F** stand for an assigner of **f**
         c.   Let **C** stand for a constituent specified without a vari-
              able
     B.  An operation which affects the assignment of **f** to **C**, such
         that it is not subject to any condition exterior to the prop-
         erties of **F**, **f**, or **C** is an **inflectional** rule (Borer 1984:20).

In the light of these definitions, we would propose the following insertion
rule for French:

(30) *de*-Insertion:        ø → *de*  / [$_{NP}$ NP+quant. ___ N'].

This insertion rule (based essentially on Borer's *sel*-insertion in Modern
Hebrew) would guarantee the presence of *de*, a Case marker, in quantified
French NPs like \**beaucoup livres*, thus giving *beaucoup de livres* as a

grammatical output.  This insertion is guaranteed in the terms of Borer's
analysis because the particular Case assigned by *de* is an inflectional feature **f**.  The Case marker *de* corresponds to **F** and the context [$_{NP}$ NP ___ N']
is the specific constituent without a variable where *de* would be inserted.
Clearly, the condition put forward in (29B) of Borer's definition is met, in
that there is no operation external to the properties of **C**, **F** and **f** involved
here.  In the structure which results from the operation of the insertion rule,
the two NPs involved would each have an abstract Case and, as a consequence, there would be no violation of the Case filter.[11]

## 2.3. Concerning 'la quantification à distance'

One interesting consequence of the analysis of pseudo-partitive structures
given in §2.2 is that it provides, in a very straightforward manner, an insightful account of the QAD configuration.  Consider again the structures
(12a'), (12b'), (12c'), repeated here as (31a-c) for convenience:

(31)  a.  *J'ai beaucoup lu de romans.*
          'I've many read of novels.'
      b.  *J'ai assez mangé de gâteaux.*
          'I've enough eaten of cakes.'
      c.  *J'ai trop fait de gaffes.*
          'I've too-many made of gaffes.'

The best way to begin an exposition of our account of the grammaticality
of these structures is to clarify the internal structure of the NP in direct object position in a QAD configuration.  Consider, to this end, this structure:

(32)  *J'ai beaucoup lu* [$_{NP}$ e *d'articles*].
      'I've many read of articles.'

Now the question which immediately springs to mind here is: what is the
status of the empty category *e* in (32)?  It is our proposal that this empty
category should be treated as a variable in Chomsky's sense of the term:

(33)  a.   $\alpha$ is a variable if and only if
           (i)    $\alpha = [_{NP}$ e ]
           (ii)   $\alpha$ is in an A-position (hence bears an A-GF)
           (iii)  there is a $\beta$ that locally A'-binds $\alpha$
                  (Chomsky 1981:185).
      b.   [$_{NP}$ e ] is a variable if and only if it has Case (*ibid.*:175).

Can we claim that the empty category in (32) is Case marked? Following our analysis of pseudo-partitive structures in §2 of this study, the reply is positive. The presence of the Case marker in the configuration *d' articles* implies that the head noun *articles* takes its Case feature not from the verb (i.e., *lire*) but from the Case marker *de*. The Case feature assigned by the verb is, then, available to mark the empty category in Spec N' position of the direct object NP, and so one of the conditions for the realization of a variable is satisfied in this configuration.

If we consider the other conditions set out in Chomsky's definition of what is necessary for a variable to be identified, then on two further counts no difficulties are encountered. The condition that the empty category must be of categorial status NP poses no problem. The condition that the variable should have a local A'-binder which identifies its content is also satisfied, because, as noted with respect to the example (14), those nominal quantifiers which participate in QAD can also function independently as NP adverbial constituents.[12] The use of NPs as adverbial constituents is quite common in French (but see note 12 for some consideration of the types of NP adverbials that can appear in the position between the auxiliary and the past participle). Thus it is proposed that the abstract structure of (32) should be as in (35) overleaf.[13] The condition on the realization of a variable, which says that it should have an A'-binder, is here respected. The empty Case marked NP category in the Spec N' has as its binder the NP *beaucoup*, which has been generated in an A'-position.

On the surface, at least, the last condition on the identification of a variable (i.e., that it be in an A-position) does present some problems. In the perspective of a 'classic' approach to θ-theory and argument positions (i.e., Chomsky 1981:34 and *passim*), it does seem that this particular condition is not fully satisifed. There are, however, two possible lines that might be pursued to resolve this difficulty. One is to adopt the modified definition of condition (33a(ii)) of the variable proposed by Obenauer:

>     (34)  α est une variable si et seulement si [...] α est dans une A-
>            position ou fait partie d'une A-position. (Obenauer 1983:69).

Such a modification allows the analysis of the empty category in Spec N' as a variable to be maintained, since clearly the Spec N' position in a configuration like (35) is to be considered as part of an A-position.

(35)

```
                    IP
                  /    \
             Spec I'    I'
               |       /  \
              je      I    VP
                          /  \
                         V    Scl
                         |    /  \
                        ai  NP    VP
                               /    \
                            AdvP     VP
                             |      /  \
                            NP     V    NP
                             |     |   /  \
                         beaucoup lu Spec N'  N'
                                      |      /  \
                                     NP    d'    N
                                      |          |
                                     vbl       articles
```

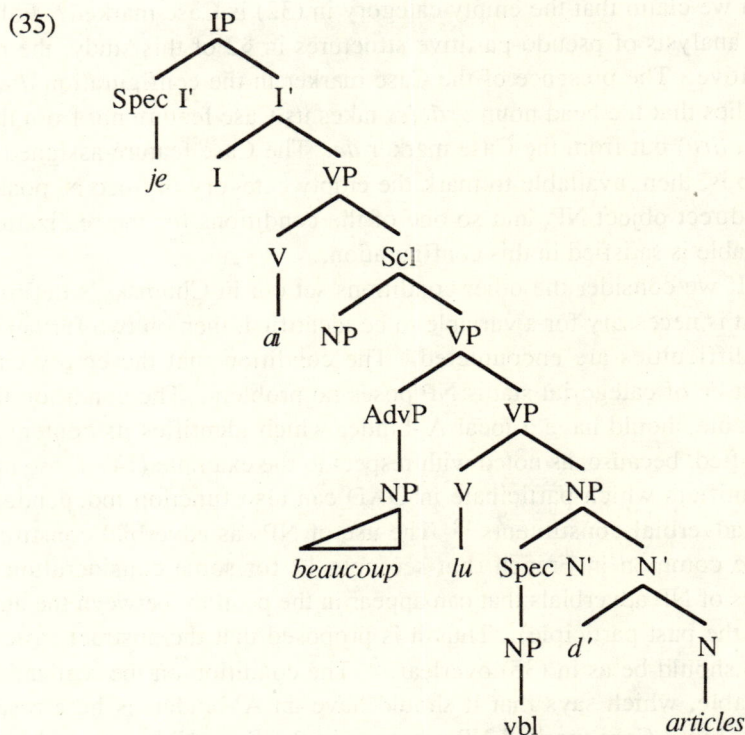

Another possible line of inquiry might be to leave Chomsky's definition of the variable unchanged and to exploit recent proposals on the nature
of Specifier positions made by Sportiche (1989). Sportiche suggests that
what we are terming the Spec N' position here should be classed as an A-
position; his arguments for this are based on data independent of the QAD
configuration. Our analysis of the QAD configuration and, in particular,
the identification of the variable within Spec N' may be considered to provide some interesting possible further corroboration of Sportiche's proposal. In the context of this study we will not pursue these issues further; it
will simply be noted that the superficial problem concerning the condition
on the identification of a variable which says that the empty category has to
be in an A-position is certainly not an insuperable one.

### 2.3.1. Some consequences of this QAD analysis

The analysis of QAD proposed in the previous subsection has a number of very interesting consequences. We will briefly consider just three of these in this part of the study. Firstly reconsider the data of (13a'), (13b'), (13c') and (13a"), (13b"), (13c"), repeated here as (36) for convenience:

(36)  a'.  *J'ai deux rencontré hommes.
           'I've two met men.'
      a".  *J'ai deux rencontré d'hommes.
           'I've two met of men.'
      b'.  *J'ai plusieurs caressé chats.
           'I've several stroked cats.'
      b".  *J'ai plusieurs caressé de chats.
           'I've several stroked of cats.'
      c'.  *J'ai quelques eu problèmes.
           'I've some had problems.'
      c".  *J'ai quelques eu de problèmes.
           'I've some had of problems.'

In these examples, all three conditions required for the identification of a variable are violated. *Deux, plusieurs*, and *quelques* are, in the context of our analysis, adjectival quantifiers, and so the empty category in Spec N' in these examples cannot be an NP. In the second place, these adjectival quantifiers cannot appear in the position of AdvPs (i.e., in A'-positions), and so they cannot function as local A'-binders. Finally, the absence of *de* in these examples leads one to conclude that abstract Case is not absorbed by the specifier, and so once again the empty category in the specifier cannot be a variable.

The absence of structures like these in (37) poses no problem for our analysis:

(37)  a.  *Tu es trop devenu gentil.
          'You are too-much become kind.'
      b.  *Le livre a peu été apprécié.
          'The book has little been appreciated.'

To account for the ungrammaticality of these sentences, we have to assume that a copula verb such as *devenir* or *être* does not assign abstract Case to the predicative AP and, in the absence of Case, the empty category in the specifier position of AP cannot be identified as a variable, despite the presence of a potential A'-binder.

A further set of data which find an interesting explanation in the context of these proposals are strings like the following:

(38)  a.  *Des cerises, tu en as trop mangé de vertes.*
          'Some cherries you of-them have too-many eaten of
          greens.'

      b.  *Des chevaux, j'en ai beaucoup vu d'absolument
          magnifiques.*
          'Some horses I of-them have many seen of absolutely
          magnificent.'

What is characteristic of these structures is the configuration of *de* plus adjective. The presence here of the Case marker *de*, despite the fact that no noun is present, can be accounted for as follows. The pronominal form seen here is the *en-partitif* form referred to in §2.1 — this is a pronominal form which is linked to an N' position. Bearing in mind that N' must be a recursive node in the Romance NP in order to generate structures such as (39):

(39)  [$_{NP}$ *les* [$_{N'}$ *beaux* [$_{N'}$ *petits* [$_{N'}$ [$_{N}$ *jardins*] *anglais*]]]]
      'the lovely little gardens English'

it is clear then that the structures of the NP objects in (38) could be analysed as here:

(40)    a.

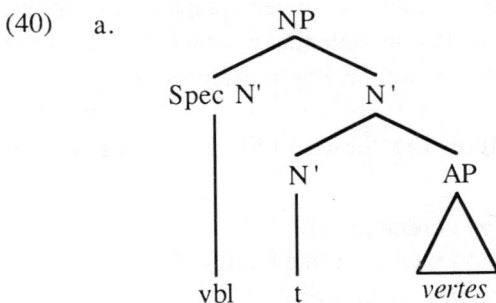

b.

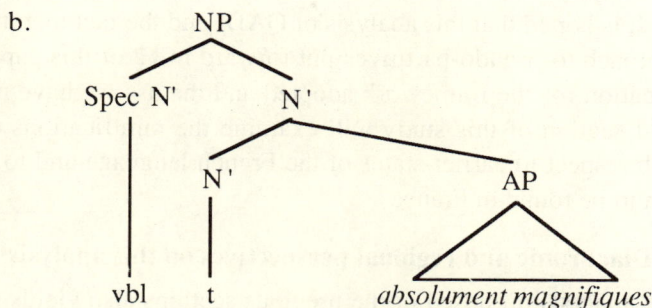

Now from these analyses, it can be seen that, even after the pronominalization of the N', the context for the *de*-Insertion rule (see (30)) is met. A further possible argument in favour of the necessity of *de* here is that attributive adjectives need to be able to be marked with the Case of the head N of the NP in which they are generated. Since in (38) the vbl absorbs the Case assigned by the verb, it must be concluded that the Case marker *de* is inserted in order to provide a Case feature for the adjectives still left within NP.

A third and final consequence of this proposed analysis of QAD is that it provides an account of the ungrammaticality of structures such as

(41) a.  ?**Ce livre m'a beaucoup coûté* [NP vbl *d'argent*]
'This book me has much cost of money.'

b.  **Combien a pesé ce colis* [NP vbl *de grammes*]?
'How-much has weighed this parcel of grams?'

The above data contrast noticeably with their non-QAD equivalents:

(42) a.  *Ce livre m'a coûté* [NP *beaucoup d'argent*]
'This book me has cost much of money.'

b.  [NP *Combien de grammes*] *a pesé ce colis?*
'How-much of grams has weighed this parcel?'

Quite simply, in the context of the analysis proposed here, the NPs shown in (42), which are traditionally analysed as adverbial in nature, will not be considered to be in an A-position (or to form part of an A-position), in the sense that the NP does not receive a θ-role from the verb (see Smith (1991; 1992)). Therefore, one crucial part of the definition of the variable fails to be met in the structures (41), and so QAD cannot result.

It is hoped that this analysis of QAD, and the fact that it is based on the approach to pseudo-partitives put forward in §2 of this paper, provide justification for the framework adopted and the use we have made of it. The final section of this study will examine the ramifications of this analysis with respect to earlier states of the French language and to dialectal variation to be found in France.

## 3. Diachronic and regional perspectives on this analysis

The analysis proposed in the previous sections also yields some insightful perspectives with respect to diachronic data from French (§3.1) and data from regional variation in French and other Gallo-Romance dialects (§3.2). In as much as our approach to the problem of quantifiers offers an account of the empirical data of Old French and regional varieties of Gallo-Romance, we include the following sections as useful corroboration of the framework which has been proposed in the previous discussion.

### 3.1. Quantification in Old French

If we consider the phenomenology of quantification in a diachronic perspective with respect to French, then two features appear: first, that there has been a definite shift from adjectival to nominal quantification during the Old French period; and, second, that the group of nominal quantifiers is, at present, a locus of lexical productivity.

Examples of the change from adjectival to nominal quantifiers are most clearly exemplified in Old French by the behaviour of the word *tant* and *assez*,[14] as in the following, roughly contemporaneous examples:

(43) a. *Sire Alexis, tanz jurz t'ai desirrat.*
         'Lord Alexis many days you-have (I) wished-for.'
         (*Saint Alexis*, cit. Aspland 1978:16)

     b. *J'ay assas robes, car de joliveté ne me chault.*
         'I've enough clothes for of fashion not me bothers.'
         (Rychner (ed.) 1964:24)

     c. *Et voit assez gent amassee ! qui a grant mervoille*
         *l'esgardent.*
         'And (he) sees enough people gathered / who in great
             marvel him-watch.'
         (Chrétien de Troyes, cit. Foulet 1928:66)

(44) a. *Par foi ... ge oi / tant d'eise com ge avoir poi.*
'By faith I have / so-much of pleasure as I can have.'
(Chrétien de Troyes, cit. Foulet 1928:64)

b. *De cers, de biches, de cheveus / ocist asez par le boscage.*
'Of deer, of hind, of horses / (he) killed enough in the
wood.'
(Béroul, cit. Foulet 1928:64).

We propose that *tant* and *assez* in (43) behave as adjectives; this is clear
from the number and gender agreement seen with *tant*, but is more theory-
internal with *assez*, where no overt indication of agreement is seen. In
(44), the same items appear to have been reclassified lexically as nominal
in status in the terms of our analysis, because of the presence of the Case
marker *de*. Interestingly, the same shift of lexical classification can be
identified in the now defunct lexical item *molt/mout*. This is usually considered to be an adjective and certainly it is in this guise that it is usually
attested in the Old French period, as example (45) shows:

(45) *[D]esus un fort puncel, / U mult home periseient*
'Upon a strong little-bridge / Where many men perished
(*The Voyage of St Brendan*, cit. Aspland 1978:17).

However, in the context of this study, it is worth noting that in the Middle
French period *molt/mout* does appear to have undergone a degree of lexical
reclassification before it finally disappears from the language:

(46) *... pluseurs aultres ont travaillé en mout de manieres a
moustrer la douleur qui y est.*
'... several others have worked in many of ways to show the
sorrow that in-it (there)is.'
(Rychner (ed.) 1964:3-4)

Besides the change in lexical categorization of the items *assez, tant* and
probably *mout/molt*, there has also been the 'eviction', as it were, of other
quantifier adjectives such as *quant*, and *maint*[15] as in:

(47) a. *Quantes heures sont?*
'How-many hours are?'
(Rabelais, cit. Grandsaignes d'Hauterive 1947:487)

    b.  *[O]t Erec mainz presanz.*
       'Had Eric many gifts.'
       (Chrétien de Troyes, cit. Aspland 1978:78).

But, of course, the most noticeable aspect of these diachronic shifts in the
lexical classification of quantifiers is the influx of what are clearly nouns
into the group of words used as quantifiers in Old French (e.g, *point, pas,
mie*). The last three of these are clearly nominal in character and the ety-
mology of *beaucoup* (*beau* plus *coup*) is again clearly nominal. Indeed the
class of nominal quantifiers still appears today to be an area where new
lexical creativity (or reanalysis) is taking place — hence the underlined
(new?) forms in the following examples:

    (48)  a.  <u>*Grand/bon nombre d'interprétations*</u> *sont possibles.*
          'Many/good number of interpretations are possible.'
        b.  *Le bateau a déplacé* <u>*quantité d'eau*</u>.
          'The boat has displaced lots of water.'
        c.  *Nous avons acheté* <u>*pas mal de livres*</u> *cette année.*
          'We have bought not bad of books this year.'
          (i.e., quite a few).
        d.  *J'y ai consacré* <u>*un paquet de temps*</u>.
          'I to-it have given a lot of time.'

Also interesting, but perhaps more problematic to account for precisely in
the context of this study, is what appears to be the reanalysis of adverbs as
nominal items (requiring Case marking, in the terms of our analysis) in the
following examples:

    (49)  a.  *J'ai lu énormément de livres.*
          'I've read enormously of books.'
        b.  *Pierre veut éliminer tellement de papiers qu'on va les
            brûler dans le jardin.*
          'Peter wants to-eliminate so-many of papers that one is
            going them to-burn in the garden.'
        c.  *Davantage d'articles seront publiés l'année prochaine.*
          'More of articles will-be published the next year.'
        d.  *Nous avons déjà suffisamment de problèmes.*
          'We have already sufficiently of problems.'

Another reanalysis that has taken place is the reclassification of *plein* as a nominal quantifier as in :

(50)  *Elle m'a donné plein de conseils.*
       'She me-has given full of advice.' (i.e., lots of advice)

Thus the shift towards nominal quantifiers in French seems to be very strong, and contrasts quite strikingly with the more conservative nature of quantification in many other Romance languages, such as Italian and Spanish.

## 3.2. Quantification in other Romance varieties in France

Further corroboration of the point of view adopted in this study can be adduced from data taken from regional varieties of Romance spoken within France. If one examines closely the lexical items in some of these varieties, what is most striking is the variety of different expressions which exist and the general trend for there to be both adjectival and nominal quantifiers to some, but different, extents in these varieties. Consider first data from the Picard dialect (taken from Debrie 1983):

(51) a.  *Yo gramin d' chirtchulasyon din l' vile.*
          'There-is a lot of traffic in the town.'
     b.  *Si t' avwé in molé d' jinjin...*
          'If you had a little of intelligence...'
     c.  *I n' yo pu tan d' armano din ché famile.*
          'There not are any longer so-many of almanacs in families.'
     d.  *Quéqu' geins fin riches.*
          'Some people very rich.'

Here it would seem that *gramin de*[16] corresponds to *beaucoup de* in Standard French; *in molé de* to *un peu de*, and *tan de* to *autant de*. There is, of course, adjectival quantification in the form of *quéque* (corresponding to *quelque* in Standard French). In this Romance variety it would appear (admittedly from rather scant evidence) that nominal and adjectival quantifiers are to be found, and basically they seem to be distributed over the same semantic field, although in the case of *gramin* and *molé* their etymological source is different.

If attention is turned to Romance varieties spoken in Southern France, then the picture becomes more complex. In Gascon the following data are attested (examples from Grosclaude 1977):

(52) a. *Un païs ou i a hèra de petitas proprietas.*
        'A village where there are many of little farms.'
     b. *Quant de dias i a dens ua setmana?*
        'How-many of days there are in a week?'
     c. *Pas pro d'espitaus tanpoc.*
        'Not enough of hospitals either.'

In these data *hèra de* corresponds to *beaucoup de*; *quant de* to *combien de*; and *pro de* to *assez de*. From the sources consulted, no adjectival quantifiers could be found, but this is not to imply that they do not exist. What is of interest here is that there is a similar lexical distribution of nominal quantifiers as in French, but clearly their origins are different.

Occitan again shows a different array of lexical items, but here the presence of adjectival quantifiers is more in evidence (data from Nouvel 1975):

(53) a. *La lenga nòstra s'ensenha dins força països.*
        'The language ours is-taught in many villages.'
     b. *Es aquí qu'estudiet Rabelais e un fum de grands omes
         coma Paul Valéri.*
        '(It) is here that-studied Rabelais and a lot of great men
         like Paul Valéry.'
     c. *I a plan d'autres meravilhas a Tolosa.*
        'There are lots of other marvels in Toulouse.'
     d. *Quanta ora es?*
        'How-many hour is-it?'
        (i.e., What time is it?)
     e. *Quant monde!*
        'How-many people!'

These examples show that *quant* (as in Old French) is still adjectival in nature and has not undergone reanalysis as a noun (as it has in the Gascon example (52b)). Similarly, we find the opposite tendency to the one identified in Standard French; instead of an adjective becoming a noun, *força* (a noun) appears in (53a) to have been reanalysed as an adjective (at least in the sense that it neither absorbs the Case of the verb nor requires insertion of the Case marker *de*; but the lack of agreement may be considered a problem for this kind of approach).

The broad aim of this subsection has been met in pinpointing the lexical diversity to be found within this semantic field in Romance varieties spoken in France. This diversity can be accounted for within the framework of this study by making reference to the shift from adjectival-type quantifiers to nominal-type quantifiers — a type of lexical variation which seems, in the context of the Romance languages, to be more or less unique to the Gallo-Romance linguistic area.[17]

## 4. Conclusions

This paper has sought to motivate an analysis of pseudo-partitive structures in French within the context of Government-Binding theory. Central to its argumentation is the contention that QP is, as Bresnan said, a 'temporary convenience', and that, in fact, treating quantifier items as being syntactically heterogeneous and, in particular, the proposal that some quantifiers be classed as nouns yields insights into the QAD structures of Modern French, as well as into diachronic and geographical variation in French and closely related Romance varieties.

## Notes

\*   This paper has been presented in a couple of versions; the first of which was at a conference entitled 'Le français dans sa diversité géographique et sociale' held at the University of Salford in March 1989 and the second at the Manoir de Brion conference on 'The Romance Languages and Current Linguistic Theory'. I would like to thank the participants in Salford and at the Manoir de Brion for their stimulating remarks. I have tried to take account of the comments made as far as is possible. I would like to express a particular word of thanks to J.-P. Watbled and Marie-Anne Hintze for their patient help with the data. All errors and misinterpretations are my own.

1.   A detailed study of the question of the syntactic status or otherwise of the category QP (Klein 1980) has much influenced my thinking about the status of the so-called quantifiers in Romance. I do not wish to imply, however, that Klein would endorse my interpretation of his ideas.

2.   Jackendoff (1977:31-3) does propose a different set of primitive syntactic features to distinguish the four lexical categories A, N, P, V. These features also succeed in defining the 'minor' lexical categories of English. I shall not, however, pursue the possibilities offered by Jackendoff's framework here. See also Abney (1987) for a similar *mise en cause* of the classic Chomskyan lexical primes.

3.   Although it should be noted that Gérard (1980), in her study of exclamative structures in French, has proposed a very extensive expansion of a class of exclamative complementizers, but her ideas remain an isolated example of an analysis which allows major

lexical creativity to take place in this class of grammatical formatives. It should also be noted that Radford (1983) has argued at some length against Gérard's proposals.

4. Present day orthographical conventions can generally reflect the suffixal nominal morphology of earlier states of the French language (see Pope 1952:302-315).

5. An anonymous reviewer of this article has pointed out that in Italian NPs containing a possessive (e.g., *il mio professore* (lit., 'the my teacher'), *la mia spada* (lit., 'the my sword'), etc.) might be interpreted as containing two determiners. We would argue that such an interpretation would be wrong as in Italian the possessives (i.e., *mio, tuo,* etc.) are adjectives and not determiners, hence the possibility of the collocations shown here.

6. In addition to the problem of the difference in the interpretation of the scope of the quantifier, it would seem that other conditions affect the realization of QAD structures. Consider the following examples drawn from Obenauer (1983:70-71):

    (i)  a.   *Le critique a apprécié peu de films.*
             'The critic has appreciated few of films.'
        b.   *Son regard a impressionné beaucoup de minettes.*
             'His glance has stunned many of chicks.'
        c.   *La réorganisation a accéléré beaucoup de procédures.*
             'The reorganization has speeded-up many of procedures.'
    (ii)  a.   *\*Le critique a peu apprécié de films.*
        b.   *\*Son regard a beaucoup impressionné de minettes.*
        c.   *\*La réorganisation a beaucoup accéléré de procédures.*

For the purposes of this study, Obenauer's account of these ungrammatical structures will be accepted. He proposes (*op. cit.*) that the interpretation of a QAD structure is subject to the following principle: 'Dans la structure ... QP V [NP [QP e] de ... ] ..., la quantification est obtenue "indirectement", à savoir, via V, et plus précisément via QP V.' (*ibid.*:74). Thus the ungrammaticality of the sentences in (ii) derives from the nature of the verb contained in the predicate and does not have a direct influence on my analysis of QAD.

7. This remark does not preclude the class of quantifiers of which *beaucoup, trop* and *assez* are members from being generated under the determiner position in NP, however.

8. The 'classic' study of N' pronominalization in the generative tradition is probably Belletti & Rizzi's (1981) study of the phenomenology of *ne* in Italian. Their arguments with respect to *ne* in Italian are, for the most part, equally applicable to French *en*.

9. It was suggested at the Manoir de Brion conference that *beaucoup des cheminées* (a true partitive structure) appears not to give rise to *en-avant* configurations. This is problematical for the argument put forward in the text. However Milner (1978:69) gives the following contrasting data (admitting though that 'les exemples [sont] peu clairs' (*loc. cit.*)) in favour of *en-avant* from partitive structures headed by items such as *beaucoup* and *deux*, but not from pseudo-partitive structures containing the same items:

    (i)    *\*Des pommes, beaucoup/deux en sont jetées.*
         'Some apples many/two of-them are rotten.'
    (ii)   *Ces pommes, beaucoup/deux en sont jetées.*
         'These apples many/two of-them are rotten.'

10. The more orthodox version of the filter is: '\*NP if NP has no phonetic content and has no Case' (Chomsky 1981:42). The use of this version of the filter to explain the ungrammaticality of examples like *\*J'ai beaucoup livres* in the context of the analysis I am proposing would be no simple matter. My analysis would have to study the prob-

lem of Case percolation within NP and the repercussions of absorption of Case on percolation. Such a topic would be material for another article!

11. For further reflections on the ramifications of this analysis on Theta theory and the Projection Principle, see Battye (1987:19-20).

12. A full account of those lexical items which can participate in QAD is beyond the scope of this article, but it would seem that there are three types of nominal quantifier: those that can participate in QAD; those that have to participate in QAD, and those that cannot.

Examples of the first group would be: *beaucoup, tant, peu, trop, assez, plus, moins, énormément, tellement, davantage, vachement, suffisamment*. Some slightly problematical cases are to be found, as with the following which not all informants accept:

    (i)    *??J'ai autant lu de livres que toi.*
            'I've as-many read of books as you.'

    (ii)   *??J'ai tout autant lu de livres que toi.*
            'I've just as-many read of books as you.'

    (iii)  *??J'ai très peu vu d'erreurs.*
            'I've very few seen of errors.'

    (iv)  *??J'ai beaucoup moins vu de films cette année.*
            'I've many less seen of films this year.'

In the second class of nominal quantifiers, we find *pas, point,* and *plus* (negative), which are ungrammatical here:

    (v)   *Je n'ai lu pas de livres.*
            'I not-have read not of books.'

    (vi)  *Je n'ai lu point de livres.*
            'I not-have read not of books.'

    (vii) *Je n'ai lu plus de livres.*
            'I not-have read more of books.'

The nominal quantifiers which are not mobile are: *quantité, bon/grand nombre, un paquet, plein, un kilo,* etc.

    (viii) *J'ai quantité mangé de pommes.*
            'I've a-lot eaten of apples.'

    (ix)  *J'ai bon/grand nombre mangé de pommes.*
            'I've good/large number eaten of apples.'

    (x)   *J'ai un paquet mangé de pommes.*
            'I've a lot eaten of apples.'

    (xi)  *J'ai plein mangé de pommes.*
            'I've full eaten of apples.' (i.e., many)

    (xii) *J'ai un kilo mangé de pommes.*
            'I've a kilo eaten of apples.'

Before the restrictions on QAD structures can be fully understood, much more work needs to be done on the distribution of adverbial constituents in general, and, in particular, the precise conditions governing the intervention of adverbial constituents between auxiliaries and past participles in Romance need to be looked into.

I thank both J.-P. Watbled and Marie-Anne Hintze for their help in sorting out the data presented in this note.

.3. This structure is based on notes taken during Richard Kayne's syntax seminar held at the Salzburg Summer school in August 1985.

.4. A further quantifier related to *tout* and *assez* is *trop*, which according to Bloch-Wartburg (cit. Grevisse 1980:477) derives from the Frankish word *\*throp*. It offers a dif-

ferent but none the less interesting perspective in the context of this study, since in
French this quantifier item is nominal in status:

    (i)    *Trop de problèmes se sont posés.*
           'Too-many of problems themselves have posed.'

but the same reflex of the Frankish original gives an adjectival quantifier in Italian:

    (ii)   *Si sono presentati troppi problemi.*
           'Themselves have presented too-many problems.'

15. Of course, *maint* still survives in certain *formes figées*, such as *à maintes reprises*.
16. Marie-Anne Hintze (personal communication) has suggested that the Picard form
    *gramin* is related to the standard French from *grandement*. Considering our observa-
    tions in the previous section concerning *énormément*, etc., in Standard French, this
    adverb-to-noun reanalysis in quantifier structures is not at all surprising.
17. But see Battye (1990) for some reflections on this area of syntax in two Northern
    Italian dialects.

# References

Abney, S. 1987. *The English Noun Phrase in its Sentential Aspect.*
    Unpublished Ph.D. dissertation, MIT.

Aspland, B. 1978. *A Medieval French Reader.* Oxford: Oxford
    University Press.

Battye, A. C. 1987. Quantificatori nominali in francese. *Ipotesi e
    applicazioni di teoria linguistica dal XIII incontro di grammatica
    generativa,* ed. P. Cordin, 9-27. Trento: Università di Trento.

———. 1990. La quantificazione nominale: il veneto e l'italiano a
    confronto con il genovese e il francese. *Annali di Ca' Foscari* 29, 27-
    44.

———. 1991. Partitive and pseudo-partitive revisited: reflections on the
    status of *de* in French. *Journal of French Language Studies* 1, 21-43.

Belletti, A. & Rizzi, L. 1981. The syntax of *ne*: some theoretical
    implications. *The Linguistic Review* 1, 117-154.

Borer, H. 1984. *Parametric Syntax.* Dordrecht: Foris.

Bresnan, J. 1973. Syntax of the comparative clause construction in
    English. *Linguistic Inquiry* 4, 275-343.

Chomsky, N. 1970. Remarks on nominalization. *Readings in English
    Transformational Grammar,* ed. R. Jacobs & P. Rosenbaum, 11-61.
    Waltham, Mass: Ginn.

————. 1974. The Amherst Lectures, presented at 1974 Linguistics Institute. Documents Linguistiques, Université de Paris VII.

————. 1977. On *wh*-movement. *Formal Syntax*, ed. P. W. Culicover, T. Wasow & A. Akmajian, 71-132. New York: Academic Press.

————. 1981. *Lectures on Government and Binding*. Dordrecht: Foris.

————. 1986. *Barriers*. Cambridge, Mass.: MIT Press (*Linguistic Inquiry Monographs* 13).

Debrie, R. 1983. *Eche pikar bèl a rade*. Paris: Omnivox.

Foulet, L. 1928. *Petite Syntaxe de l'ancien français*. Paris: Champion.

Gérard, J. 1980. *L'Exclamation en français*. Tübingen: Niemeyer (Linguistische Arbeiten 85).

Grandsaignes d'Hauterive, R. 1947. *Dictionnaire d'ancien français*. Paris: Larousse.

Grevisse, M. 1980. *Le Bon Usage* (11ème édition). Paris & Gembloux: Duculot.

Grosclaude, M. 1977. *Lo gascon lèu e plan*. Paris: Omnivox.

Hall Partee, B. 1975. Comments on C. J. Fillmore's and N. Chomsky's papers. *The Scope of American Linguistics*, ed. R. Austerlitz, 197-209. Lisse: Peter de Ridder.

Hark, I. 1982. On clitic *en* in French. *Journal of Linguistic Research* 1, 134-175.

Jackendoff, R. 1977. *X-bar Syntax: a study of phrase structure*. Cambridge, Mass: MIT Press (*Linguistic Inquiry* Monographs 2).

Klein, E. 1980. Determiners and the category Q. Ms, University of Sussex.

Longobardi, G. & Giorgi, A. 1991. *The Syntax of NPs: configurations, parameters and empty categories*. Cambridge: Cambridge University Press.

Milner, J.-C. 1978. *De la Syntaxe à l'interprétation*. Paris: Seuil.

Nouvel, A. 1975. *L'Occitan sans peine*. Chennièvres-sur-Marne: Assimil.

Obenauer, H.-G. 1983. Une quantification non-canonique: La quantification à distance. *Langue française* 58, 66-88.

————. 1984. On the identification of empty categories. *The Linguistic Review* 4, 153-202.

Pinkham, J. 1982. The formation of comparative clauses in French and English. Mimeo, Indiana University Linguistics Club.

Pollock, J.-Y. 1986. Sur la syntaxe de *en* et le paramètre du sujet nul. *La Grammaire modulaire*, ed. M. Ronat & D. Couquaux, 211-246. Paris: Minuit.

Pope, M. K. 1952. *From Latin to Modern French.* Manchester: Manchester University Press.

Radford, A, 1983. The status of exclamative particles in Modern French. Ms, Università di Padova.

————. 1988. Small children's small clauses. *Transactions of the Philological Society* 86, 1-43.

Rouveret, A. & Vergnaud, J.-R. 1980. Specifying reference to subject: French causatives and conditions on representations. *Linguistic Inquiry* 11, 97-202.

Ruwet, N. 1972. *Théorie syntaxique et syntaxe du français.* Paris: Seuil.

Rychner, J. (ed.) 1964. *Les XV Joyes de mariage.* Paris: Champion.

Selkirk, E. 1977. Some remarks on Noun Phrase structure. *Formal Syntax*, ed. P. W. Culicover, T. Wasow & A. Akmajian, 285-316. New York: Academic Press.

Smith, J. C. 1991. Themacity and 'object'-participle agreement in Romance. *New Analyses in Romance Linguistics: papers from the Linguistic Symposium on Romance Languages 18*, ed. D. Wanner & D. A. Kibbee, 335-352. Amsterdam: Benjamins.

————. 1992. Circumstantial complements and direct objects in the Romance languages: configuration, Case, and thematic structure. *Thematic Structure: its role in grammar*, ed. I. M. Roca, 293-316. Berlin: Foris.

Sportiche, D. 1989. Syntactic movement: constraints and parameters. Handout for talk, GLOW Colloquium, Utrecht.

Stowell, T. 1981. *Origins of Phrase Structure.* Unpublished Ph.D. dissertation, MIT.

Tranel, B. 1987. *The Sounds of French.* Cambridge: Cambridge University Press.

Vergnaud, J.-R. 1974. *French Relative Clauses*. Unpublished Ph.D. dissertation, MIT.

Wheeler, M. This volume. 'Underspecification' and 'misagreement' in Catalan lexical specifiers. 201-229.

# The prepositional accusative in Sardinian: its distribution and syntactic repercussions

## Michael Allan Jones
*University of Essex*

## 0. Introduction.

This paper is concerned with the use of the preposition *a* before certain types of direct object NPs in Sardinian. Our discussion of this phenomenon is divided into three sections. Firstly, we shall investigate the conditions under which 'accusative' *a* occurs, primarily in terms of the internal properties of the direct object NP. In the second section we shall discuss the implications of this analysis for the categorial status of certain items which have a 'pronominal' function. The third section is devoted to an examination of a range of cases where the distinction between accusative and dative complements is somewhat blurred, possibly as a result of the prepositional accusative phenomenon.

The evidence on which this study is based was elicited from a number of native informants from the Central-Eastern area of Sardinia. We have also consulted various contemporary prose texts from different dialect areas in order to check our findings against a wider empirical base. Our investigation reveals some degree of variation in the use of accusative *a* and related phenomena, which we have noted, but without attempting to identify the geographical, social, or stylistic correlates of this variation, our main concern being to isolate the grammatical factors which determine the phenomena under discussion.

The orthographic conventions which we have adopted are broadly in line with those advocated by Pittau (1978), adapted somewhat to reflect the phonology and morphology of the dialect of our principal informants (from the Bitti-Lula area); see Jones (1993) for details. Attested examples from our written corpus are, however, cited in their original spelling.

## 1. Distribution of accusative *a*

The prepositional accusative phenomenon is illustrated in (1):

(1) a. *Appo vistu a Juanne.*
       'I saw John.'
    b. *Appo vistu solu a isse.*
       'I saw only him.'
    c. *Appo vistu a frate tuo.*
       'I saw your brother.'
    d. *Appo vistu a babbu.*
       'I saw father.'
    e. *Appo vistu a duttore Ledda.*
       'I saw Doctor Ledda.'
    f. *Appo vistu a Nápoli.*
       'I have seen Naples.'

In these examples, the object NP must be introduced by the preposition *a*, which normally indicates an indirect object relation, even though the verb *vídere* 'see' is quite clearly transitive, as can be seen from the examples in (2) where the object NP cannot be preceded by *a* (or indeed any other preposition):

(2) a. *Appo vistu (\*a) su frore/su cane/sa mákkina.*
       'I saw the flower/the dog/the car.'
    b. *Appo vistu (\*a) unu pastore.*
       'I saw a shepherd.'
    c. *Appo vistu (\*a) metas sordatos.*
       'I saw many soldiers.'

In the above examples, we have used the same verb throughout in order to show that the presence or absence of *a* before a direct object is due to properties of the object NP rather than to properties of the verb. However, the same facts hold for all transitive verbs, including the verb *áere* 'have' and verbs which take an indirect object in addition to the direct object:

(3) a  *Jeo so tottu solu, ma tue as a Maria.*
       'I am all alone, but you have Maria.'
    b. *Amus mandatu a Juanne a Núgoro.*
       'We sent John to Nuoro.'
    c. *Amus presentatu a Pretu a Maria.*
       'We introduced Peter to Mary.'

(4) a. *Jeo so tottu solu, ma tue as (\*a) una mudzere.*
'I am all alone, but you have a wife.'

b. *Amus mandatu (\*a) sa líttera a Núgoro.*
'We sent the letter to Nuoro.'

c. *Amus presentatu (\*a) unu cumpandzu a Maria.*
'We introduced a friend to Mary.'

The examples in (1-2) are representative of clear-cut cases where the use of the prepositional accusative is either obligatory or excluded. There is a further, intermediate range of cases where judgements are much less certain; namely NPs with human reference which are introduced by a definite or demonstrative article. For some speakers, the use of accusative *a* with NPs of this type is possible, but not obligatory, with varying degrees of acceptability (the symbol '%' is used here and throughout to indicate acceptability for some but not all speakers):

(5) a. *Appo vistu (%a) su mere/su duttore/su re.*
'I saw the boss/the doctor/the king.'

b. *Appo vistu (%a) su duttore de Rosaria.*
'I saw Rosaria's doctor.'

c. *Appo vistu (%?a) cudd'ómine.*
'I saw that man.'

d. *Appo vistu (%??a) s'ómine k'at iscrittu cussu libru.*
'I saw the man that wrote that book.'

e. *Appo vistu (%?a) sas pitzinnas.*
'I saw the girls.'

In these cases, the use of *a* tends to be most natural with singular NPs which have a minimal descriptive content; i.e., the information conveyed by the head noun (and possibly its complement) is sufficient to identify the intended referent (as in (5a,b)). Accusative *a* occurs much less readily with plural NPs (as in (5e)) and in cases where deictic cues (e.g., the demonstrative in (5c)) or additional descriptive information (e.g., the relative clause in (5d)) are required in order to establish reference. Broadly speaking, the NPs which allow accusative *a* most readily are those which can be construed as 'titles', with a function similar to that of proper names.

From the examples we have looked at so far it seems clear that the distribution of accusative *a* cannot be defined in terms of a single property or combination of properties of the direct object NP. There is, to be true, a strong correlation between the presence of accusative *a* and definite, human reference of the object NP, but this correlation cannot be stated as a necessary or sufficient condition. The fact that accusative *a* is obligatory before a place name (example (1f)) shows that human reference is not a necessary condition for the occurrence of accusative *a*. Similarly, we may note that accusative *a* is obligatory before a proper name referring to an animal, as in (6), where *Ercole* may be taken as referring to a horse:

> (6)   *Appo vistu a Ercole.*
>       'I saw Hercules.'

Within an approach based on the features [±human] and [±definite], examples like (1f) and (6) would have to be treated as special cases subject to a separate condition; e.g., 'Accusative *a* occurs before definite NPs with human reference and before proper names regardless of their reference.'. A further problem with this approach is that it fails to distinguish between the obligatory uses of accusative *a* exemplified in (1) and the more marginal and, at best, optional uses in (5). The difficulty is that the marginal, optional cases are subsumed under the condition which covers a subset of the obligatory cases, whereas the remaining obligatory cases (non-human proper names) are treated as falling under a quite separate condition. In other words, not only does this approach require the distribution of accusative *a* to be defined in terms of a disjunction of conditions, but this disjunction is orthogonal to the distinction between obligatory and optional cases.

An alternative approach is to define the distribution of accusative *a* in terms of structural properties of the object NP. Note in this connection that all the direct object NPs in (1) lack a determiner. Obviously, this property cannot provide the basis for a uniform account of the prepositional accusative in Sardinian any more than the semantically based approach envisaged above, because of the examples in (5). Nevertheless, this approach does draw the line between the clear, obligatory cases in (1) and the more marginal, optional cases in (5) in a way which is consistent with native speakers' judgements. Thus, it may be argued that the obligatory use of accusative *a* is triggered by the absence of a determiner, whereas the more peripheral uses in (5) are governed by other factors (e.g., definite human reference).

A difficulty for this approach is raised by the indefinite use of plural or non-count nouns without a determiner, as in (7):

(7)  a.  *Appo vistu (\*a) dzente.*
         'I saw people.'
     b.  *Appo bitu (\*a) latte.*
         'I drank milk.'
     c.  *Appo mandicatu (\*a) meleddas.*
         'I ate apples.'

As indicated, accusative *a* is totally excluded with these NPs, even though they fulfil the structural criteria envisaged above. One way round this problem would be to reintroduce the notion of definiteness into our characterization of the core cases; e.g., 'Accusative *a* is obligatory before definite NPs which lack a determiner.'. Alternatively, one might postulate that there is a structural difference between the NPs in (7) and those in (1) in that the former may be held to contain a null determiner, whereas the latter lack a determiner position altogether, as shown in (8):

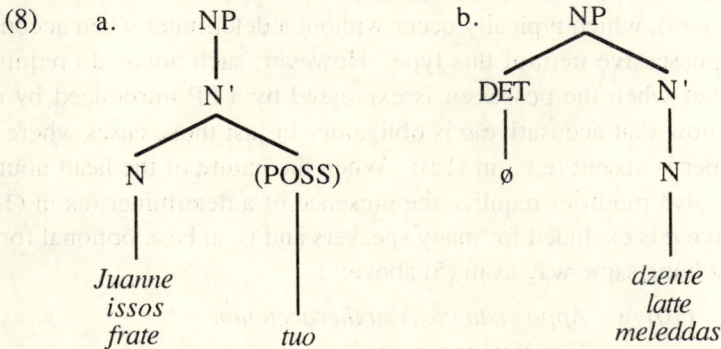

(8)  a.              NP                    b.              NP
                    /  \                                 /  \
                        N'                          DET       N'
                      /   \                           |        |
                    N    (POSS)                        ø        N

               *Juanne*                                      *dzente*
               *issos*                                        *latte*
               *frate*              *tuo*                    *meleddas*

If the structural distinction in (8) is valid, accusative *a* can be defined as occurring obligatorily before NPs which lack a determiner position. An advantage of this approach is that it allows the core cases of accusative *a* to be accounted for in purely structural terms, without need to refer to semantic criteria such as definiteness. Nevertheless, we should point out that there are other semantic restrictions, which cannot plausibly be recast in terms of syntactic properties. In particular, metalinguistic and metonymic uses of proper nouns do not allow accusative *a*:

(9)   a.   *Li nan (\*a) Marieddu.*
           'They call him Marieddu.'
           (Lit. 'They say to him Marieddu.')
      b.   *Appo lessu (\*a) Marx.*
           'I have read Marx.'

We shall not attempt to choose between these two approaches to cases of
the type in (7). For the purposes of exposition, we shall assume the approach based on the structural distinction in (8).

Positive support for the hypothesis that the absence of a determiner
plays a crucial role in the distribution of accusative *a* is provided by cases
involving possessive items such as *tuo* 'your', as in (1c). We assume that
such items are not determiners but modifiers of some sort, akin to adjectives. Unlike determiners, they normally follow the noun, as do adjectives.
Moreover, with most types of noun, they must be accompanied by a determiner in the prenominal position (e.g., *su libru tuo* [the book your] 'your
book'). The principal exceptions to this generalization are kinship nouns,
such as *frate* 'brother' in (1c), and terms of endearment (e.g., *amore meu*
'my love'), which typically occur without a determiner when accompanied
by a possessive item of this type. However, such nouns do require a determiner when the possessor is expressed by a PP introduced by *de* 'of'.
Note now that accusative *a* is obligatory in just those cases where the determiner is absent (e.g., in (1c)). When the nature of the head noun or the
possessive modifier requires the presence of a determiner (as in (10)), accusative *a* is excluded for many speakers and is, at best, optional for others,
in much the same way as in (5) above:

(10)  a.   *Appo vistu (%a) su theraccu tuo.*
           'I saw your servant.'
      b.   *Appo vistu (%a) su frate de Lukia.*
           'I saw Lucy's brother.'

Clearly, the contrast between (1c) and (10) cannot be attributed to semantic
properties such as humanness or definiteness, nor can it be explained in
terms of the type of head element (as one might be tempted to conclude for
cases involving proper nouns or disjunctive pronouns). Thus, in these
cases, the absence of a determiner is the only factor which characterizes the
obligatory use of accusative *a*.

Returning now to the marginal cases in (5), it is important to recall that, for some speakers, the variants with *a* are totally excluded. Consequently, for these speakers, a condition formulated in terms of the absence of a determiner provides an adequate account of all uses of accusative *a*. Moreover, even for those speakers who do accept these instances of the prepositional accusative, the variants without *a* are always possible and are generally preferred, hence our conclusion that these cases fall under a set of conditions different from those which define the core cases. We submit that it is only in these cases (NPs with a definite determiner) that human reference is a relevant factor, though the vast majority of NPs which satisfy the core condition also happen to refer to human beings (e.g., disjunctive pronouns, kinship terms and, for the most part, proper nouns). Our earlier observation that accusative *a* tends to occur most readily with definite NPs which function as 'titles' suggests that the prepositional accusatives in (5) may be due to a process of analogy whereby some speakers have extended the use of accusative *a*, optionally, to NPs which do not satisfy the structural condition which defines the core cases, but which do have the semantic or referential properties which are typical of the core cases (i.e., definite human reference with a minimum of descriptive content).

Our conclusions concerning the conditions under which accusative *a* may or must occur are summarized in (11):

(11) I.  Accusative *a* is obligatory before direct object NPs which lack a determiner position (structure (8a)).

II.  For some speakers, accusative *a* occurs optionally before direct object NPs introduced by a definite or demonstrative article which refer to human beings, particularly NPs which function as 'titles'.

The rules in (11) apply regardless of the surface position of the direct object. Thus, accusative *a* is obligatory before fronted or dislocated direct object NPs which conform to the condition in (11.I):

(12) a.  *A Maria appo vistu.*
'Mary I saw.'

b.  *A isse, non l' appo vistu.*
'Him, I have not seen.'

c.  *Non l' appo vistu, a frate tuo.*
'I have not seen him, your brother.'

For the marginal cases covered by (11.II) the optional use of *a* appears to be more prevalent when the direct object is fronted or left dislocated; e.g., for the relevant speakers, *a* tends to occur more readily in cases like (13) than in comparable examples like (5a), where the direct object is in the canonical postverbal position:

> (13)  a.  *(%A) su duttore appo vistu.*
> 'The doctor I saw.'
> b.  *(%A) su mere, non l'at vistu neune.*
> 'The boss, nobody has seen him.'

We suggest that this is due to the fact that *a* serves a functional purpose in these cases, indicating that the initial NP is to be parsed as an object rather than a subject.

The prepositional accusative phenomenon is not restricted to direct objects of verbs, but occurs also with the objects of some prepositions, notably the 'comparative' prepositions *comente* 'like', *ke* 'as' and *cantu* 'as much as':[1]

> (14)  a.  *Lukia est bella cantu/comente/ke a Maria.*
> 'Lucy is as beautiful as Mary.'
> b.  *Lukia est bella cantu/comente/ke (*a) su sole.*
> 'Lucy is as beautiful as the sun.'

Such examples can be accommodated by assuming that accusative *a* occurs with NPs (of the appropriate type) which bear accusative Case rather than specifically with NPs which function as direct objects. Thus, we postulate that the prepositions in (14) assign accusative Case to their objects, whereas others, like those in (15), which do not allow accusative *a* according to our informants (but see below, examples (19-20)), are specified as assigning some other Case:

> (15)  a.  *L'appo fattu pro (*a) Maria.*
> 'I did it for Mary.'
> b.  *Juanne est innamoratu de (*a) Lukia.*
> 'John is in love with Lucy.'
> c.  *Cussu libru fit iscrittu dae (*a) babbu meu.*
> 'This book was written by my father.'
> d.  *Gavini est issitu kin (*a) Pretu.*
> 'Gavino went out with Peter.'

Direct evidence that Sardinian prepositions differ in terms of the Case which they assign is provided by examples with first- and second-person singular disjunctive pronouns. With most prepositions, including those in (15a-c), these pronouns assume the 'oblique' forms *me, te* (dialectal variants: *mene, tene*), which can occur only after prepositions. *Kin* 'with' requires the 'comitative' forms *mecus, tecus*, which are exclusive to this preposition. The forms used with the prepositions in (14) are *mie, tie* (variants: *mime, tibe*), which are also used as direct or dative objects of verbs:

(16)  a.  *Lukia est bella cantu/comente/ke a tie.*
          'Lucy is as beautiful as you.'
      b.  *Appo vistu a tie.*
          'I saw you.'
      c.  *Juanne at datu su dinari a mie.*
          'John gave the money to me.'

Note that these forms are always preceded by *a*, which either serves to indicate the indirect object relation, as in (16c), or occurs obligatorily before accusatives by virtue of condition (11.I) above.

The fact that the three prepositions in (14) systematically take the accusative can perhaps be elucidated in terms of the distinction between 'inherent' and 'structural' Case proposed by Chomsky (1981). Inherent Cases are those which are assigned as a lexical property of the governing predicate and generally correlate, albeit rather loosely, with particular semantic roles (e.g., in many languages, dative Case tends to correlate with a role of the 'possessor' or 'experiencer' type), whereas structural Cases are assigned to NPs by virtue of their being governed by an appropriate item, regardless of the semantic relation involved (e.g., nominative is assigned to the subject of a finite clause whatever its semantic role may be) — cf. Chomsky (1981:171). Assuming now that the oblique and comitative Cases mentioned above are inherent whereas accusative is a structural Case, the obligatory use of the accusative with *cantu, ke*, and *comente* may be related to the fact that the complement of these prepositions is not assigned a consistent θ-role but inherits the θ-role of the entity with which it is compared. Thus, in (14) and (16a) the complement of the preposition takes its semantic role from the subject *Lukia* whereas in (17) it can be construed as parallel to either the subject or the direct object ('John loves

Lucy as much as Mary does' or 'John loves Lucy as much as he loves Mary'), though there appears to be some preference for the latter interpretation:

> (17)  *Juanne istimat a Lukia cantu/ke/comente a Maria.*
> 'John loves Lucy as much as Mary.'

It is tempting to conclude that these prepositions cannot assign an inherent Case precisely because they do not assign a consistent θ-role to their complement. This argument is weakened by the fact that comparative *de* normally assigns oblique Case even though it shows the same variability with respect to the θ-role of its complement. Thus, (18) is potentially ambiguous in the same way as (17), though the preference appears to work in the opposite direction (i.e., the preferred reading is 'John loves Lucy more than I do'):

> (18)  *Juanne istimat a Lukia prus de me.*
> 'John loves Lucy more than me.'

However, it is interesting to note that, in some local dialects, comparative *de* does assign accusative Case, as in the following attested example from *Boghes Sardas* ...(Comitato San Paolo 1986:116):

> (19)  *... ca nde ischit prus de a nois.*
> '... for he knows more about it than us.'

For the record, we may also note that in some dialects *pro* 'for' takes the accusative (as opposed to the more standard oblique Case as in (15a)), even though it assigns a consistent (benefactive) θ-role, as in the following example (Enna 1984:210):

> (20)  *Cras potes bennere a tribagliare pro a mie.*
> 'Tomorrow you can come to work for me.'

Consequently, the correlation between assignment of structural, accusative Case by prepositions and variability of the θ-role of the complement cannot be regarded as more than a tendency. However, this observation does not invalidate our hypothesis that the prepositional accusative in Sardinian is linked to accusative Case rather than to the direct object relation.

This hypothesis is consistent with an analysis of the following constructions whereby *Juanne* is thematically and structurally (at least at an underlying level in the case of (21b)) a subject of the complement verb *cantare* rather than the direct object of the matrix verb, but is nevertheless assigned accusative Case by the matrix verb:

(21) a. *Appo intesu a Juanne cantande.*
'I heard John sing(ing).'
b. *Faco cantare a Juanne.*
'I (will) make John sing.'

In these constructions, accusative *a* is obligatory. The accusative status of the NP in question is clearly indicated by the fact that *a* does not occur when the NP does not meet the conditions in (11):

(22) a. *Appo intesu (\*a) unu pitzinnu cantande.*
'I heard a boy singing.'
b. *Faco cantare (\*a) unu pitzinnu.*
'I (will) make a boy sing.'

On the other hand, this hypothesis makes the wrong predictions for 'accusative + attribute' constructions with epistemic verbs such as *crédere* in (23):

(23) a. *?Credio Juanne maláidu.*
b. *\*Credio a Juanne maláidu.*
'I believed John (to be) sick.'

Generally, such constructions are much more natural with an accusative clitic (e.g., *Lu credio maláidu.* 'I believed him (to be) sick.'), but to the extent that a 'full' NP (such as a proper name) can occur, our informants have clear judgements that this NP must not be introduced by *a*. We shall not attempt to solve this problem here, except to note that the claim that *Juanne* is not an argument of the main verb is intuitively more plausible in (23) than in (21). In (21a), it can be inferred that I heard John as well as the event of his singing and in (21b) one can deduce that John was acted upon in some way, but in (23) the content of my belief is clearly the proposition that John was sick rather than the person named 'John'. Whether these inferential differences should be represented in syntactic structure or at some level of semantic representation, or whether they should be accounted for in purely pragmatic terms is a question which we leave open. For present purposes we simply note that they play a role in the distribution of accusative *a*, which we characterize informally in (24):

(24) Subject to the conditions in (11), accusative NPs which can be construed as arguments of the Case-assigning predicate are introduced by *a*.

In this section, we have investigated the distribution of accusative *a* from two viewpoints: the internal properties of NPs which allow or require the presence of *a* and the external or contextual conditions under which the prepositional accusative phenomenon occurs. With regard to the internal properties of the NP, we have argued that they are primarily structural, based on the absence of a determiner. Definiteness also appears to play a role, though given certain assumptions (which we have tentatively adopted) this property can be expressed in structural terms, as in (8). Human reference, though a typical characteristic of NPs which take accusative *a*, appears to play only a marginal role in so far as the occurrence of accusative *a* with NPs introduced by a definite determiner is only possible for some speakers and tends to be restricted to NPs which have referential properties analogous to proper nouns. With regard to the external conditions, we have argued that the prepositional accusative is linked to the accusative Case feature rather than to the direct object relation, largely on the basis of the use of accusative *a* with certain prepositions, though we have noted certain problems concerning cases where accusative Case does not coincide with argumenthood (cf. (21-23)). Moreover, we have noted that the occurrence of accusative *a* is independent of the actual structural position of the accusative NP, as can be seen in the case of fronted or dislocated direct objects in (12).

## 2. Prepositional accusatives with pro-forms.

Our conclusion that human reference plays only a marginal role in the distribution of accusative *a* appears to be undermined by the behaviour of demonstratives when they are used with a pronominal function without an accompanying noun. In this case, these items must be preceded by accusative *a* if they refer to human beings, but do not allow *a* otherwise:

(25) a. *Appo vistu a custu/cussu/cuddu.*
       'I saw this/that (person).'
     b. *Appo vistu custu/cussu/cuddu.*
       'I saw this/that (thing, event).'

The same situation is found with the universal quantifier *tottu* 'all' when used on its own:

> (26) a. *Appo vistu a tottu.*
>         'I have seen everybody.'
>     b. *Appo vistu tottu.*
>         'I have seen everything.'

Moreover, the interrogative and negative pronouns which are used to refer to human beings (*kie* 'who' and *neune, nemos* 'nobody') systematically require accusative *a*, whereas their non-human counterparts (*itte* 'what' and *nudda* 'nothing') never take accusative *a*:

> (27) a. *A kie as vistu?*
>         'Who did you see?'
>     b. *Itte as vistu?*
>         'What did you see?'
> (28) a. *No' appo vistu a neune/nemos.*
>         'I did not see anyone.'
>     b. *No' appo vistu nudda.*
>         'I did not see anything.'

This evidence might be taken as indicating that the importance of human reference in determining the occurrence of accusative *a* is much greater than we claimed in the preceding section. Note, however, that the contrasts in (25-28) are clear in the sense that they involve obligatory versus prohibited uses of *a* and, as far as we can ascertain, are valid for all speakers, unlike the marginal cases discussed earlier. Consequently, rather than revising the conditions proposed in (11) to accommodate these cases, it might be more appropriate to postulate a separate condition (as in (29)) to account for the prepositional accusative with pro-forms of this type:

> (29) Accusative pro-forms are introduced (obligatorily) by *a*, iff they refer to human beings.

The postulation of a further condition, in addition to the two which we have already proposed in (11), is obviously undesirable in itself. Moreover, the condition envisaged in (29) does not account for the whole range of facts. In particular, it does not account for the behaviour of the interrogative pro-form *cale* 'which', which never takes accusative *a*, even when used to refer to humans:

(30)  *Cale as vistu?*
      'Which (thing, person) did you see?'

A clue to the exceptional behaviour of *cale* is provided by the fact that this item is more typically used as a determiner followed by a noun, as in (31):

(31)  *Cale pitzinna/frore as vistu?*
      'Which girl/flower did you see?'

Consequently, *cale* in (30) might plausibly be analysed as a determiner which is followed by a null N', as in (32):

(32)  [$_{NP}$ DET [$_{N'}$ ø]].

If condition (29) is taken as applying only to pro-forms which occupy the head N position within the NP, the absence of *a* is accounted for.

Interestingly, the non-human interrogative and negative items *itte* and *nudda* can also be used, albeit rather marginally, as determiners in the same way as *cale* in (31):

(33)  a.  *Itte dzente/frore as vistu?*
          'What people/flower did you see?'
      b.  *No' appo vistu nudda dzente/frores.*
          'I saw no people/flowers.'

However, the human counterparts *kie* and *neune/nemos* cannot be used in this way:

(34)  a.  *\*Kie pitzinna est vénnita.*
          Lit. 'Who girl came.'
      b.  *\*No' appo vistu (a) neune/nemos pitzinna.*
          Lit. 'I saw nobody girl.'

In view of the examples in (33), we may extend the analysis of 'bare' *cale* proposed in (32) to cases where *itte* and *nudda* occur without a following noun. Thus, these items in (27b) and (28b) can be analysed as occupying the DET position in the structure (35a), whereas *kie* and *neune/nemos* occur in the PRONOUN position in (35b):

(35)  a.  [$_{NP}$ DET [$_{N'}$ ø]]
      b.  [$_{NP}$ [$_{N'}$ [$_{N}$ PRONOUN]]].

Note now that if this approach is adopted, the special condition (29) becomes redundant for the interrogative and negative items under discussion, since NPs of the type in (35b) clearly conform to the structural condition

(11.I) which determines the obligatory use of accusative *a* (they lack a determiner position), whereas those of type (35a) do not.

Let us now consider the categorial status of *tottu* and the demonstratives in the light of the above discussion. It is clear that demonstratives have the status of determiners in phrases like *custu frore* 'this flower' and *cudda pitzinna* 'that girl', for which we assume the structure [NP DET [N' N ]]; but for 'bare' demonstratives either of the analyses in (35) is a priori possible. *Tottu* is slightly different in that it is normally followed by a full NP, containing a determiner, rather than an N' (e.g., *tottu sas pitzinnas* 'all the girls', *tottu custos frores* 'all these flowers'); but for the 'bare' use of this item we can envisage a similar choice between (35b) and the structure in (36), where *tottu* retains its status as a quantifier, but the quantified NP is null:

(36)  [NP Q [NP ø]].

If we adopt the analyses in (35a) and (36) for all cases, our rules predict (incorrectly) that accusative *a* should never occur with these items, as with *cale*. On the other hand, if we adopt analysis (35b) for all cases, we must invoke the special condition (29), since otherwise condition (11.I) would predict the obligatory occurrence of accusative *a* even when reference is to a non-human entity, as in the case of proper nouns. An alternative approach is to analyse these items as pronouns when they refer to humans, but as determiners or quantifiers modifying an empty category otherwise. The advantage of this approach is that it allows us to eliminate the special condition (29) entirely, since the facts concerning accusative *a* can now be accounted for directly by condition (11.I). On the negative side, this approach involves a slight complication of the categorial status of these items. Note, however, that even if we retain condition (29), we must still assume that these items are pronouns as well as determiners or quantifiers, since we argued earlier that this condition can apply only to pronouns, because of the 'exceptional' behaviour of *cale*. Thus, the issue is not whether these items belong to more than one syntactic category, but whether their categorial status is sensitive to properties of the referent. Nevertheless, this approach would carry greater conviction if we could show that it is supported by independent evidence or that the categorization of these items can be determined from more general principles.

The correlations between syntactic and referential properties of the
items discussed in this section are summarized in Table 1 overleaf.

**TABLE 1**

|                 | DET+N' Q+NP | DET+∅ Q+∅ | PRONOUN |
|-----------------|-------------|-----------|---------|
| demonstratives  | ±human      | –human    | +human  |
| *itte*          | ±human      | –human    | _____   |
| *kie*           | _____       | _____     | +human  |
| *nudda*         | ±human      | –human    | _____   |
| *neune/nemos*   | _____       | _____     | +human  |
| *cale*          | ±human      | ±human    | _____   |
| *tottu*         | ±human      | –human    | +human  |

Firstly, we may note that whenever such items function as determiners or
quantifiers with an overt N' or NP, they are [±human]. This generalization
appears to hold for all items of this class (e.g., *su* 'the', *unu* 'a', *meta(s)*
'much, many', etc.) — i.e., there are no determiners or quantifiers which
specifically select either a [+human] or a [–human] noun. Consequently,
the fact that *itte* and *nudda* can occur with a [+human] noun (cf. the
examples in (33)), even though they are exclusively [–human] when used
alone, need not be stipulated as a property of these particular items.

The second systematic generalization we may make is that whenever
such items function as pronouns, they are always interpreted as [+human].
Again, this generalization extends beyond the items under discussion here,
in so far as personal disjunctive pronouns (e.g., *isse* 'him', *issa* 'her') are
used almost exclusively with human reference, unlike their accusative clitic
counterparts (e.g., *lu* 'him, it (MASC.)', *la* 'her, it (FEM.)'). A corollary of
this generalization is that *kie* and *neune/nemos* need not be specified as
having exclusively human reference, since this can be derived from their
status as pronouns. Moreover, we no longer need to stipulate that *tottu* and
the demonstratives cannot be analysed as pronouns when used with non-
human reference, hence the absence of accusative *a* in these cases.

The complementary generalization that determiners and quantifiers
with a null N' or NP are [–human] also appears to hold, except in the case
of *cale*. Note that if this generalization were absolute, we could treat
[–human] as an intrinsic property of a null N' or NP governed by a determiner or quantifier. This in turn would automatically account for the dif-

ference in the referential properties of *itte* and *nudda* in (27b), (28b) and (33) according to whether the modified N' is null or overt. Moreover, it would provide a principled basis for our hypothesis that 'bare' *tottu* and demonstratives with human reference must be analysed as pronouns, which we have so far justified only in terms of the obligatory occurrence of accusative *a* in these cases. Unfortunately, however, the exceptional behaviour of *cale* undermines this generalization. If [$_{N'}$ ø] can be [+human] with *cale*, there is no obvious reason why the same should not be true with *tottu* and the demonstratives, thus invalidating our hypothesis that [+human] instances of these items must be pronouns and, therefore, introduced by accusative *a*. With this problem in mind, let us now consider some further facts concerning *tottu* and the demonstratives which may shed light on their categorial status and on the exceptional behaviour of *cale*.

Our first piece of evidence concerns 'floating' of *tottu* to a position between the auxiliary and main verb, as in (37):

(37)  a.  *Appo tottu vistu.*
          'I have seen everything/*everybody.'
      b.  *\*Appo a tottu vistu.*

Note that in this position *tottu* cannot refer to humans, nor can it be introduced by *a*. Both of these restrictions can be accounted for by making the natural assumption that the 'floating' rule applies only to the quantifier *tottu*, not to the homophonous pronoun, thus obviating the need to appeal to a semantic condition on this process. Note, however, that the semantic restriction illustrated in (37a) does not hold when the element quantified by *tottu* is expressed as a clitic pronoun:

(38)  a.  *Los appo vistos tottu.*
      b.  *Los appo tottu vistos.*
          'I saw them all (persons, things)'

Our general approach forces us to treat *tottu* as a quantifier in this case, even when interpreted as [+human], because 'floating' is possible and also because of the (obligatory) absence of accusative *a*. This conclusion is corroborated by theoretical considerations in so far as a clitic, such as *los*, must bind an empty category in a position appropriate to its semantic interpretation, which is provided by the position ø in (36) but is not accommodated in the pronoun structure (35b). The fact that *tottu* in (38) can be associated with human reference, even though it is a quantifier, can plausibly be attributed to this binding relation. Indeed, if we adopt a movement analysis of clitic pronouns, *los* in (38) occupies the same position at D-structure as a 'full' NP, as in *tottu sos pitzinnos* 'all the boys', and can thus be treated as underlyingly analogous to the cases in the first column in Table 1.

Our second range of data involves the use of *átteru* 'other' with various determiners and pronouns, particularly demonstratives. Typically, this item occurs as as a prenominal adjective (e.g., *un'átteru frore* 'another flower', *sas átteras pitzinnas* 'the other girls'), adjoined, we assume, to the N', as in (39):

(39) [NP DET [N' *átteru* [N'... N ...]]].

It can also occur without an overt head noun, as in *un'átteru* 'an other (MASC.)', *sas átteras* 'the others (FEM.)'. For these cases, two possible analyses might be envisaged. We could treat *átteru* either as an adjective modifying a null N', as in (40a) (i.e., the same structure as (39) except that the N' is null), or as the head noun, as in (40b):

(40) a. [NP DET [N' *átteru* [N' ø]]]
b. [NP DET [N' [N *átteru*]]].

Apparent support for (40b) is provided by the fact that definite articles, unlike demonstratives, cannot occur with a completely null N' (e.g., we cannot say *\*Appo vistu su* 'I saw the (one)'). However, definite articles can occur in headless NPs containing modifiers (e.g., an AP, PP or relative clause), which clearly cannot be analysed as head nouns:

(41) a. *Appo vistu su prus mannu.*
'I saw the biggest one.'
b. *Appo vistu sos de Juanne.*
'I saw John's ones.'
c. *Appo vistu sos ki sun arrivatos.*
'I saw the ones that arrived.'

A further observation is that phrases such as *sos átteros* can have human reference:

(42) *Appo vistu sos átteros.*
'I saw the others (persons, things).'

A simple way of accounting for this under analysis (40b) would be to assume that the noun *átteru* is unmarked for the [±human] feature. However, the headless NPs in (41) also allow human reference (e.g., out of context, *sos de Juanne* in (41b) would normally be interpreted as referring to John's family). Moreover, the use of *átteru* with the interrogative and negative determiners is not compatible with human reference, in contrast to clear cases where these items are used with an overt noun (cf. (33)):

(43) a. *Itte átteru as vistu?*
'What/*who else did you see?'
b. *No' appo vistu nudda átteru.*
'I did not see anything/*anybody else.'

In other words, the referential properties of the phrases in (43) follow the pattern which we have associated with 'DET + ø' constructions rather than full NPs of the type 'DET + N'. From this evidence we conclude that there is nothing to be gained by treating *átteru* as a noun, and we therefore adopt the analysis in (40a). A consequence of this conclusion is that examples like (42), and indeed those in (41), provide further counterevidence to the hypothesis that [N' ø] is always [–human], alongside the cases involving *cale*.

Before we discuss this problem further, we may note that *átteru* can also be used as a post-modifier with certain pronouns:

(44) *An vistu a nois/vois átteros.*
'They saw us/you others.'

For these cases, we propose that *átteru* is adjoined to the right of the N', as in (45):

(45) [NP [N' [N' PRONOUN] *átteru*]].

The same structure is assumed for the phrases with interrogative and negative pronouns in (46):

(46) a. *A kie átteru as vistu?*
'Who else did you see?'
b. *No' appo vistu a neune/nemos átteru.*
'I did not see anybody else.'

However, for reasons which we shall not attempt to explain here, there are some pronouns which cannot be modified in this way, notably the third-person forms of personal pronouns:

(47)  *Appo vistu a issos átteros.
       Lit. 'I saw them others.'

Note now that the distribution of accusative *a* in (43), (44) and (46) is exactly the same as in similar examples without *átteru*, as we would expect, since adjunction of *átteru* to the N' does not affect the presence or absence of a determiner position. Curiously, however, demonstratives accompanied by *átteru* do not normally take accusative *a*, even when human reference is intended, as in (48a):

(48)  a.  *No' appo vistu a isse, ma appo vistu cudd' átteru.*
          'I have not seen him, but I have seen that other (person).'
      b.  *No' appo lessu custu libru, ma appo lessu cudd' átteru.*
          'I have not read this book, but I have read that other one.'

The absence of *a* in (48a) can be reconciled with condition (11.I) if we assume that *cuddu* is a determiner, in spite of its human reference. This approach raises two crucial questions. Firstly, why does the presence of *átteru* impose determiner status on the demonstrative? Secondly, why can [$_{N'}$ ø] refer to a person in this case, whereas in all other cases this item must be [–human] when governed by a demonstrative determiner?

A possible answer to the first question is that the restriction illustrated in (47) applies also to demonstrative pronouns; e.g., this restriction might be formulated as in (49):

(49)  *[$_{NP}$ PRONOUN *átteru*], where PRONOUN is third person and definite.

Thus, *cuddu* in (48a) must be a determiner, since the filter in (49) precludes modification of the pronoun *cuddu* by *átteru*. With regard to our second question, we suggest that the possibility of human reference for NPs of the type [DET ... ø...] is linked in some way to the impossibility of using an appropriate pronoun. As a first hypothesis, we propose the principle in (50):

(50)  [$_{N'}$ ø] governed by a determiner is [–human] unless the use of a [+human] pronoun with the same semantic properties is excluded.

This principle will also account for the possibility of human reference for *sos átteros* in (42) given that the corresponding pronoun with third-person plural features (i.e., *issos* in (47) is excluded by (49)). It also extends to the cases in (41) in so far as personal pronouns cannot be modified by such phrases (e.g., we cannot say \**isse su prus mannu* 'him the biggest', except perhaps as an appositive construction). In the case of *cale* we suggest that the possibility of human reference is related to the absence of a [+human] pronoun which corresponds to this item in the same way as *kie* and *neune/nemos* correspond to *itte* and *nudda*. Note that *cale*, like English *which*, differs from *itte* and *kie* in that it questions the identity of an element from a restricted set which is contextually determined, whereas the potential reference of the latter forms ranges over all things or persons. Our claim then is that there is no interrogative pronoun which operates over a restricted set of human beings. Given this observation the difference between *cale* and the other interrogative and negative items can be derived from the generalization in (50). In cases of unrestricted interrogation or negation the use of a determiner necessarily entails non-human reference, since a pronoun with the same semantic properties (i.e., [–restricted]) is available when human reference is intended, but in cases of interrogation over a restricted set the absence of a pronoun with the feature [+restricted] allows human reference by virtue of the 'unless...' clause in (50).

Finally, we may note that the possibility of human reference for the quantifier *tottu* when accompanied by a clitic, as in (38), is consistent with the generalization in (50), extended to cover [NP ø] governed by a quantifier. In this case, we argued earlier that the pronoun *tottu* is excluded, since it fails to provide an empty NP for the clitic to bind. Consequently, the 'unless...' clause in (50) becomes operative because of a general syntactic requirement. On the other hand, in the absence of a clitic, the quantifier *tottu* (identifiable by the absence of accusative *a* and the possibility of 'floating' — cf. (26) and (37)) must be [–human], since there is nothing to prevent the use of the homophonous pronoun in this case.

The general pattern which emerges from the above discussion is that the referential possibilities of ø governed by a determiner or quantifier cannot be defined as an intrinsic property of this element but that they complement those of bona fide pronouns. Given our earlier observation concerning the semantic properties of pronouns, restated in (51), the conditions

governing the use of determiners or quantifiers as pro-forms can be stated
as in (52):

(51) Pronouns (occupying the head N position) must be interpreted
as [+human].

(52) The use of the null element ø governed by a determiner or
quantifier is possible in just those cases where the intended
reference cannot be expressed by means of a pronoun.

It follows from (51) that all pro-forms which are interpreted as [–human]
must be of the determiner or quantifier type, though this is not part of the
definition in (52). In addition, (52) allows for the residue of miscellaneous
cases where the use of a pronoun is excluded for other reasons; e.g., the absence of a pronoun with the requisite semantic properties (as in the case of
*cale*), modification by an item such as *átteru* which is incompatible with
the corresponding pronoun (demonstrative and definite articles), the obligatory presence of an empty NP node bound by a clitic (*tottu*). Taken together, (51) and (52) correctly predict that human reference for determiner
or quantifier pro-forms is possible in these, and only these, cases.

In this section we have looked at a range of cases involving various
pro-forms which appear to undermine the conclusion reached in §1 that the
distribution of accusative *a* is determined primarily by structural properties
of the NP (absence of a determiner position) rather than in terms of human
reference. In spite of a strong tendency for accusative *a* to correlate with
human reference in these cases, we have shown that this correlation does
not provide an adequate basis for an account of accusative *a* with the items
in question. On the contrary, we have argued that these cases can be accommodated within the structural approach advocated in §1 provided that
we make a distinction between 'genuine' pronouns (occupying the head N
position) and pro-forms which occupy the determiner or quantifier position
governing a null projection of the head N. This distinction is empirically
justified to the extent that all the items which we have classified as determiners or quantifiers can be used as such with an overt nominal expression,
whereas those which we have classified exclusively as pronouns cannot.
Empirical justification is at its weakest for those items which which we
have assigned to both categories (*tottu* and the demonstratives). Nevertheless, we have offered evidence to show that the categorial distinction motivated by the distribution of accusative *a* is consistent with other syntactic

phenomena, such as quantifier floating and modification by items like *átteru*. We have also argued that there is a significant correlation between the 'determiner vs. pronoun' distinction and the [±human] distinction, though it cannot be formulated on a simple one-to-one basis. Specifically, human reference is a necessary, but not sufficient, condition for pronoun status, whereas 'bare' determiners and quantifiers function as pro-forms in all cases where the use of a pronoun is prohibited, either because the intended referent is non-human or because the use of a pronoun is excluded for independent reasons.

The idea that so-called 'pronouns' can or should be analysed as determiners is not new. It was first proposed within a generative framework by Postal (1966) and has been subsequently developed by various linguists (e.g., Emonds (1985) and Abney (1987)). However, in the works just cited, the status of such items is treated as a largely theoretical issue, the argument being that all items traditionally classified as pronouns should be analysed as intransitive determiners of some sort rather than as a subclass of nouns. To the extent that the arguments presented in this section are valid, they indicate that the categorial status of nominal pro-forms is not determined once and for all by syntactic theory or Universal Grammar, but that both options are potentially available within a single language.

At this point, it should be emphasized that we do not wish to imply that this distinction is relevant to all languages, still less that it is always determined in the manner which we have proposed for Sardinian. For instance, though it might be reasonable to postulate a categorial distinction in English somewhere along the continuum *the*, *this*, *it*, *him*, there is little reason to suppose that *it* and *him* belong to different categories as would be required if (50) were a principle of Universal Grammar. Nevertheless, it is possible that our conclusions may shed light on parellel phenomena in languages which are closely related to Sardinian but do not exhibit the prepositional accusative phenomenon which forms the basis for our discussion. For example, in French, the fact that *cela* can have only non-human reference might be accounted for in terms of an abstract analysis of the type [$_{NP}$ *ce* [$_{N'}$ ø] *là*], whereas *celui-là*, which is neutral with respect to the [±human] distinction, can be analysed as containing an overt head *lui* ([$_{NP}$ *ce* [*lui*] *là*]), and *lui* on its own, which we may analyse as a pronoun occupying the head N position, is normally interpreted as [+human], like the genuine pronouns in Sardinian. Similarly, the facts which we have re-

ported concerning 'floating' of *tottu* and co-occurrence with a clitic apply
also to the French counterparts *tout* and *tous*, except for the incidence of
the prepositional accusative.

As a postscript to this section, it may be useful to consider how our
conclusions might be formulated within Abney's (1987) approach to the
structure of noun phrases. The essence of Abney's thesis is that determiners are not generated as part of the NP but head their own maximal projection, Determiner Phrase (DP), and select an NP as complement: e.g.,
[DP [D' [D *the* ] [NP *old man* ]]]. Within this framework, pronouns are determiners which simply do not select a complement NP, thus obviating the
need for the ø element which we have postulated (on the grounds that the
head node is obligatory, though complements are not): e.g.,
[DP [D' [D *him* ]]]. For our purposes, this would be an attractive analysis for
those pro-forms which we have classified as determiners, but it is not clear
how our class of 'genuine' pronouns could be distinguished from these in a
manner consistent with a unified account of the obligatory cases of the
prepositional accusative. The main problem is the assumption that all so-
called 'noun phrases' are dominated by a DP node, which is presumably
headed by a DET node, even when no overt determiner is present (e.g.,
with proper names). Consequently it is difficult to see how our condition
(11.I) could be stated within this framework. However, if we were to
abandon this assumption and treat proper nouns, kinship nouns (optionally
modified by a possessive) and 'genuine' pronouns simply as NPs, with the
internal structure proposed in (8a), we could reformulate condition (11.I) in
a rather simple fashion; i.e., accusative *a* is obligatory before all accusative
complements of the category NP (as opposed to DP). An obvious general
problem with this approach is that it leaves us with two distinct categories
(DP and NP) which have the same distribution and which behave in the
same way with respect to other syntactic phenomena (e.g., Case-marking
and agreement). Note also that for this analysis to work, we would have to
assume that indefinite NPs of the type in (7) are DPs headed by a null determiner. A further problem concerns the adjective *átteru* which, under the
revised analysis, would have to be treated as part of the DP in a phrase like
*sos átteros* 'the others' but as part of the NP in *nois átteros* 'we others' —
it is not clear what its structural position would be in *sos átteros pitzinnos*
'the other boys'. We shall not pursue these questions here, but merely observe that if our account of the prepositional accusative in Sardinian is on

the right track, it has interesting ramifications for Abney's approach. For the remainder of this paper, we shall revert to the 'classical' analysis of NP structure.

## 3. Prepositional accusatives and grammatical Case.

Throughout our discussion so far, we have assumed that there is a clear distinction between the accusative use of *a* and its use as an indirect object (dative) marker. For the most part this assumption is well-founded. However there are a few cases where the distinction between accusatives and datives is not clear-cut.

Before we discuss these cases, let us briefly review the criteria according to which direct and indirect objects can be distinguished, taking the direct object of *vídere* 'see' and the second object of *dare* 'give' as representative examples. Although both types of object are introduced by *a* with NPs of the type defined in (11) above, as in (53), the presence of *a* clearly indicates an indirect object relation with other types of NP, as in (54):

(53)  a.  *Appo vistu a Maria.*
          'I saw Mary.'
      b.  *Appo datu unu frore a Maria.*
          'I gave a flower to Mary.'
(54)  a.  *Appo vistu una pitzinna.*
          'I saw a girl.'
      b.  *Appo datu unu frore a una pitzinna.*
          'I gave a flower to a girl.'

When the direct object is realized as a third-person clitic, it assumes one of the accusative forms *lu* (MASC. SG.), *la* (FEM. SG.), *los* (MASC. PL.) or *las* (FEM. PL.) and triggers obligatory number and gender agreement of the past participle in compound perfective tenses, whereas datives are realized as *li* (SG.) or *lis* (PL.) with no agreement of the past participle:

(55)  a.  *Las appo vistas.*
          'I saw them (FEM.)'
      b.  *Lis appo datu frores.*
          'I gave them flowers.'

Note that the final vowel of the singular forms of these clitics is always elided before another vowel, resulting in neutralization of the 'accusative vs. dative' distinction except when there is overt evidence of participle agreement:

(56) a. *L'appo vistu/vista.*
'I saw him/her.'
b. *L'appo datu unu frore.*
'I gave him/her a flower.'

This neutralization is complete with first- and second-person clitics, whose accusative and dative forms are identical and which (unlike third-person clitics) never trigger agreement of the participle, even when they function as direct objects:

(57) a. *Nos an vistu.*
'They saw us.'
b. *Nos an datu frores.*
'They gave us flowers.'

The reflexive/reciprocal clitic *si* is likewise used for both the accusative and the dative, but the distinction is evident in sentences with compound perfectives, since accusative *si* selects the auxiliary *éssere* 'be' with agreement of the participle, as in (58a), whereas dative *si* selects *áere* 'have' without participle agreement, as in (58b):

(58) a. *Sas pitzinnas si sun vistas.*
'The girls saw each other.'
b. *Sas pitzinnas s'an datu frores.*
'The girls gave each other flowers.'

The choice of *áere* in (58b) could be attributed either to the fact that *si* is dative (rather than accusative) or to the fact that *dare* also takes a direct object; i.e., the data in (58) are consistent with either of the hypotheses in (59):

(59) a. Reflexive clitics select *éssere* iff they function as direct objects.
b. Reflexive clitics select *éssere* unless the verb also takes a direct object.

From a theoretical point of view, the hypothesis in (59a) is the more interesting in so far as it offers the possibility of a uniform account of auxiliary selection which would also cover the use of *éssere* with so-called 'unaccusative' or 'ergative' verbs, as in (60):

(60) a. *Sas pitzinnas sun arrivatas.*
'The girls have (lit. 'are') arrived.'
b. *Custu libru m'est piághitu.*
'This book pleased me.' (lit. '... is pleased to me.')

If, following the arguments presented by Burzio (1986) for Italian, we assume that the superficial subjects of verbs of this type are represented underlyingly as direct objects and are 'promoted' in much the same way as the superficial subjects of passives, we may envisage the possibility that selection of *éssere* in Sardinian correlates with some sort of identity between the superficial subject and the underlying direct object, which is realized as 'promotion' of the direct object in (60) and by binding of the direct object by the subject in (58a). A more precise formulation of this hypothesis raises a number of issues which are beyond the scope of this paper. However, it seems clear that the descriptive statement in (59a) is compatible with this hypothesis, whereas (59b) is not. Note in particular that absence of a non-reflexive direct object is not a sufficient condition for selection of *éssere*, since many intransitive verbs, principally those which denote activities and whose subject is generally assumed to be base-generated as such, take *áere*: e.g., *Appo travallatu* 'I have worked'.

Leaving theoretical considerations aside, an obvious way of deciding which of the statements in (59) is empirically correct would be to see what happens when the indirect object of an intransitive verb is reflexivized — (59a) predicts that we should have *áere* as perfective auxiliary, whereas (59b) predicts *éssere*. Unfortunately, it is difficult to find clear cases of genuinely intransitive verbs which take a dative complement. There are abundant examples of double object verbs (such as *dare*) whose second object conforms systematically to the criteria for dativehood proposed above. Also, there are a few ergative verbs (identified as such by selection of *éssere* as perfective auxiliary) which can take an object which behaves consistently as a dative with respect to our criteria, as shown in (61):

(61) a. *Cussa cathone est piághita a meta dzente.*
'That song pleased many people.'
b. *Cussa cathone lis est piághita.*
'That song pleased them.'

    c.  *Est pássitu a su duttore ki Maria ésseret maláida.*
       'It seemed to the doctor that Mary was ill.'
    d.  *Lis est pássitu ki Maria ésseret maláida.*
       'It seemed to them that Mary was ill.'

However, with verbs which select a single underlying object, this object either behaves consistently as a direct object according to our criteria (as in the case of *vídere*) or, in the case of a small number of verbs which we might expect to take a dative object on semantic or cross-linguistic grounds, the object exhibits a mixed behaviour with respect to these criteria.

    Consider first the verb *faeddare* 'talk' in (62):

    (62)  *Appo faeddatu a Maria.*
        'I talked to Mary.'

From this example, we cannot determine whether *Maria* is a direct or indirect object, since it belongs to the class of NPs which take *a* obligatorily even with a direct object function. According to Pittau (1972), *faeddare* is a transitive verb, as evidenced by the accusative form of the clitic and agreement of the participle in (63), a judgement which is corroborated by many of our informants and the written texts which we have consulted and which appears to represent the 'standard' situation:

    (62)  *Los appo faeddatos.*
        'I talked to them.'

However, some of our informants require a dative clitic (with no participle agreement) with this verb:

    (63)  *%Lis appo faeddatu.*
        'I talked to them.'

On the basis of this evidence we might simply conclude that there is some dialectal or idiolectal variation in the Case-marking properties of this verb. However, we have found no speakers (including those who opt for (62)) who accept the use of an object NP without *a* with this verb:

    (64)  a.  *\*Appo faeddatu sas pitzinnas.*
          'I talked to the girls.'
      b.  *\*Appo faeddatu unu duttore.*
          'I talked to a doctor.'

In such cases, *a* is used even though the NP in question does not have the properties which normally allow accusative *a*; or, more commonly, the problem is avoided by using the alternative construction with *kin* 'with', particularly when the NP is indefinite:

      (65)  a.   *Appo faeddatu a/kin sas pitzinnas.*
               'I talked to/with the girls.'
          b.   *Appo faeddatu ?a/kin unu duttore.*
               'I talked to/with a doctor.'

Thus, even for those speakers who require an accusative clitic as in (62), this verb does not behave like a straightforward transitive verb. For the version of (65) with *a* we must conclude either that the range of NPs which show the prepositional accusative is extended with objects of *faeddare* or that this verb is perceived as taking the dative when the object is not a clitic. In reflexive constructions, this verb requires the auxiliary *éssere* with obligatory agreement of the participle:

      (66)  a.   *Sas pitzinnas si sun faeddatas.*
          b.   *\*Sas pitzinnas si sun/an faeddatu.*
               'The girls talked to each other.'

This is precisely what we would expect if *si* is analysed as a direct object — (66a) is exactly parallel to (58a) with the transitive verb *vídere*. However, for those speakers who appear to treat the complement of *faeddare* as dative (cf. (63)), the data in (66) are somewhat problematic in so far as they force us to adopt the (theoretically undesirable) hypothesis given in (59b) above. Moreover, we must also conclude that dative *si* induces participle agreement in the same way as accusative *si*. An alternative approach is to assume that *si* in (66) is treated as accusative even for those speakers who favour the dative form of the non-reflexive clitic in (63), just as we suggested earlier that full NP complements appear to act more like datives even for those speakers who require the accusative clitic in (62).

With the verb *telefonare* 'telephone', *a* is optional (though generally preferred) before NPs of the type which do not normally allow the prepositional accusative:

      (67)   *Appo telefonatu (a) unu duttore.*
           'I telephoned a doctor.'

Similarly, this verb allows both accusative and dative clitics:

(68)  a.  *Los appo telefonatos.*
      b.  *Lis appo telefonatu.*
          'I telephoned them.'

Essentially, accusative and dative forms appear to be in free variation with this verb, perhaps with individual preferences one way or the other. However, in the reflexive construction we again find the properties which are characteristic of transitive verbs, but which are somewhat problematic if they hold also of dative-taking verbs; i.e., *éssere* with obligatory participle agreement:

(69)  a.  *Sas pitzinnas si sun telefonatas.*
      b.  *\*Sas pitzinnas si sun/an telefonatu.*
          'The girls telephoned each other.'

Following the approach tentatively suggested for *faeddare*, we might conclude that, while *telefonare* allows either dative or accusative complements when they are full NPs or non-reflexive clitics, the dative option is not available in the reflexive construction.

The verb *pessare* 'think' differs from the others discussed so far in that it can readily take inanimate as well as animate complements. In both cases, the object NP must be introduced by *a* whatever its structural properties, a fact which strongly suggests that this verb takes an indirect object:

(70)  a.  *So pessande a custu problema.*
          'I am thinking about this problem.'
      b.  *So pessande a una pitzinna.*
          'I am thinking about a girl.'

When the object of this verb is represented by a clitic, the locative form *bi* 'there' is used for inanimate entities, but the accusative forms are used to refer to animate beings:

(71)  a.  *Non bi pesso prus.*
          'I do not think about it any more.'
      b.  *Non la/\*li pesso prus.*
          'I do not think about her any more.'

Examples (70b) and (71b) show quite clearly that the grammatical function of a complement is not necessarily determined 'once and for all' as a property of the governing verb but may depend on the syntactic type of the complement (e.g., indirect object with a full NP, but direct object with a clitic). This observation gives indirect support to our suggestion that the reflexive clitic *si* in (66) and (69) should be analysed exclusively as a direct object even though the verbs in question allow complements of other types which appear to function as indirect objects. As we might expect on the basis of (71b), *pessare* takes *éssere* with obligatory participle agreement in the reflexive construction:

> (72) a. *Sas pitzinnas si sun pessatas.*
> b. **Sas pitzinnas si sun/an pessatu.*
> 'The girls thought about each other.'

The clearest example we have been able to find of an intransitive verb which takes a dative object is *sorrídere* 'smile', which requires *a* before all types of NP and systematically takes a dative clitic:

> (73) *Appo sorrísitu a una pitzinna.*
> 'I smiled at a girl.'
> (74) a. *Lis appo sorrísitu.*
> b. **Los appo sorrísitos.*
> 'I smiled at them.'

In the reflexive construction, the perfective auxiliary is *éssere*, but some informants found it difficult to decide whether agreement of the past participle was obligatory in this case:

> (75) a. *Si sun sorrísitos/?sorrísitu.*
> b. **S'an sorrísitu.*
> 'They smiled at each other.'

For the version of (75a) with participle agreement we might appeal to the variability of grammatical functions noted above and conclude that *si* is in fact accusative, as we have suggested for (66) and (69), thus allowing us to maintain the 'theoretically desirable' hypothesis given in (59a). However, if the version without agreement is grammatical, we must conclude that *si* is dative in this case, and that dative *si* induces selection of *éssere* in the absence of a direct object (as envisaged in (59b)), but differs from accusative *si* in that it does not trigger participle agreement.

At this point, we should mention that our informants appeared to have considerable difficulty in arriving at judgements for the reflexive constructions (particularly (75), but also to varying degrees (66) and (69)). Generally they arrived at the judgements which we have reported by a process of

elimination in the sense that they were reluctant to accept examples with
*éssere* with participle agreement until they were confronted with the alternative logical possibilities (*áere* or *éssere* without participle agreement), at
which point they concluded that *éssere* with participle agreement was the
'correct' construction.   Our supposition that *éssere* without participle
agreement may be acceptable in (75) is based on the observation that our
informants took longer to make this decision and, in some cases, could not
commit themselves one way or the other.   Moreover, our informants frequently offered periphrastic alternatives to the construction with *si* which
are neutral with respect to the accusative-dative contrast (e.g., *An faeddatu
tra issos* 'They talked among themselves') or which contain a direct object
which requires *si* to be construed as a dative (*S' an datu unu sorrisu* 'They
gave a smile to each other').   Interestingly, they showed no hesitation in
accepting reflexive or reciprocal constructions with simple tense forms:
e.g., *Non si faeddan prus* 'They do not talk to each other any more', *Si
sorridian* 'They used to smile at each other'.   Although this evidence is
anecdotal, it may be significant in so far as it suggests that native speakers
face an artificial task when pressed to make judgements concerning auxiliary choice and participle agreement in these cases, in the sense that they
cannot rely on their intuitions about what they would say in spontaneous
discourse, but base their judgements on a grammatical 'logic' extrapolated
from analogous cases involving genuinely accusative reflexive clitics.

Leaving aside the factors on which native informants may base their
judgements when interrogated by linguists, our conclusions concerning the
accusative versus dative distinction can be summarized in terms of the
continuum represented in Table 2:

**TABLE 2**

| **Full NP** | [–def] | [+def] |

$$ACC \longleftrightarrow DAT$$

| **Clitic** | [+refl] | [–refl] |

The use of *a* before definite NPs is obligatory with all of the verbs discussed except *telefonare*, where it nevertheless appears to be preferred.   It
is in this sense that definite NPs are more 'dative-like' than the other cases.

At the opposite end of the spectrum, reflexive clitics with these verbs have exactly the same properties as accusative reflexives with respect to auxiliary selection and participle agreement, except possibly for *sorrídere* if the version of (75a) without agreement is grammatical. The accusative versus dative contrast is at its most apparent with third-person, non-reflexive clitics, where we find a variety of patterns: free variation with *telefonare*, dialectal variation with *faeddare*, whereas *sorrídere* consistently requires the dative and *pessare* consistently requires the accusative for animates but a locative form for inanimates. Our reasons for placing indefinite NPs in the intermediate zone are rather different. In (65b) (*Appo faeddatu ?a/kin unu duttore* 'I talked to/with a doctor') we noted that the use of *a* with indefinite complements of *faeddare* is rather marginal and tends to be avoided in favour of the construction with *kin* 'with', though no such restriction is apparent with 'true' datives (e.g., *Appo datu unu frore a una pitzinna* 'I gave a flower to a girl'). Thus, with *faeddare* at least, indefinite object NPs do not conform to the normal dative pattern.

In order to gain insight into the situation represented in Table 2, let us briefly consider our earlier claim that the only clear instances of verbs which take a dative object are double-object verbs and ergative verbs. Given the assumption that the subject of an ergative verb occupies the direct object position in the underlying structure, this claim can be generalized as in (76):

(76) In Sardinian, dative Case is predominantly associated with the second object of the verb in underlying structure.

It is easy to imagine how (76) as a statistical generalization (i.e., there are very few verbs whose only complement is dative) might become integrated as part of the speaker's grammar restricting the use of dative forms to verbs which also take an underlying direct object. Note now that, in a substantial proportion of cases, dative and accusative complements are identical in form because of the prepositional accusative phenomenon and also because of neutralization of the Case distinction with many clitic pronouns. Moreover, since the elements which are affected by this neutralization are predominantly human (e.g., proper names, kinship terms, 'genuine' pronouns and first- and second-person clitics), the proportion of instances where the grammatical function of a complement is not identifiable by its form will be significantly higher for those verbs which require their object to be human for semantic reasons (including most of the verbs which take a dative object in other related languages). Furthermore, since the vast majority of two-place verbs are syntactically transitive, most of these neutral forms will, in fact, be direct objects. In view of these circumstances, it would be natural for speakers to treat all such neutral forms as direct objects (and hence to classify the governing verb as transitive) unless there is some other complement which already fulfils the direct object function. At the same time, one might postulate a countervailing tendency (hinted at above) for certain types of verb to select a dative complement by virtue of their semantic properties; e.g., as in (77):

(77)  Human NPs which have a 'goal' interpretation typically function as dative objects.

What we would like to suggest is that the mixed pattern of judgements summarized in Table 2 can be elucidated in terms of the conflict between the tendencies in (76) and (77).

Note firstly that on a purely empirical level, this conflict does not arise with the neutral forms mentioned above. For instance, in cases like *Appo faeddatu a Maria* 'I talked to Mary' or *Nos an faeddatu* 'They talked to us' the speaker does not have to decide whether the 'goal' expression is dative (in accordance with (77)) or accusative (by virtue of (76)), since the result is the same in either case. Consequently, our observation that definite NPs appear to be more consistently dative-like than other expressions may reflect the fact that for many NPs of this type (e.g., proper names and pronouns, but also a wider range of NPs introduced by a definite determiner for some speakers) the presence of *a* is compatible with either dative or accusative status. However, as we move further away from the class of NPs which require or allow the prepositional accusative, the presence or absence of *a* must be construed as reflecting a decision as to the grammatical function of the complement. Our earlier observation concerning the avoidance of *a* with indefinite NPs as complements of *faeddare*, in favour of the construction with *kin* 'with', and the complete impossibility of a prepositionless NP with this verb (cf. (64-65)) may be taken as evidence that speakers are reluctant to make this decision if an alternative construction is readily available. With the other verbs, no such alternative is available, so a decision has to be made, the general tendency being to extend the use of *a* to NPs of all types (perhaps by analogy with those NPs which require *a* in any case).

With third-person clitics, a decision regarding morphological Case is likewise imposed, and appears to be resolved in a fairly arbitrary fashion. In particular, our evidence concerning *pessare* (cf. (70b), (71b)), and to a lesser extent *faeddare* (cf. (62-65)), indicates that the choice of Case with clitics is largely independent of the decision made for full NPs. In other words, speakers do not subclassify such verbs as inherently 'dative-taking' or 'accusative-taking' but appear to make piecemeal decisions concerning the Case-morphology of clitics and the presence or absence of *a* for any given verb. Nevertheless, the fact that *sorrídere* consistently selects the dative forms of both clitics and NPs may be significant in so far as there is no obvious sense in which the 'goal' is a semantic argument of this verb. Intuitively, 'smile' is a one-place predicate denoting an action, whereas 'talk', 'telephone' and 'think (about)' are arguably two-place relations. Consequently, it is perhaps natural that the semantic principle (77) should outweigh the effects of (76) in this case, given that we are dealing with a 'goal' adjunct rather than a complement and accusative Case is not generally available for adjunct NPs.

In reflexive constructions with simple tense forms, such as *Si faeddan* 'They talk to each other/themselves', decisions as to the Case of the reflexive clitic are immaterial in the sense that they do not affect the surface form. However, with compound perfective tenses, the Case of the reflexive clitic has potential consequences for the choice of auxiliary and for agreement of the participle. If *si* is taken to be accusative, these consequences are clear, since there is abundant evidence from sentences with bona fide transitive verbs that accusative *si* selects *éssere* and triggers obligatory agreement of the participle. However, these consequences are much less evident if *si* is taken to be dative. In so far as the only clear examples of dative complements are those which occur with double-object or ergative verbs, the native speaker (like the linguist) has no sound empirical basis on which to choose between the hypotheses in (59) (i.e., whether selection of *éssere* is determined by the accusative status of *si* or by the absence of another direct object in the reflexive construction). Given our observation that the Case-assigning properties of these verbs are not uniform (e.g., *pessare* takes an accusative clitic but a dative NP), it is reasonable to suppose that speakers are free to decide on the Case of *si* independently of the

Case which they have ascribed to other complement types. The fact that
speakers appear to treat *si* as accusative, even with verbs which tend to
favour dative complements of other types, may be attributed to the fact that
this choice enables them to determine the selection of the auxiliary and
participle agreement on the basis of a well-established pattern based on the
behaviour of genuine transitive verbs, whereas treatment of *si* as a dative
poses a dilemma for which the speaker's grammar offers no clear solution.
Our informants' hesitation over such examples and their willingness to
suggest alternative paraphrases (e.g., *An faeddatu tra issos* 'They talked
among themselves', *S'an datu unu sorrisu* 'They gave each other a smile')
may be symptomatic of a tension between the 'easy option' of treating *si* as
accusative and the intuitive feeling that this element should really be analysed as dative according to (77) (particularly with *sorrídere* and for those
speakers who favour a dative clitic with *faeddare* as in (63)). Similarly,
the fact that some informants entertain the possibility that the past participle of *sorrídere* need not show agreement (cf. (75a)), even though it requires *éssere* in the reflexive construction, may not reflect actual usage, but
possibly represents a semi-conscious attempt on the part of our informants
to fit this example into the established pattern of reflexive verbs without a
direct object (with respect to auxiliary selection) while recognizing that *si*
is not a plausible direct object because of its adjunct status.

## 4. Conclusion

In §1 we investigated the distribution of accusative *a* along two dimen-
sions, firstly the internal properties of NPs which manifest the prepositional accusative, and secondly the external contexts which determine the
occurrence of this phenomenon with NPs of the appropriate type.

   With regard to the first question, we noted that the obligatory use of accusative *a* correlates systematically with NPs which lack a determiner.
Although some speakers also allow accusative *a* with certain types of definite human NPs with an overt determiner, the use of *a* in such cases is
never obligatory and is not accepted by all speakers. From this evidence
we concluded that the NP-internal conditions which determine the use of
accusative *a* are structural and that semantic properties play a very
marginal role. The prepositional accusative occurs with direct objects of
all transitive verbs regardless of their semantic role and regardless of their
actual position in the sentence. Moreover, the prepositional accusative also

occurs with certain prepositions which can be classified as assigning accusative Case (as shown by the form of first- and second-person pronouns)
rather than oblique Case, which is more typical with objects of prepositions. We thus concluded that the prepositional accusative is associated
with the Case feature [accusative] rather than with the direct object relation, though we pointed out that this conclusion raises some interesting
problems (which we left unresolved) in connection with certain types of
'small clause' constructions.

In §2 we returned to the NP-internal properties relevant to the prepositional accusative, concentrating on a range of cases involving pronoun-like
elements, which appear to contradict the conclusions reached in §1, in that
they show a strong correlation between human reference and the presence
of accusative *a*. However, detailed investigation of these cases reveals that
the [+human] feature cannot be analysed as the factor which directly conditions the occurrence of accusative *a*. Rather, we argued that the link
between human reference and accusative *a* is mediated by a categorial distinction between pronouns (occupying the head N position) and determiners which lack an overt nominal element. Our classification of items into
these two categories was based on two principal criteria: the distribution of
accusative *a*, as defined by the structural condition proposed in §1, and the
ability of items to function as determiners with an overt nominal element.
As well as providing a coherent account of the prepositional accusative
which is consistent with our original structurally-based proposal, this approach also revealed an interesting correlation between the syntactic category of the items in question and their semantic properties; namely that all
items which qualify as pronouns according to these criteria are [+human],
while 'bare' determiners occur only in cases where a corresponding pronoun cannot be used (including all cases of non-human reference and miscellaneous instances where the use of a pronoun is prohibited for syntactic
reasons or because there is no corresponding pronoun). Thus, the
'syntactic repercussions' of the prepositional accusative discussed in this
section are rather abstract, in that they relate to a question (the syntactic
status of so-called 'pronouns') which has hitherto been regarded as a
largely theoretical issue. In particular, the evidence of the prepositional accusative in Sardinian suggests that discussions as to whether 'pronouns' as
a whole should be treated as heads of NP or as determiners are misplaced,
since in this language at least, both types must be available.

The 'syntactic repercussions' discussed in §3 are more directly concerned with the way in which the prepositional accusative phenomenon has influenced the syntax of Sardinian. Our central hypothesis is that the prepositional accusative, along with the absence of an overt Case contrast with certain clitics, has led to such widespread neutralization of the accusative versus dative distinction, which is irrecoverable unless a direct object is also present (possibly underlyingly), that dative has come to be perceived almost exclusively as the Case of the second object. At the same time, we have recognized a tendency to treat animate 'goal' NPs as datives, particularly if they function as adjuncts rather than subcategorized complements (e.g., *sorrídere*), thus giving rise to a conflict for verbs which allow a 'goal' phrase but do not take a direct object as well. Our evidence is that such verbs behave erratically in this respect, sometimes assigning one Case to a full NP but a different Case to the corresponding clitic, with some degree of free or dialectal variation. We have thus postulated that these verbs are, in effect, indeterminate with respect to the Case of their complements. Because of the widespread neutralization mentioned above, this indeterminacy has no adverse effect for a wide range of nominal expressions, the form of the complement (and indeed the sentence as a whole) being exactly the same whether it is treated as accusative or dative. For other expressions which do not exhibit neutralization of the Case distinction, speakers appear to cope with this indeterminacy in an essentially ad hoc manner, e.g., by extending the use of *a* to NPs which do not normally allow accusative *a* and, independently, opting for one Case or the other with third-person clitics. However, this indeterminacy raises more far-reaching problems in reflexive constructions, since the Case assumed for the clitic has potential consequences for the choice of perfective auxiliary and agreement of the past participle. Here, the linguist faces a dilemma; since the Case of the reflexive cannot be reliably determined by referring to the Case of other complement types, because of the erratic behaviour noted above, we have no direct basis on which to form a rule for auxiliary selection and participle agreement with a dative reflexive which is not accompanied by a direct object. Our evidence suggests that native speakers face the same dilemma, since they show considerable difficulty in making intuitive judgements on such examples, favouring paraphrases wherever possible, and, when pressed for a judgement, decide in favour of the construction which follows the well-established pattern for accusative reflexives. If we are right in thinking that perfective reflexive constructions with these verbs lie outside the intuitive linguistic competence of native speakers, we are led to the interesting conclusion that one of the indirect consequences of the prepositional accusative (and other instances of Case neutralization) is a gap in the grammar which effectively precludes perfective counterparts of reflexive constructions which are perfectly acceptable with simple tense forms.

## Note

1.   For discussion of other potential cases, see Jones (1993:186-187).

## References

Abney, S. P. 1987. *The English Noun Phrase in its Sentential Aspect.* Unpublished Ph.D. dissertation, MIT.

Burzio, L. 1986. *Italian Syntax.* Dordrecht: Reidel.

Chomsky, N. 1981. *Lectures on Government and Binding.* Dordrecht: Foris.

Comitato San Paolo. 1986. *Boghes Sardas de e sa Zittade.* Sassari: Stamperia Artistica. (An anthology of poems and short stories entered for the San Paolo literary prize)

Emonds, J. 1985. *A Unified Theory of Syntactic Categories.* Dordrecht: Foris.

Enna, F. (ed.) 1984. *Sos Contos de Foghile.* Sassari: Gallizzi.

Jones, M. A. 1993. *Sardinian Syntax.* London: Routledge.

Pittau, M. 1972. *Grammatica del sardo-nuorese.* Bologna: Pàtron.

———. 1978. *Pronuncia e scrittura del sardo logudorese.* Sassari: Dessì.

Postal, P. 1966. On so-called pronouns in English. *Modern Studies in English*, ed. D. Reidel & S. Schane, 201-224. Englewood Cliffs, N.J.: Prentice-Hall.

# Voice, Aspect, and Arbitrary Arguments*

Christopher Lyons
*University of Salford*

## 1. Introduction

### 1.1. Constructions with *se*

My purpose in this paper is to examine, from a comparative perspective, a
number of related constructions in Spanish and French — those which involve a pronominal clitic descended historically from the Latin reflexive
paradigm — and, more particularly, to consider a constraint affecting one
of them. In certain of these constructions, such as the purely reflexive use,
where the clitic is most obviously analysed as part of a chain with the bind-
ing-theory status of an anaphor, this modern clitic is still part of a complete
paradigm; in others, only the third-person form occurs. For both cases I
refer to this clitic or clitic paradigm by the modern reflex of the Latin third-
person form, *se*, as it appears (orthographically) in Spanish and French. I
will also have occasion to look at the 'canonical' passive construction,
which shares some syntactic and semantic characteristics with certain of
the *se* constructions. I will argue that most uses of *se* can be reduced to a
single construction — a passive construction — in which the clitic behaves
syntactically in a uniform manner, with no need of parametrization. Observed differences between the various *se* constructions considered follow
from differences in the lexically represented argument structures of the
verbs involved. And the constraint affecting one *se* construction, involving
aspect, is due to the 'arbitrary' nature of the implicit agent argument of one
interpretation of this unified *se* passive.

Modern Romance *se* has a much wider range of uses than did its ances-
tor, Latin SE, which was purely a reflexive/reciprocal anaphor. In addition
to this use, verb forms with *se* have taken the place of the Latin deponent
verbs, in the form of 'inherent reflexives' like French *s'évanouir* 'to faint'.
The loss of the Latin deponent paradigm (in its original form, since *s'é-*

*vanouir* can reasonably be regarded as exemplifying a modern deponent construction) is to be seen in terms of the loss of the synthetic passive paradigm in general. The place of this has been taken in the modern languages by two constructions: a compound passive involving an auxiliary corresponding to English *to be* (Spanish *ser*, French *être*) plus the past participle of the verb in question; and the *se* construction, as in Spanish *Estos sombreros se venden muy baratos aquí* 'These hats are sold very cheaply here'. Of these, the former tends to be regarded as the canonical passive, while the latter tends to be thought of as **resembling** a passive rather than **being** one. But it seems clear that both these constructions display the properties typically associated with passive morphology: an underlying object moves to subject position, because (on the usual account) it cannot get Case in complement position, accusative Case being 'absorbed' by passive morphology; subject position, where nominative Case is to be had, is free for it to move to on the assumption that passive morphology also 'absorbs' the external θ-role, making it impossible for a D-structure subject argument to appear. I shall adopt the name 'passive *se*' to denote this particular *se* construction.

Burzio (1986) assimilates 'inherent *se*', exemplified above by *s'é-vanouir*, to the 'ergative *se*' construction. Ergative *se* (also known as 'neutral *se*' following Ruwet (1972)) is exemplified by Spanish *La puerta se cerró* 'The door closed', French *La branche s'est cassée* 'The branch broke'. The superficial subject of this construction, like that of the passive, corresponds to the direct object of the transitive use of the same verb (*Juan cerró la puerta* 'Juan closed the door', *J'ai cassé la branche* 'I broke the branch'), so the subject of ergative *se* looks like a derived subject. But the interpretation of the ergative *se* construction differs from that of the passive in that an agent argument (corresponding to the absorbed external θ-role) is implicit in the case of the passive, and may indeed be expressed in the compound passive by the equivalent of an English *by*-phrase (*La puerta fue cerrada por Juan* 'The door was closed by Juan', *La maison a été achetée par des étrangers* 'The house has been bought by some foreigners'); whereas with ergative *se* there is no implicit agent — the interpretation of *La puerta se cerró, La branche s'est cassée* is that the door closed, the branch broke, spontaneously, or at least with no deliberate human agency being involved. It is frequently pointed out that the ergative *se* construction is subject to various constraints of an idiosyncratic and lexical character, and is not productive (Ruwet 1972, Burzio 1986), though this has been disputed by Lyons (1982) and Zribi-Hertz (1987).

Similar in certain respects to the passive use of *se* is the 'impersonal' use, exemplified by Spanish *Se vende manzanas aquí* 'Apples are sold here', *Se trabaja mucho en este país* 'One works/They work hard in this country'. The verb may be intransitive (*trabajar* 'to work'), and where it is transitive (*vender* 'to sell') it does not agree with the following NP which satisfies its subcategorization requirement; the verb is always invariant, in its third-person singular form. So the subcategorized argument, if there is one, is in object position, suggesting that impersonal *se* does not have the property of absorbing accusative Case. But it does appear to absorb the external θ-role, with the result that no subject can be expressed. A subject or agent is implicit, however, with an indefinite interpretation which can be rendered in English by *one*, *they*, *someone*, *people*, etc. In apparently absorbing the external θ-role but not accusative Case, impersonal *se* resembles, in varying degrees, impersonal passives in such languages as German (*Es wurde getanzt* 'There was dancing/People danced'), Irish (*Dúnadh an fhuinneog ar a seacht* 'The window was closed at seven/Someone closed the window at seven'), and possibly French (*Il a été écrit une lettre* 'A letter was written') — though for a different analysis of this French construction, according to which the object receives an inherent Case rather than structural accusative, see Belletti (1986) and Cinque (1988).

Finally there is 'middle *se*', as in Spanish *Esta habitación se limpia en diez minutos* 'This room cleans/is cleaned in ten minutes', French *Cette chemise se lave facilement* 'This shirt washes easily/is easily washed'. This construction resembles both passive and ergative *se* in that the subcategorized object appears in subject position. But it differs from ergative *se* in that it does involve an implicit agent — there is no implication that the shirt or the room will clean itself without the owner/user lifting a finger. Middle *se* is also generally accepted to be fully productive. It differs also from passive *se*, in that it is subject to an aspect restriction whereby it occurs only in habitual or generic contexts, and in that it is understood as predicating a property of the subject (such as that of being easily washable) rather than describing an event or process.

But while the Romance languages as a whole show a wide range of constructions involving the reflex of SE, they also exhibit a considerable amount of variation. All the uses discussed above are found in Spanish, but French shows a more limited distribution.[1] The constructions which occur freely in French are the inherent, ergative, and middle ones. It may be that French also has passive *se*, but this use appears to be restricted to a small number of verbs; I return to this point below. French also appears to have the impersonal use, though again somewhat marginally and with rather severe constraints:

(1)   a.   *Il s'est confirmé qu'ils arriveront ce soir.*
           'It has been confirmed that they will arrive this evening.'
      b.   *Il s'est commis un crime ce matin.*
           'A crime was/has been committed this morning.'
      c.   *\*Il s'est commis ce crime ce matin.*
           'This crime was committed this morning.'
      d.   *\*Il se travaille beaucoup ici.*
           'One works hard here.'

The construction is essentially restricted to transitive verbs, and shows a definiteness effect whereby the complement can be a clause or an indefinite NP, but not a definite NP.

## 1.2. Standard analyses

Much of the by now vast literature on *se* is devoted to the attempt to unify the different constructions or uses. It seems impossible to avoid the conclusion that there is more than one *se*, or use of *se*, on the surface, so any unified analysis must be at a deeper level. The question then comes down to the level of abstraction at which the *ses* can be unified, and the parameter(s) or feature(s) whose differing settings or values produce the more superficial divergences. For example, Grimshaw (1982), working in a lexical framework, treats all occurrences of French *se* as a grammatical morpheme, with no argument or pronominal status, resulting from the operation of certain lexical rules on the verb. Essentially, this morpheme marks the verb as a derived intransitive, but a different rule is involved in the derivation of each *se* construction. Manzini (1983, 1986) proposes that Italian *si* is a single lexical item with optionality in the value-setting of certain features. It is a variable, but may be either a free variable (in the impersonal construction, for example) or a dependent variable (as in the reflexive use); and it has, optionally, a passivizer property, which is present in the middle use but absent in the impersonal and reflexive uses. Some of the differences between Italian and French are accounted for by the assumption that the passivizer property is obligatory in French. Cinque (1988), while not offering a completely unified account, contributes to the search for one by proposing that many aspects of the behaviour of Italian *si* (and *se* in the other Romance languages) can be accounted for in terms of the setting of a feature [±argument]. The idea is that *se* is optionally either an argument or a non-argument, and this dichotomy interacts with other features to yield the various types of *se* observed.

The present paper is also intended as a contribution to this debate, but I confine my attention to the passive, middle and ergative uses of *se*. Let us examine more closely the basic points of the analysis generally assumed for these constructions.

Chomsky (1981) takes passive *se* to share a common underlying form with impersonal *se*. This is as in (2) (substituting a Spanish example for Chomsky's Italian one):

(2)   [NPe] *se come* [NP*las manzanas*]
       e   CL eats      the apples

The clitic *se* is in Infl in D-structure and is 'related to the subject' — that is, it governs and is coindexed with the subject position. Its property of absorbing the accusative Case normally assigned by the verb is an optional one, and the impersonal construction is the result of this option not coming into effect — impersonal *se* is thus an active structure, its semantic similarity to passives deriving from the arbitrary or indefinite interpretation of *se*. In most accounts along these lines, *se* is taken to be an argument with nominal category status, and thus requiring Case (or to be in a chain assigned Case); see, for example, Belletti (1982). This requirement is met by the clitic's coindexation with the subject position, which receives nominative Case at S-structure either directly, under government by Infl, or indirectly, by membership of a chain. As an argument, *se* also requires a θ-role, and the one it receives is the external θ-role normally assigned to the subject. One way to achieve this result would be to assume that the external θ-role is assigned as normal to the subject position, and then associated with the clitic via the latter's coindexation with the subject. But the usual assumption is that *se* withholds the subject θ-role, preventing it being assigned to subject position. A way of conceiving the difference between this and the property of passive morphology of 'absorbing' the external θ-role is to see the latter process as preventing assignment of this θ-role by the verb, while with *se* the θ-role is 'emitted' by the verb but intercepted (outside VP) before reaching the subject. Belletti & Rizzi (1986) suggest that this is effected by assignment of the external θ-role first to Infl; it would then normally be transmitted by Infl to subject position (governed by Infl), but a *se* in Infl absorbs it at this point.[2]

If, on the other hand, *se* is allowed to absorb accusative Case, the result is passive *se*. This possibility is, of course, limited to clauses containing transitive verbs, since only with such verbs is there an accusative Case feature to absorb. The complement NP, *las manzanas* in (2), deprived of accusative Case, has to move to a Case-marked position to satisfy the Case Filter. Subject position is open to it because this position is empty, and is one that will receive Case; this is because, since *se* has absorbed the accusative Case, it cannot also take nominative Case. *Se* does, however, still absorb the external θ-role — another necessary factor if the complement NP is to be able to move to subject position; for *las manzanas* has been assigned the object θ-role at D-structure and carries this with it to subject position, which would not be possible if subject position was already marked with a distinct θ-role. An important point to note here is that, generally, adjunct agent phrases such as regularly accompany the canonical passive (corresponding to the English PP with *by*) do not occur with passive *se*; this indicates that *se* retains the external θ-role it has absorbed, while passive morphology can reassign it. Once *las manzanas* is in subject position, the verb must agree with it in person and number (through combination of the Agr element of Infl with V); hence the contrast between the impersonal construction (3), where there is no agreement between the verb and the theme argument (the verb generally being taken here to be in a non-inflected, stem form), and the passive *se* construction (4) and (5), which shows subject-verb agreement.

(3)   *Se come las manzanas.*
(4)   *Las manzanas se comen.*
(5)   *Se comen las manzanas.*

The variant (5) differs from (4) only in that it has undergone an essentially stylistic process of inversion, an option often taken to be a characteristic of null-subject languages. An alternative view is that the complement remains in its D-structure position and a mechanism is available for it to get nominative Case; see Burzio (1986), Jaeggli (1986). The analysis outlined, relating passive to impersonal *se*, is a useful starting point, though it is far from being unproblematic. As Cinque (1988) points out, the idea that when the verb is transitive *se* can freely absorb (or be associated with) either nominative or accusative Case is odd.

The derivation of middle *se* is similar to that of passive *se*. The clitic absorbs accusative Case and the external θ-role, and the complement NP (θ-marked as theme by the verb) is therefore compelled to move to subject position, where it receives nominative Case and triggers subject-verb agreement. The main difference between middle and passive *se* is that, as noted, the former construction seems to predicate a property of the derived subject, relegating the implicit agent to the background, and only occurs in generic contexts. These properties are shared by the English middle (*This material washes easily, That table transports easily*), which, however, is limited to a smaller range of verbs, those taking 'affected' objects (Jaeggli 1986). The absence of an overt clitic or other morphology has led some writers to propose at least partially lexical accounts for the English middle (Williams 1981, Cinque 1988), though syntactic analyses have also been advanced (Keyser & Roeper 1984, Roberts 1987); Keyser & Roeper go so far as to propose that English middles involve a phonologically null clitic with the properties of *se*. The Romance middle is generally taken to have a syntactic derivation, because of the overt clitic and because the construction is not apparently subject to Jaeggli's (1986) Affectedness Constraint, limiting the (lexical) elimination of a head's external θ-role to heads with 'affected' theme complements — roughly, complements which undergo a change of state. Thus, note the contrast between Spanish and English in (6), where the verb appearing is one of perception, and does not take an affected complement:

(6)  a.  *Las montañas se ven fácilmente aquí.*
     b.  *The mountains see easily here.

A striking property of the middle, in Spanish, French and English, is that it requires some form of modification, typically by a manner adverbial:

(7)  a.  *Este tejido se lava fácilmente/bien/con dificultad/en cinco minutos.*
     b.  *Ce tissu se lave facilement/bien/avec difficulté/en cinq minutes.*

c. This material washes easily/well/with difficulty/in five minutes.

Moreover, middles are not compatible with adverbials which require an agent, and are awkward with purpose clauses:

(8) a. *El salón se limpia (rápidamente) de propósito.
b. *Le salon se nettoie (vite) exprès.
c. *The lounge cleans (quickly) deliberately.

(9) a. ?El salón se limpia (rápidamente) para impresionar a los visitantes.
b. ?Le salon se nettoie (vite) pour faire impression sur les visiteurs.
c. ?The lounge cleans (quickly) to impress the visitors .

In (8), de propósito, exprès, deliberately select an agentive argument, and the purpose clauses in (9) require an agent in the matrix clause to control their PRO subject. The difficulty in both cases clearly stems from the lack of a suitable agent, and this suggests that the unexpressed agent of the middle is (to some extent) syntactically inert. The middle contrasts strikingly in this with the passive, where an implicit argument can license agentive adverbs and control the PRO of a purpose clause. Note that the Spanish examples (8a) and (9a) are in fact acceptable if the construction is interpreted as passive rather than middle se (with the meanings 'The lounge is (being) cleaned (quickly) deliberately', 'The lounge is (being) cleaned (quickly) to impress the visitors').

Ergative se has in common with passive and middle se that the subject satisfies the verb's subcategorization requirements, as does the object when the verb is not accompanied by se. So one can assume that here, too, the external θ-role fails to be assigned to subject position and accusative Case to object position. But it is almost universally assumed that this suspension of the normal θ- and Case-marking is a lexical rather than a syntactic process. This is principally because of the observation that the construction is much more restricted than the other se constructions, and idiosyncratically restricted, as argued by Ruwet (1972). In probably the most detailed treatment, Burzio (1986) proposes that se in the ergative construction is a morphological marker of the suppression of the subject θ-role, the process by which ergative lexical entries are derived from transitive ones. For him, there is no essential difference between such verbs as romperse, se casser 'to break', *cerrarse, se fermer* 'to close', and unaccusative (also known as 'ergative') verbs like *mejorar* 'to improve', *couler* 'to sink', which can also occur transitively; the question whether the ergative member of a transitive-ergative alternation takes *se* is one of lexical idiosyncrasy. This is because, on the 'unaccusative hypothesis' (Perlmutter 1978), verbs like *mejorar*, *couler*, and *llegar*, *arriver* 'to arrive' (with no transitive alternant), also take only one argument, which is VP-internal, and assign no external θ-role; this internal argument then moves to subject position to get nominative Case, since these verbs also fail to assign accusative Case.

## 2. The aspect constraint

### 2.1. Middle voice and generic aspect

As noted above, the middle construction is limited to generic or habitual contexts, as opposed to contexts in which individual events are expressed. This restriction is obviously connected with the intuition that the middle predicates a property of the surface subject. One manifestation of this restriction, which I will refer to as the 'aspect constraint', is that the middle does not occur in punctual tenses such as the preterite, nor with time adverbials indicating a specific point in time:

(10)  a.  (\*)*El tejido se lavó sin dificultad.*
          'The material washed without difficulty.'
      b.  (\*)*Las montañas se vieron a las nueve.*
          'The mountains saw (i.e., were visible) at nine.'
(11)  a.  \**La chemise se lava très bien.*
          'The shirt washed very well.'
      b.  \**Mes lunettes se sont nettoyées à huit heures et quart.*
          'My glasses cleaned at quarter past eight.'

Note that the examples (10) are grammatical on the passive interpretation ('The material was washed without difficulty', 'The mountains were seen at nine' — reporting an event rather than describing a property of the material/mountains), a possibility available for Spanish but generally not for French. The aspect constraint distinguishes the middle very clearly from passive *se* and the compound passive, and from ergative *se*, none of which is subject to any such restriction:

(12)  *Estos relojes se nos regalaron.*
      'These watches were given to us as presents.'

(13) a. *Mi dormitorio fue limpiado ayer.*
     'My bedroom was cleaned yesterday.'
   b. *Ma chemise a été lavée hier.*
     'My shirt was washed yesterday.'
(14) a. *La puerta se cerró hace tres minutos.*
     'The door closed three minutes ago.'
   b. *Cette branche s'est cassée hier à huit heures et quart.*
     'This branch broke yesterday at quarter past eight.'

This aspect constraint is characteristic also of the English middle, as noted. In English, both the middle and the ergative uses of verbs are indistinguishable morphologically from the transitive use of the same verbs; but the aspect constraint clearly distinguishes the middle use from the ergative and transitive (as well as from the morphological passive). A further manifestation of this constraint in English is that the middle is generally excluded from the progressive construction:

(15) a. ?The chairs are positioning quite easily.
   b. ?This old copper lamp is polishing up without effort.

This is to be expected, since the progressive denotes an event in progress, not a state or characteristic. French has no progressive aspectual form, but the expression *en train de* is close in meaning to the English progressive, and also fails to occur with the middle construction. Spanish has a progressive aspectual form, similar in structure to that of English, and this too is excluded with middle *se*. These facts are illustrated in (16-17):

(16) (*)*La puerta se está pintando sin dificultad.*
     'The door is painting without difficulty'.
(17) **Ces lunettes sont en train de se nettoyer (facilement).*
     'These glasses are (in the process of) cleaning (easily).'

(Again (16) is acceptable on a passive reading.)

The most detailed attempt to explain the aspect constraint is that of Roberts (1987), in relation to English, though the account would carry over equally to Romance — as is obviously required, since the same constraint is shared by Spanish, French and English (and Italian, as is clear from the substantial literature on Italian middle *si*). Roberts observes that the middle has much of the behaviour of stative verbs, and he makes this the basis of his account. He proposes that the middle results from a process of stativization, which consists of 'the temporal obviation of V with respect to Infl'; that is, the normal, though optional, coindexation between V and the Tense component of Infl, which is responsible for the verb receiving an event reading, does not take place. The result is that the verb must receive a state interpretation. Other consequences also follow, which I shall return to below.

## 2.2. Agentive ergatives

The aspect constraint affects middle *se* only, not passive or ergative *se*. On the other hand, middle *se* agrees with passive *se* in being agentive, while ergative *se* is non-agentive. For, while the agent of the middle may be felt as backgrounded, there is still felt to be an agent involved, as in the passive. The ergative, however, is interpreted as agentless — or at least as not involving any human agency. For example, contrast (18) with (19):

(18)  a.  *Estas gafas se limpian fácilmente.*
      b.  *Ces lunettes se nettoient facilement.*
      c.  These glasses clean easily.
(19)  a.  *La taza se rompió en el agua caliente.*
      b.  *La tasse s'est cassée dans l'eau chaude.*
      c.  The cup broke in the hot water.

In (19) the interpretation is (or can be) that the cup simply broke, as it were spontaneously, as a result of the temperature it was subjected to, but in (18) one assumes that the cleaning will only occur if someone deliberately performs it.

The middle differs from the ergative on two counts, therefore. But there are cases where a *se* construction is agentive, and therefore apparently middle, yet shows the aspectual behaviour of ergatives, appearing in event contexts, in punctual tenses for example. Such cases are more clearly observed in French, because in Spanish they can always be argued to be instances of passive *se*, despite the apparent backgrounding of the agent. The following discussion is therefore limited to French, which (largely) lacks the complicating factor of passive *se*. It is interesting to note, too, that the same phenomenon is readily observable in English, where middle and ergative are morphologically identical, and distinct from the passive. Consider (20-22):

(20) *J'ai nettoyé ces deux chemises avec deux détergents dif-*
    *férents; celle-ci s'est bien nettoyée, mais pas celle-là.*
    'I cleaned these two shirts with two different detergents; this
    one has cleaned well, but that one hasn't.'

(21) *Quel hôtel! Les chambres sont sales, on vous sert du pain*
    *rassis, de la bière éventée. Ce matin le café s'est bu froid;*
    *ce soir il se boira peut-être tiède.*
    'What a hotel! The rooms are dirty, you get stale bread and
    flat beer. This morning the coffee was/was drunk cold;
    perhaps this evening it will be/be drunk lukewarm.'

(22) *On m'a dit que ces malles ne se transportent pas facilement,*
    *mais celle-ci s'est transportée sans difficulté.*
    'I've been told that these trunks don't transport easily, but this
    one has transported with no difficulty.'

For comparison, note the example (23), from Roberts (1987), of an English
middle in the progressive; further English examples with punctual tenses,
as in (24), are easy to construct.

(23) Bureaucrats are bribing more than ever in Reagan's second
    term.

(24) I spent the whole day trying to paint the bathroom wall, but it
    didn't paint easily.

These examples seem to indicate that the aspect constraint on the
middle is not absolute. Notice that in (22) *se transportent* is clearly a
middle, which strongly favours the assumption that the occurrence in the
following clause of the same verb, again with *se*, *s'est transportée*, is also
middle, despite the punctual tense. Such event uses of apparent middles
are admittedly exceptional (more so in French than in English), but the exception requires explanation. It is clear that a non-exceptional use of the
construction, respecting the aspect constraint, can make an exceptional use
in a succeeding clause more acceptable; this is the case in (22) and (24). In
(20), it is a normal use of a verb in a non-clitic construction that somehow
legitimizes the exceptional use of the same verb in the *se* construction in
the next clause. One might suggest that in cases like (22) and (24), a repetition in the second clause of the same verb in the same construction is felt
to be desirable for stylistic reasons, despite the different aspectual context,
and that such stylistic factors permit a relaxation of the aspect constraint.

But it seems unlikely that a constraint which in general is a very strong one would give way to a stylistic preference in this way. A more plausible approach is to see the event uses of *se* in (20-22), while certainly being occasioned by stylistic or pragmatic factors, as involving a change in interpretation. That is, the agency is pushed further into the background so that the construction becomes ergative rather than middle. Of course, if one is saying that sentences like (22) stem from a desire to use the same construction in two clauses, but the result is that middle *se* is followed by ergative *se*, then the question arises of whether middle and ergative *se* are really two distinct constructions or uses. Moreover, while it is intuitively plausible to argue that the agent is further backgrounded in (20-22) (and (23-24)), it is clear that the agency is not eliminated. While verbs like *casser* 'to break', *fermer* 'to close', readily admit an ergative use with *se* because they can be easily conceived of as denoting an agentless event, such a conception is less available with *nettoyer* 'to clean', and probably not available with *boire* 'to drink' and *transporter* 'to transport'. Certainly in the examples (20-22) the interpretation is not that the events are agentless. The conclusion is either that the ergative construction need not be agentless, or that *se* can express a degree of prominence/backgrounding of agency between that of the middle and that of the ergative. Either way, the distinction between middle *se* and ergative *se* becomes rather hazy.

The agent demotion accompanied by non-observance of the aspect constraint illustrated in (20-22), where it occurs as an exceptional phenomenon, is found regularly with certain verbs, of which the clearest instance is perhaps *vendre* 'to sell':

(25) *Notre dernier modèle s'est vite/bien vendu.*
'Our last model sold quickly/well.'

(26) *Sa voiture s'est vendue 40.000 francs.*
'His/Her car sold for 40,000 francs.'

(27) *Toutes les actions de notre compagnie se sont vendues en une heure.*
'All our company's shares sold in an hour.'

*Vendre* is like *boire* and *transporter* in not allowing, or not easily allowing, a complete lack of agency: selling necessarily involves a seller. But *se vendre*, unlike these other verbs, freely admits a use in which the aspect constraint is not respected, and, as the glosses to (25-27) show, the same is

true of English *sell*. Keyser & Roeper (1984) show that the syntactic behaviour of *sell* in its intransitive use is precisely that of an ergative, despite
its being necessarily agentive in some degree; the same is clearly true of *se
vendre*. These are clear instances of a verb whose argument structure logi-
cally includes an agent, necessarily, but with which the agency can be
minimized or backgrounded, to a greater degree than in the middle, to the
point where the construction becomes syntactically ergative. As (20-22)
indicate, this possibility is in principle available for all agentive verbs,
given certain 'exceptional' pragmatic conditions; but for *vendre* it is conventional.

   As already noted, French does not, in general, permit a passive use of
*se*. But what looks like a passive — in that it is agentive and appears in
punctual tenses — does occur with a limited range of verbs:

   (28)  *Les vols vers la lune vont s'espacer.*     (Ruwet 1972)
         'Flights to the moon are going to get spaced out.'
   (29)  *La question s'est vite décidée.*
         'The matter was quickly decided.'
   (30)  *Cette question se discutera demain.*
         'This matter will be discussed tomorrow.'
   (31)  *Le crime s'est commis ce matin.*     (Zribi-Hertz 1982)
         'The crime was committed this morning.'

The verbs *décider, discuter,* and *commettre* denote events or activities
which necessarily involve an agent, and at least in (28) *s'espacer* too seems
agentive. But if (28-31) are taken to exemplify passive *se*, it is unclear
why very few verbs allow this construction. A neater solution would be to
assimilate these verbs to the class represented by *vendre* — agentive verbs
permitting an ergative use of *se* with severe backgrounding of the agent.
(Ruwet (1972) takes such uses to be ergative, though he regards *se vendre*
in examples like (25-27) as middle.) I shall adopt this position, which
makes it possible to say that French does not have passive *se*.

   The position we have now reached is as follows. Ergative *se* is for the
most part limited to verbs denoting an event which can be seen as agentless, and *se* presumably signals non-assignment or suppression of the external θ-role. However, some essentially agentive verbs can appear with
ergative *se*, their agency being severely backgrounded; what precisely is
happening to the agent θ-role in these cases is far from obvious, but it does

not seem to be totally suppressed. Middle *se* is available to agentive verbs, and absorbs (or demotes in some other way) the external θ-role. The agent with this construction is still present implicitly, though it is generally taken to be backgrounded — more so than with the passive construction, but apparently less so than with agentive ergatives like *se vendre*, *se décider*. The aspect constraint applies consistently to middle *se*, but ergative *se* is not subject to it. Given this rather subtly graded continuum, it may turn out that the distinction between ergative and middle *se* cannot be maintained — a desirable result. But this can be decided only when it is established what *se* is doing (specifically, what is happening to the external θ-role) in the different cases discussed.

## 3. The implicit argument

### 3.1. Arbitrary and indefinite arguments

All the constructions discussed (compound and clitic passive, middle, agentive and non-agentive ergative) involve some degree of subject or agent demotion; but the picture sketched of four different degrees of demotion (the agent being most prominent in the passive, more backgrounded in the middle, severely backgrounded in the agentive ergative, and completely absent in the non-agentive ergative) is hardly plausible. It can be simplified, however, and I will argue in this section that there is no difference in degree of backgrounding between middle *se* and passive *se*. The intuition that the agent is pushed to the background in the middle construction is a mistaken one, resulting from a difference in the nature of the implicit agent in the two constructions. I will suggest subsequently that the difference between agentive and non-agentive ergatives, and between these and middles and passives, can be explained fully in terms of the different lexically represented thematic structures of the verbs involved, and has nothing to do with varying behaviour on the part of *se*.

The idea that the agent of the middle is less to the fore than that of the passive is supported by its being syntactically inert, as observed above (examples (8-9)), and has been expressed formally in different ways. Roberts (1987) argues for a process of subject 'dethematization' — in effect suppression, since on his account the agent is not structurally present, whereas it is in the passive. For Roberts, middle formation is a process of stativization — V fails to be coindexed with the Tense element of Infl, and

the result is a state, rather than event, reading.  But the indices of this temporal binding are also involved in 'structural' θ-role assignment (agent and
theme being 'structural' θ-roles — an idea inspired by the distinction between structural and inherent Cases), so the agent θ-role also fails to be assigned.  (It hangs around, however, with 'chômeur' status, to be interpreted
at LF.)  Applied to the Romance *se* constructions, these ideas can be interpreted as follows.  Passive *se* absorbs the agent θ-role, which continues to
be present structurally (though it cannot in general be reassigned to an adjunct agent phrase as it can with the compound passive).  In the middle
construction, the agent θ-role simply fails to be assigned as a result of stativization, so it is not there to be absorbed by *se* (as I have so far assumed
happens); *se* therefore serves as a signal of dethematization, much as in the
ergative.

I believe that this view is mistaken, and that middle *se* absorbs the external θ-role exactly as passive *se* does.  To see why, let us examine the interpretation given to the implicit agent argument in each case.  Roberts
claims that the implicit argument of both the passive and the middle is
'arbitrary' in interpretation, having a meaning something like that of the
English pronoun *one*.  But compare (32) with (33) and (34) with (35):

(32)  a.  *Este cuarto se limpia fácilmente.*
          'This room cleans easily.'
      b.  *Aquellos policías se sobornan sin dificultad.*
          'Those policemen bribe without difficulty.'
(33)  a.  *Este cuarto fue limpiado ayer.*
          'This room was cleaned yesterday.'
      b.  *Aquellos policías son sobornados a menudo.*
          'Those policemen are bribed often.'
(34)  a.  *Ma chemise se lave vite.*
          'My shirt washes quickly.'
      b.  *Ce vin se boit très frais.*
          'This wine is drunk very cool.'
(35)  a.  *Ma chemise est lavée très souvent.*
          'My shirt is washed very often.'
      b.  *Ce vin a été bu très frais.*
          'This wine was/has been drunk very cool.'

In the passive examples, (33) and (35), the agent is real but unspecified. It is of course possible to identify the agent by means of a '*by*-phrase' such as *por atracadores* 'by gangsters', *par mon oncle* 'by my uncle'; but this is optional, and I am concerned only with the implied agent when such a phrase is not added. This implied agent, then, can be thought of as something like *someone, I'm not saying who*, or *some people, it doesn't matter who* — in other words, a (generally human) indefinite. In (33) I use the compound passive to make the passive-middle contrast clear, but the interpretation of the implied agent is the same with passive *se*:

(36) a. *Ese problema se solucionó ayer.*
'That problem was solved yesterday.'
b. *Estos problemas se discuten a menudo.*
'These problems are often discussed.'

But in the middle examples, (32) and (34), the implied agent is not so much *someone* as *anyone* — anyone who wishes to or has to wash the shirt or clean the room, whoever wishes to enjoy the wine or has an interest in bribing the police. In other words, the agent is non-specific rather than unspecified; arbitrary or potential rather than unidentified. It is also always understood as human.

Arguments of these two types are also distinguished by Cinque (1988), who terms them, respectively, 'quasi-existential' and 'quasi-universal'. But he sees the two as contextual variants of a single 'arbitrary' argument. I believe them to be independent of each other, and I shall refer to them as 'indefinite' (with the passive) and 'arbitrary' (with the middle). It is important to note that the implicit argument of the passive may have an arbitrary interpretation:

(37) a. *Mis gafas son fácilmente limpiadas.*
'My glasses are easily cleaned.'
b. *Este juez es fácilmente sobornado.*
'This judge is easily bribed.'
(38) a. *Ce tissu est vite lavé.*
'This material is quickly washed.'
b. *Ce vin est bu très frais.*
'This wine is drunk very cool.'

This indicates that indefinite may be a superordinate category which includes arbitrary. The implicit argument of the middle is always arbitrary.

It is instructive to compare the syntactic behaviour of the middle construction with that of the compound passive and passive *se* when the latter have an arbitrary implicit agent. Notice first of all that the arbitrary passives (as I shall term them for convenience) in (37-38) are exactly synonymous with the corresponding middles:

(39)  a.  *Mis gafas se limpian fácilmente.*
      b.  *Este juez se soborna fácilmente.*
(40)  a.  *Ce tissu se lave vite.*
      b.  *Ce vin se boit très frais.*

It turns out that they are also subject to the same syntactic restrictions. First, the arbitrary passive respects the aspect constraint, as (41-42) show. Again I use only the compound passive for Spanish because passive *se* showing this behaviour could always be claimed to be middle *se*; but this of course simply proves my point, that passive *se* with an arbitrary agent is indistinguishable from middle *se*.

(41)  a.  *Los vestidos de los campesinos medievales eran hechos bastante rápidamente.*
      b.  *Les vêtements des paysans médiévaux étaient faits assez rapidement.*
          'The clothes of medieval peasants were made rather rapidly.'
(42)  a.  *El hierro fue descubierto hace tres mil años.*
      b.  *Le fer fut (a été) découvert il y a trois mille ans.*
          'Iron was discovered three thousand years ago.'

The implicit arguments of the passives in (41), where the imperfect tense may be interpreted as expressing past generic aspect, are understood as arbitrary. Those in (42), where the tense is punctual and where there is an adverbial expressing a more or less precise point in time, may not be so understood.

The modification requirement on the middle also applies equally to the arbitrary passive; (43-44), without an appropriate adverbial modifier, cannot be interpreted as having an arbitrary implicit agent, even though the context is generic:

(43) *Aquellos policías son sobornados (a menudo).*
  'Those policemen are bribed (often).'
(44) *Ces lunettes sont nettoyées (une fois par semaine).*
  'These glasses are cleaned (once a week).'

Arbitrary passives also agree with middles in being incompatible with agentive adverbials:

(45) a. *El salón es limpiado (rápidamente) de propósito.*
  b. *Le salon est (vite) nettoyé exprès.*
  'The lounge is (quickly) cleaned deliberately.'

These passives cannot be interpreted as having arbitrary agents, though this interpretation becomes possible if *de propósito* and *exprès* are removed.

Finally, arbitrary passives, like middles, are not readily followed by purpose clauses in which PRO must be controlled by an agent:

(46) a. *El salón es limpiado (rápidamente) para impresionar a los visitantes*
  b. *Le salon est (vite) nettoyé pour faire impression sur les visiteurs.*
  'The lounge is (quickly) cleaned to impress the visitors'

The sentences (46) are perfectly grammatical, but the implicit arguments of the passives are most naturally interpreted as indefinite, not arbitrary. Thus the sense is that someone, or some team of people, cleans the lounge to impress the visitors, rather than that the lounge can be quickly cleaned by whoever may wish to do so in order to impress the visitors.[3]

The conclusion to be drawn from these observations is that the distributional limitations discussed (the aspect constraint, the modification requirement, incompatibility with agentive adverbials and agent-control purpose clauses) are not characteristics of the middle construction, as generally assumed, but characteristics of verbs with arbitrary implicit agents. The difference in behaviour frequently pointed out in relation to these constraints between the middle and the passive stems from the fact that the implicit agent of the passive is generally not arbitrary, while that of the middle has to be.[4]

A remaining difference between the middle and the compound passive in Spanish and French (and English) is that passive morphology can transmit the absorbed agent θ-role to a *by*-phrase, whereas middle *se* (and the English middle) retains it. This difference does not seem to depend on the arbitrary-indefinite distinction (as suggested in Lyons (1989)), because the arbitrary passive allows an (appropriate) agent phrase:

(47) a. *Estas gafas son limpiadas fácilmente por cualquiera.*
     b. *Ces lunettes sont facilement nettoyées par n' importe qui.*
     'These glasses are easily cleaned by anyone.'

But the significant point is that the inability to reassign the absorbed θ-role to a *by*-phrase applies to passive *se* as well as middle *se*. In fact the data are not altogether straightforward on this point; some speakers of Spanish do accept reassignment in some cases. Otero (1986) gives the following example:

(48) *Las normas se dictarán por el gobierno.*
     'The regulations will be dictated by the government.'

This possibility is stylistically limited, but it is interesting to note that speakers accepting it also accept the possibility of an agent phrase, given the same stylistic context, in examples such as (49), where the agent is arbitrary:

(49) *Tal trabajo se efectúa rápidamente por cualquier persona calificada.*
     'Such a task is quickly carried out by any qualified person.'

Of course (49) could be claimed to be an example of arbitrary passive *se*, but, again, the point is that there is no way one could distinguish arbitrary passive *se* from middle *se* — they are evidently the same thing.

So ability versus inability to reassign the absorbed θ-role (insofar as this distinction is valid for Spanish) is a defining feature not of the passive-middle opposition, but rather of the opposition between the participial (that is, compound) passive and *se* constructions. Baker (1988:334-337) observes that it is not unusual cross-linguistically for passive morphemes to be unable to transmit the external θ-role to an agent phrase, and that a number of languages have two passive morphemes, one with, and the other without, this property. So it is not an invariant property of the passive to be able to take a *by*-phrase, but rather an idiosyncratic property of individual passive morphemes. One can conclude, then, that Spanish has two passive constructions, one able to transmit the external θ-role freely, the other having this capacity only to a very limited extent as a stylistically marked option.

Of more immediate importance is the conclusion that middle *se* can be completely assimilated to passive *se*. The essential difference between the middle and the passive is that the implicit agent of the former is arbitrary while that of the latter may be either arbitrary or indefinite (arbitrary arguments perhaps being a subset of indefinite ones). Now, when Spanish passive *se* has an implicit agent interpreted as arbitrary, it is totally indistinguishable from middle *se*. The conclusion that, for Spanish, middle *se* is nothing more nor less than passive *se* with the arbitrary option, is compelling.

What, then, of the French middle? Since I have assimilated possible instances of passive *se*, as in (25-31), to the ergative, French differs from Spanish in having middle, but not passive, *se*. But it is natural to maintain that French middle *se*, too, instantiates a passive construction, exactly as in Spanish. The difference is that the *se* passive of French, by contrast with the participial passive, is constrained to take only an arbitrary implicit agent. This was not always the case; Old French had a fully productive passive *se* construction with indefinite implicit agent (Stéfanini 1962). With the historical restriction of the construction to arbitrary use, it may be that the uses exemplified in (29-31) are relics of the earlier indefinite use which have now been reanalysed as ergatives.

The frequently noted intuition that the middle involves backgrounding of the implicit agent to a greater degree than in the passive, reflected syntactically in the restrictions illustrated in (8-9), is a consequence of the fact that the agent is arbitrary. This is shown by the fact that when the 'canonical' passive (in both Spanish and French) has its implicit argument interpreted as arbitrary, it is exactly synonymous with the middle, as shown by (37-40), and is subject to precisely the same syntactic restrictions, as seen in (45-46).

## 3.2. Other arbitrary arguments

The arbitrary interpretation discussed is not limited to implicit agents of passive constructions, nor even to null arguments. Let us briefly survey some other nominal elements having this interpretation.

PRO is the null pronominal anaphor which occupies the ungoverned subject position of non-finite clauses. It is often referentially dependent on an antecedent, which may be the subject (as in (50-51)) or the object (as in (52-53)) of the higher clause, depending on the verb of this clause. PRO may also be pragmatically controlled, as in (54-55), where its reference is determined by the context.

(50)  *María quiere* [PRO *volver a casa*].
      'María wants to go home.'

(51)  *J'ai envie de* [PRO *sortir ce soir*].
      'I feel like going out this evening.'

(52)  *No permite a su hijo* [PRO *acompañarla*].
      'She doesn't let her son go with her.'

(53)  *Je lui ai demandé* [*de* PRO *m'attendre*].
      'I asked him to wait for me.'

(54)  [PRO *reparar el coche a ciegas*] *no fue fácil.*
      'Mending the car in the dark wasn't easy.'

(55)  *Il faut* [PRO *partir tout de suite*].
      'It is necessary to leave right away.'

But where there is no syntactic or pragmatic controller, the reference of PRO is not fixed and it receives an arbitrary interpretation:

(56)  *Es casi imposible* [PRO$_{arb}$ *hallar un empleo en Madrid*].
      'It's almost impossible to find a job in Madrid.'

(57)  [PRO$_{arb}$ *boire une telle quantité de vin*] *n'est pas bon pour la santé.*
      'Drinking such a lot of wine is not good for the health.'

The interpretation of PRO$_{arb}$ is in fact identical to that of the implied agent of the middle. The three sentences in each of (58) and (59) are synonymous:

(58)  a.  *Tales promesas no se cumplen fácilmente.*
          'Such promises are not easily kept.'

      b.  *No es fácil* [PRO$_{arb}$ *cumplir tales promesas*].
          'It isn't easy to keep such promises.'

      c.  *Tales promesas no son fáciles* [*de* PRO$_{arb}$ *cumplir* t].
          'Such promises are not easy to keep.'

(59)  a.  *Cette fenêtre s'ouvre facilement.*
          'This window opens easily.'

b. *Il est facile [d' PRO$_{arb}$ ouvrir cette fenêtre]*.
   'It's easy to open this window.'
c. *Cette fenêtre est facile [à PRO$_{arb}$ ouvrir t]*.
   'This window is easy to open.'

An overt expression with this same arbitrary human reference is the English pronoun *one*. There is a more specific use of *one*, as an oblique way of referring to oneself, the speaker (*The mechanic was awfully slow, and one didn't want to wait all day*), but in its usual use *one* is synonymous with PRO$_{arb}$ and the agent of the middle. Spanish has the form *uno* with the same sense, though it is much less commonly used than *one*. *Uno* tends to occur, for example, when the constraint banning two sequential occurrences of *se* rules out the middle:

(60) *Si uno se preocupa, empeora la situación.*
     'If one worries, it makes things worse.'

Now, PRO$_{arb}$, *one* and *uno* respect the aspect constraint, being restricted to non-event contexts. Since PRO$_{arb}$ occurs only as the subject of non-finite verb forms, punctual tenses are not available in its clause, so I use time adverbials to set the aspectual context:

(61) *Fue difícil [PRO*$_{arb}$ reparar el coche a ciegas anoche]*.
     'Mending the car in the dark last night was hard.'

(62) *Il sera plus facile [de PRO*$_{arb}$ déchiffrer cette écriture demain matin]*.
     'It will be easier to make out this handwriting tomorrow morning.'

PRO in (61-62) can be interpreted only as pragmatically controlled. In (63), *one* is to be understood as having its normal sense, not the (frequently ridiculed) specific one mentioned above; (63) and (64) are uninterpretable.

(63) *After driving around for two hours after dark last night, one was lost.

(64) *Al recibir este informe a las diez, uno se deshizo en lágrimas.*
     'On receiving this news at ten o'clock, one burst into tears.'

With French *on* we have a different situation. As is well known, *on* is used colloquially as a first-person plural pronoun; but even when it does not have this definite sense, it is broader in possible reference than *one* and *uno*, being similar to the implied agent of the passive rather than to that of the middle. That is, its reference can be arbitrary, but it can equally well be indefinite, designating an unidentified subject rather than a generic one. This is clear in (65):

> (65) a. *On frappe à la porte.*
>         'Someone's knocking at the door.'
>      b. *On m'a dit que vous comptez partir ce soir.*
>         'I've been told that you plan to leave this evening.'

Note that in (66), where the context is generic, *on* may be arbitrary; but in (67), with an event context, it may not.

> (66) *Pendant les années soixante on s'amusait beaucoup.*
>      'During the sixties one/we had a good time.'
> (67) *Mardi dernier on a mangé trois kilos de chocolat.*
>      'Last Tuesday we ate three kilos of chocolate/three kilos of chocolate were eaten.'

The position is similar with the Spanish indefinite third person plural. In a generic context, as in (68), the null subject may have an arbitrary interpretation, but in an event context, as in (69), only an indefinite reading is available.

> (68) *En el mundo antiguo, trabajaban mucho menos que hoy.*
>      'In the ancient world, one/people worked a lot less than today.'
> (69) *Arrestaron a Paco ayer.*
>      'They arrested Paco/Paco was arrested yesterday.'

Of course, a definite third-person plural reading is also possible, but the indefinite use of the third person plural (in which the indefinite referent need not even be understood as plural) is close to the passive in interpretation.

The observations made in this section make it clear that the aspect constraint is not specifically a feature of the middle, but rather of sentences with arbitrary subjects or agents, whether implicit or overt.

### 3.3. Arbitrary reference and aspect

A link between generic aspect and arbitrary reference is also discussed by Cinque (1988), who claims that the 'quasi-universal' (arbitrary) and 'quasi-existential' (indefinite) interpretations are two contextual variants of a single 'generic', 'arbitrary' or 'indeterminate' reading. This variation is a function of the aspect of the sentence, generic aspect triggering the arbitrary reading, and specific (event) aspect the indefinite reading. The evidence for this claim, based on Italian distributions, is that the arbitrary interpretation is compatible with generic but incompatible with specific time reference, and compatible with contexts suspending the specificity of time reference; the indefinite interpretation, on the other hand, is compatible with specific but incompatible with generic time reference, and incompatible with contexts suspending the specificity of time reference. In support of this view, Cinque points to the literature on generics, where it has been observed that English bare plurals and singular indefinites get a universal quantifier interpretation in generic aspectual contexts and an existential quantifier interpretation in specific aspectual contexts. The implication that the indefinite-arbitrary contrast discussed here can be subsumed under the more general distinction between specific and non-specific indefinites is an attractive one.

But the alleged complementary distribution between arbitrary and indefinite arguments does not hold, at least for the languages investigated here. Non-arbitrary, indefinite implicit arguments are perfectly compatible with generic aspect, as in the passive sentences (43-44), repeated as (70-71):

(70) *Aquellos policías son sobornados a menudo.*
    'Those policemen are bribed often.'
(71) *Ces lunettes sont nettoyées une fois par semaine.*
    'These glasses are cleaned once a week.'

The same applies to the *se* construction. Spanish passive *se* with the implicit agent interpreted as non-arbitrary can occur in a generic context:

(72) a. *Varias tonterías se dicen todas las semanas.*
       'Several silly things are said every week.'
    b. *Ese asunto se discute regularmente.*
       'That matter is discussed regularly.'

And French *on* can be interpreted non-arbitrarily in generic contexts:

(73) a. *On frappe à la porte tous les soirs à sept heures.*
       'There's a knock at the door every evening at seven o'clock.'

    b.  *Partout où elle va on la reconnaît.*
       'Everywhere she goes she is recognized.'

It is true that an arbitrary agent requires a generic context, but the converse is not the case.[5]

    If arbitrary and indefinite are not in complementary distribution, a plausible suggestion is that the difference between them is a matter of semantic vagueness. This would mean that, again, they both represent a single, indefinite, argument, but that in generic contexts indefiniteness is vague between a specific and an arbitrary or generic reading; which interpretation was appropriate would be determined by pragmatic considerations. But this approach runs into a problem with the French middle. The implicit argument of French middle *se* (alias French passive *se*) can be interpreted only as arbitrary, not as specific indefinite — unlike the compound passive and the *on* construction. It is hard to see how this constraint could exist if arbitrary and indefinite were merely variant interpretations of a single, vague entity.

    Taking it, then, that arbitrary and indefinite are semantically distinct (though retaining the possibility that the former is hyponymous to the latter), the aspect constraint amounts to the requirement that arbitrary agents appear in generic contexts. The mechanism underlying this requirement will not be discussed here, but for proposals of a coindexing or matching between non-arbitrary arguments and Infl see Roberts (1987) and Cinque (1988). What I want to do is examine the requirement itself more closely in descriptive terms.

    The arbitrary agent triggering the aspect constraint may be overt and syntactically the subject (*uno, on, one*), or it may be implicit (the agent of the *se* construction or the compound passive), with subject position being filled in S-structure by a non-agent. But the arbitrary argument need not even be an agent. In the following examples, $PRO_{arb}$ and *uno/on* are derived subjects of passives and therefore not agentive:

    (74)  [$PRO_{arb}$ *ser obligado a trabajar tanto*] *es escandaloso.*
         'To be forced to work so hard is scandalous.'
    (75)  *Il est désagréable* [*d'* $PRO_{arb}$ *être réveillé tôt le matin par un avion qui passe au-dessus*].
         'It is unpleasant to be woken early in the morning by a plane going overhead.'

(76) a. ?*Después de diez horas de interrogatorio, uno es soltado.*
    b. *Après dix heures d'interrogation, on est libéré.*
       'After ten hours of interrogation, one is released.'

The aspect constraint applies nevertheless. Notice that in (76) the context admits both a generic and an event interpretation ('is released' and 'is being released'); but in (76a) the presence of *uno* imposes the generic reading,[6] and in (76b) the arbitrary, 'one', interpretation of *on* equally requires the generic reading. Similarly, in the English example (77), the past passive form *was released* can in principle be either generic or specific, but the non-agentive subject *one* imposes the generic reading:

(77) After ten hours of interrogation, one was released.

While PRO$_{arb}$ and *on* occur only in subject position, *one* and *uno* can appear as complements. So these pronouns allow us to observe the behaviour of arbitrary arguments which are neither subjects nor agents. As (78) and (79) show, they still trigger the aspect constraint:

(78) *Es un orador tan impresionante que persuade a uno a*
      *seguirle.*
    'He is such an impressive speaker that he persuades/*is persuading one to follow him.'

(79) After three hours of interrogation (each morning/*yesterday morning), the guards led one back to one's cell.

Spanish also exhibits a null object with arbitrary reference, taken to be *pro* by Rizzi (1986), who examines its equivalent in Italian. This element, too, is compatible only with generic aspect:

(80) a. *Manuel incita* pro *a aceptar sus ideas más extrañas.*
      'Manuel encourages one to accept his strangest ideas.'
    b. **Manuel incitó* pro *a aceptar sus ideas más extrañas.*
      'Manuel encouraged one to accept his strangest ideas.'

(81) *Un tiempo tan hermoso invita* pro *a ir a la playa.*
    'Such beautiful weather makes/*is making one feel like going to the beach.'

The conclusion is that if any one of the arguments in a sentence is arbitrary, whatever its syntactic function and thematic role, and whether it is overt, null or implicit, the sentence must be generic. This is the aspect constraint.

### 3.4. Definite readings

It is well known that French *on* can have first-person plural definite reference ('we') as well as the indefinite and arbitrary interpretations discussed;
indeed, colloquially, it has virtually replaced *nous* in subject position. And
Cinque (1988) observes that the implicit argument of Italian impersonal *si*
can have the same interpretation. Where the aspectual context is specific,
the indefinite reading is available only with transitive and true intransitive
(also termed 'unergative') verbs. With other verb classes (including unaccusative, psych-movement, copulative and raising verbs) the 'we' reading
is the only one available.[7] Detailed discussion of the impersonal *se* construction is outside the scope of the present study, but a few remarks are in
order, because Cinque incorporates his observations into a more general
account of 'arbitrary' expressions.

Cinque accounts for the impossibility of the indefinite interpretation
with most verb types in event contexts in terms of the requirement that this
interpretation be matched with Infl. This matching is possible only with
transitives and intransitives because these are the only verbs which assign a
θ-role externally, to subject position. The appearance of the first-person
plural reading with the other verb types is a strategy to reconcile the requirement that the subject be referential when the aspect is specific with
the impersonal meaning of *si*. In other words, the indefinite reading is un-
available and the arbitrary one is ruled out by the event context, so a 'we'
reading is the next best thing; this is because the person and number feature
values of *we* may encompass those of all other personal pronouns, making
it the most general in reference. This is a speculative interpretation on
Cinque's part, offered tentatively. But he supports it with the striking observation that the same reading occurs in event contexts with the same verb
types for PRO*arb*.

The point I want to make is that there are problems in trying to extend
this analysis outside Italian. First, the complementary distribution Cinque
points out between the 'we' reading and the indefinite and arbitrary readings in Italian does not hold in French. He notes that *on* has the arbitrary
reading in generic contexts such as (82), the indefinite reading in event
contexts with transitive and intransitive verbs as in (83), and the definite,
'we', reading in event contexts with other verbs, like the psych-movement
and copulative verbs in (84):

(82)  *On n' est jamais content.*
      'One is never happy.'
(83)  a.  *Aujourd' hui à Beyrouth, on a tué un innocent.*
          'Today in Beirut, an innocent was killed.'
      b.  *Aujourd' hui à Beyrouth, on a tiré toute la matinée.*
          'Today in Beirut, there was shooting the whole morning.'
(84)  a.  *Aujourd' hui à Beyrouth, on préoccupe le contingent de l'ONU.*
          'Today in Beirut, we are worrying the UN contingent.'
      b.  *Aujourd' hui à Beyrouth, on est épuisé par la faim.*
          'Today in Beirut, we are worn out with hunger.'

However, the first-person plural reading is also perfectly possible in (82) and (83).

Moreover, Spanish *se* does not permit a first-person plural interpretation, despite having essentially the same constraints on the indefinite and arbitrary readings as Italian. As noted above, English *one* does permit a definite reading, marginally, but this tends to be first person singular rather than plural, or perhaps sometimes first person unspecified for number. Spanish *uno* can sometimes have a similar interpretation. German *man* 'one' does not admit a definite use.

There does seem to be a strong tendency for impersonal or indefinite expressions to develop secondary definite uses, but such uses are apparently independent of the primary use rather than being a variant of it. The coincidence between French and Italian in having a first person plural use is remarkable (particularly given that some Italian dialects have virtually replaced the first-person plural verb inflection by the *si* construction (Lepschy & Lepschy (1977), Cinque (1988, 551)), just as colloquial French has virtually replaced *nous* by *on*), and I cannot say whether it is pure coincidence, or due to borrowing, or even the result of some common early development; but I am inclined not to attribute it to anything deeper.

## 4. Voice and argument structure

### 4.1. Ergative *se*

Passive *se* (incorporating middle *se*) can be assumed to have the basic property of passive morphology, that of absorbing the external θ-role (as well, perhaps, as absorbing accusative Case). It differs from the compound passive, in Spanish and French, in not generally reassigning the absorbed θ-role to an adjunct agent phrase, and, in French alone, in that the implicit agent can only be interpreted as arbitrary. Given my suggestion in §2 that ergative and middle *se* may represent the same construction, the possible assimilation of ergative *se* to passive *se* remains to be considered. The question arising at this point is what the role of the clitic is in the ergative use.

I have argued elsewhere (Lyons 1982, 1987) that the frequently made claim that the ergative construction is lexically derived is mistaken, because, contrary to the common view, ergative *se* is almost fully productive. In common with the English ergative, it is available whenever the verb expresses an action or event which can be conceived of as not involving an agent (doors closing, plates cracking etc). There are exceptions to this but they are very few. Examples are the transitive verbs *empeorar* 'to make worse', *mejorar* 'to improve' (Spanish), and *cuire* 'to cook', *couler* 'to sink' (French), which do not admit ergative *se*, although the semantic condition for ergativity applies:

(85)  a.  *Tal problema empeora la situación general.*
          'Such a problem makes the general situation worse.'
      b.  *\*La situación general se está empeorando.*
          'The general situation is getting worse.'
(86)  a.  *Aquellos cambios mejoraron los negocios.*
          'Those changes improved business.'
      b.  *\*Los negocios se mejoraban.*
          'Business was improving.'
(87)  a.  *Pierre cuit le ragoût.*
          'Pierre is cooking the stew.'
      b.  *\*Le ragoût se cuit.*
          'The stew is cooking.'
(88)  a.  *L'ennemi a coulé le navire.*
          'The enemy sank the ship.'
      b.  *\*Le navire s'est coulé.*
          'The ship sank.'

But the reason for these exceptions is that *empeorar*, *mejorar*, *cuire* and *couler* also occur as unaccusative verbs, expressing precisely the meaning that would be expressed by the ergative:

(89)  *La situación general está empeorando.*
(90)  *Los negocios mejoraban.*
(91)  *Le ragoût cuit.*
(92)  *Le navire a coulé.*

Where the same verb form occurs as unaccusative as well as transitive, this generally blocks ergative *se* in Spanish and French. This does not happen in English, where the possibility of the ergative being in competition with a morphologically distinct unaccusative does not arise. As a result, ergative formation in English is completely free. (Indeed it is not immediately obvious whether verbs like *improve, cook,* in their non-transitive use, are unaccusatives or derived ergatives; it may be that English has no unaccusatives with transitive counterparts.)

Assuming, then, that ergative formation is productive, though subject to some more or less systematic constraints, there is no reason not to take it to be a syntactic process. The property of such verbs as *cerrar, fermer* 'to close', which readily occur in the ergative, of denoting an action which can be conceived as non-agentive, can be expressed by the assumption that they assign an external θ-role only optionally. This would make them semantically identical to unaccusative verbs when the non-assignment option is taken. But what then is the role of the *se*? It does not occur with unaccusatives like *mejorar* and *cuire, llegar* and *arriver* 'to arrive'; and in the case of *cerrar* and *fermer*, if no external θ-role is assigned, there is nothing for *se* to absorb.

To solve this problem, Lyons (1987) adopts a proposal made by Burzio (1986) and motivated on quite different grounds. Burzio is concerned to explain the fact that the passive shows implicit argument effects while the ergative does not, although in neither construction is a θ-role assigned to subject position. He proposes a distinction between 'θ-role' (expressing a purely syntactic relationship between a verb and a configurationally defined position) and 'semantic role' (a semantic function such as agent). Wherever possible, semantic roles are mediated by θ-role assignment, but it is possible for a semantic role to be present but unexpressed, when θ-role assignment has failed for some reason. If both θ-roles and semantic roles could be assigned or not assigned, independently of each other, there would be four possible combinations, as in (93):

(93) a. [+ θ-role, + semantic role]
    b. [− θ-role, − semantic role]
    c. [+ θ-role, − semantic role]
    d. [− θ-role, + semantic role].

Burzio has a use for three of these, the exception being (c). He accounts for the non-occurrence of this combination by assuming that a verb with no agent semantic role (for example) to assign cannot assign a subject θ-role either — presumably because it would be pointless. θ-role assignment is thus dependent on semantic role assignment but not vice versa, an asymmetry not convincingly explained.

My proposal is that (93c) is in fact instantiated by the ergative construction. With verbs like *cerrar*, *fermer*, what is optional, and what fails to be 'emitted' in the non-agentive use ('The door closed', etc.), is not the external θ-role, but the agent semantic role. The subject θ-role, which the verb attempts to assign in the normal way, is absorbed by the clitic *se* exactly as in the passive. (If there is no *se* present and the option of not assigning an agent role is taken, subject position will receive an 'empty' θ-role, leading to a violation of the θ-Criterion.) Verbs of this class differ, then, from unaccusatives in that the latter have neither an external θ-role nor an agent semantic role to assign, while the former do have an external θ-role and an optional agent semantic role. The intuition behind this distinction is that verbs of the *cerrar/fermer* class are in some sense primarily transitive, the secondary, ergative, use requiring mediation by *se*.

Turning to the 'agentive ergatives' discussed in §2.2, if I am right in treating them as ergatives, it follows that they are characterized by suppression of their agent semantic role, though, just as the standard ergatives, they still have an external θ-role which is absorbed by *se*. The 'exceptional' instances of this phenomenon, exemplified in (20-24), differ from standard ergatives in that their agent semantic role is not lexically specified as optional. Rather, some pragmatic factor in the context licenses its suppression, affording the optionality which is lexically provided with verbs like *cerrar* and *fermer*.

It is less clear what is going on in the conventional instances of agentive ergatives, with verbs like *vendre* and *décider*, exemplified in (25-31). But the most plausible account is probably that they are like *cerrar/fermer* in having an optional agent semantic role; this explains the conventionality of their appearance with ergative *se*. The intuition that there is a degree of agentivity present with these verbs in the ergative construction would then be accounted for in terms of the discrepancy between their lexical entries, which permit non-assignment of an agent role, and the entailments imposed by the lexical meaning of the verb concerning some agentive entity in the event described by the sentence (see Ladusaw & Dowty (1988)). The meaning of *vendre* is such that we understand the event described to involve an agent, despite the non-assignment of the corresponding semantic role; and the fact that this role is not assigned ensures that the understood agentivity is severely backgrounded.

## 4.2. Conclusion: unifying *se*

Drawing the strands of this investigation together, I claim that passive, middle and ergative *se* all represent the same construction. This is a passive construction, existing in Spanish and French alongside the participial passive, and differing from it in lacking the ability to reassign the absorbed $\theta$-role to a *by*-phrase. The clitic *se* absorbs the external $\theta$-role and prevents the assignment of accusative Case to object position. With passives and middles, the absorbed $\theta$-role is carrying a semantic role, that of agent, and this role remains as an implicit argument. It is interpreted as an indefinite in Spanish, with the possibility in an appropriate context (a generic context) of being an arbitrary indefinite (on the assumption that arbitrary is hyponymous to indefinite[8]). In French the implicit argument can only be arbitrary. In the case of ergatives, the absorbed $\theta$-role is 'empty' — it does not bear a semantic role, because verbs admitting the ergative interpretation of *se* only optionally assign an agent role. Therefore there is no implicit argument, and a degree of understood agentivity is only possible with a few verbs whose lexically represented argument structure, allowing the option of not assigning an agent role, disagrees with the argument structure entailed by their meaning. This last possibility, agentive ergatives, may apply to French only, because the corresponding expressions in Spanish are hard to distinguish from the simple passive use.[9]

If, as claimed, the role of ergative *se* is the same as that of passive *se*, to absorb the external $\theta$-role, an obvious question is: why is an ergative (non-agentive) reading impossible with the participial passive, which also absorbs the external $\theta$-role? With *cerrar* and *fermer*, it should be possible for the option of suppressing the agent semantic role to be taken, and for the empty external θ-role to be emitted, to be absorbed by passive morphology. But this does not happen; the sentences (94) cannot be interpreted as synonymous with the ergative reading of (95):

(94)  a.  *La puerta fue cerrada.*
      b.  *La porte a été fermée.*
          'The door was closed.'
(95)  a.  *La puerta se cerró.*
      b.  *La porte s'est fermée.*
          'The door closed.'

I believe this is related to the fact that the compound passive has the possibility of reassigning an agent role to a *by*-phrase. Whereas Spanish passive *se* allows this reassignment only marginally, it is always an option with the compound passive. I suggest therefore that participial passive morphology is constrained to absorb only θ-roles that come complete with semantic roles; an empty external θ-role is unacceptable. This is because a possible *by*-phrase must receive the agent semantic role as well as the external θ-role.

I have not discussed impersonal *se*, because this construction presents complexities not shared by the other uses, and is less easily assimilated to a unified account. The most striking difference is that it does not absorb accusative Case. In this it resembles passive-like constructions occurring in many languages which do not conform to Burzio's Generalization, according to which failure of θ-role assignment entails failure of accusative Case assignment. Cinque (1988) offers an account in terms of his [±argument] analysis of Italian *si*, which makes impersonal *se/si* conform to an interpretation of Burzio's Generalization. The approach outlined in §1.2 above takes accusative Case absorption to be optional, so that there are 'Burzio passives' and 'non-Burzio passives' — though what the status of the Generalization is in this case is far from clear. Both approaches are aimed at a unification, at least partial, of all *se* constructions. I have limited myself here to trying to show that three major uses of *se* can be given a fully unified account.

# Notes

*   I would like to express my gratitude to Violante Luján, Ana-Cristina Zêzere and Jean-Pierre Mailhac, for detailed discussion of the Spanish and French data appearing here.

1.  Italian too shows the full range of uses, but some Italian dialects differ considerably from the standard language: Paduan and Venetian lack passive *si* (Cinque 1988, Lepschy 1984) and Trentino has no passive or middle *si* (Zubizarreta 1982). Rumanian does not have the impersonal construction with transitive verbs (Cinque 1988, Dobrovie-Sorin 1987).

2.  On the other hand, if passive morphology is also taken to be an argument, generated in Infl, as argued by Roberts (1987), then the absorption of the external θ-role by *se* or passive *en* is essentially the same process.

3.  Control of the PRO of a purpose clause by the implicit argument of the arbitrary passive, as in (46), is by no means impossible; but it is just as possible with the middle, as in (9). Roberts (1987: 192) notes, following Jaeggli, that modification by a purpose clause is possible with the middle in Spanish, unlike English:

    (i)   *Las manzanas se comen para adelgazar.*
          'Apples are eaten to slim.'
    (ii)  *Apples eat to slim.

    In fact modification of middles by a purpose clause is possible in English too. Why (ii) is impossible is not altogether clear, but (9c) is as good as (9a) and (9b); and (iii) (suggested by a reader) and (iv) are not bad:

    (iii)  This computer turns on from the front to avoid reaching.
    (iv)   These garments machine-wash to save work.

    Jaeggli (1986) illustrates the familiar observation that English middles, unlike passives, do not allow purpose clauses with the following examples:

    (v)    The price was decreased to help the poor.
    (vi)   *The price decreased to help the poor.

    But the impossibility of (vi) is due to the fact that it is not middle, but ergative, as is clear from the fact that the aspect is most easily taken to be eventive, not generic. (Chomsky (1981), whom Jaeggli is citing, terms (vi) simply 'intransitive'.) A genuine middle like (vii) does allow a purpose clause:

    (vii)  Prices reduce easily to help the poor.

4.  Roberts (1987) discusses the alleged inertness of passive implicit arguments with respect to binding, and concludes that this inertness is only apparent, as a result of the arbitrary nature of these implicit arguments. He points out, following Rizzi, that a passive implicit argument can bind the arbitrary anaphor *oneself*:

    (i)    Such privileges should be kept to oneself.

    But this possibility is clearly due (in part) to the generic context imposed by the modal: in such contexts passive implicit arguments can be arbitrary, as I have shown. In event contexts the passive implicit argument cannot bind *oneself*:

    (ii)   *These privileges were kept to oneself.

    Since the passive is not limited to generic contexts, its implicit argument cannot be always arbitrary.

    Note also that the licensing of agentive adverbs and controlling of PRO in purpose clauses by passive implicit agents is not completely free, even when the agent is non-arbitrary. Examples like (iii)-(iv), frequent in the literature, are rejected by some speakers and marginal for others:

      (iii)  The old house was gladly sold off.
      (iv)  His tyres were let down to delay him.
5.  Even definite subjects are perfectly compatible with generic sentences:
      (i)  *Comemos siempre a las ocho.*
      (ii)  *Nous mangeons toujours à huit heures.*
      'We always eat at eight.'
6.  As already noted, *uno* is much more limited in occurrence than *one*. It is not generally favoured as subject of a passive, and (76a) is judged by native speakers to be very odd, though not ungrammatical.
7.  Cinque's Italian examples, corresponding in essentials to his French ones given in (82-84) below, are as follows (my glosses). Sentence (i) is generic, and permits the arbitrary ('quasi-universal') reading. The rest are eventive; the indefinite ('quasi-existential') reading occurs in (ii) (transitive) and (iii) (true intransitive), and the 'we' reading in (iv) (psych-movement) and (v) (copulative).
      (i)  *Non si è mai contenti.*
      'One is never satisfied.'
      (ii)  *Oggi, a Beirut, si è ucciso un innocente.*
      'Today, in Beirut, an innocent was killed.'
      (iii)  *Oggi, a Beirut, si è sparato tutta la mattina.*
      'Today, in Beirut, there was shooting the whole morning.'
      (iv)  *Oggi, a Beirut, si è preoccupato il contingente dell'ONU.*
      'Today, in Beirut, we have been worrying the UN contingent.'
      (v)  *Oggi, a Beirut, si è sfiniti dalla fame.*
      'Today, in Beirut, we are worn out with hunger.'
8.  To express this hyponymy in terms of features, the implicit agent of the passive is [–def] (equivalent to [–def, ±arb]), and that of the middle [–def, +arb].
9.  To show that Spanish too has agentive ergatives, it would be necessary to show that *vender* 'to sell', for example, used in the *se* construction with specific aspect, can involve severe backgrounding of the agency. This may be the case, and I leave the question open.

# References

Baker, M. C. 1988. *Incorporation: A Theory of Grammatical Function Changing*. Chicago & London: University of Chicago Press.

Belletti, A. 1982. 'Morphological' passive and pro-drop: the impersonal construction in Italian.' *Journal of Linguistic Research* 2, 1-34.

————. 1986. Unaccusatives as Case assigners. Lexicon Project Working Paper 8, Center for Cognitive Science, MIT.

————. & L. Rizzi. 1986. Psych-verbs and theta-theory. Lexicon Project Working Paper 13, Center for Cognitive Science, MIT.

Burzio, L. 1986. *Italian Syntax: A Government-Binding Approach*. Dordrecht: Reidel.

Chomsky, N. 1981. *Lectures on Government and Binding.* Dordrecht: Foris.

Cinque, G. 1988. On *si* constructions and the theory of *arb. Linguistic Inquiry* 19, 521-581.

Dobrovie-Sorin, C. 1987. *Syntaxe du roumain, chaînes thématiques.* Thèse de Doctorat d'état, Université de Paris VII.

Grimshaw, J. 1982. On the lexical representation of Romance reflexive clitics. *The Mental Representation of Grammatical Relations,* ed. J. Bresnan, 87-148. Cambridge, Mass.: MIT Press.

Jaeggli, O. 1986. Passive. *Linguistic Inquiry* 17, 587- 622.

Keyser, S. J. & T. Roeper. 1984. On the middle and ergative constructions in English. *Linguistic Inquiry* 15, 381-416.

Ladusaw, W. A. & D. R. Dowty. 1988. Toward a nongrammatical account of thematic roles. *Syntax and Semantics 21: Thematic Relations,* ed. W. Wilkins, 61-73. San Diego: Academic Press.

Lepschy, A. L. & G. Lepschy. 1977. *The Italian Language Today.* London: Hutchinson.

Lepschy, G. 1984. Costruzioni impersonali con *se* in veneziano. *Guida ai dialetti veneti VI,* ed. M. Cortelazzo, 69-79. Padua: Cleup.

Lyons, C. 1982. Pronominal voice in French. *Studies in the Romance Verb,* ed. N. Vincent & M. Harris, 161-184. London: Croom Helm.

————. 1987. Subject demotion devices in French. Unpublished paper delivered to the Association for French Language Studies, University of Sheffield, September 1987.

————. 1989. L'Aspect générique et la voix moyenne. *Travaux de linguistique* 19, 171-186.

Manzini, M. R. 1983. *Restructuring and Reanalysis.* Unpublished Ph.D. dissertation, MIT.

————. 1986. On Italian *si. Syntax and Semantics 19: The Syntax of Pronominal Clitics,* ed. H. Borer, 241-262. New York: Academic Press.

Otero, C. P. 1986. Arbitrary subjects in finite clauses. *Generative Studies in Spanish Syntax,* ed. I. Bordelois, H. Contreras & K. Zagona, 81-109. Dordrecht: Foris.

Perlmutter, D. M. 1978. Impersonal passives and the unaccusative hypothesis. *Proceedings of the Fourth Annual Meeting of the Berkeley Linguistics Society*, 157-189. Berkeley: University of California.

Rizzi, L. 1986. Null objects in Italian and the theory of pro. *Linguistic Inquiry* 17, 501-557.

Roberts, I. G. 1987. *The Representation of Implicit and Dethematized Subjects.* Dordrecht: Foris.

Ruwet, N. 1972. *Théorie syntaxique et syntaxe du français.* Paris: Seuil.

Stéfanini, J. 1962. *La Voix pronominale en ancien et en moyen français.* Aix-en-Provence: Ophrys.

Williams, E. 1981. Argument structure and morphology. *The Linguistic Review* 1, 81-114.

Zribi-Hertz, A. 1982. La construction se-moyen du français et son statut dans le triangle Moyen-Passif-Réfléchi. *Lingvisticæ Investigationes* 6, 345-401.

Zribi-Hertz, A. 1987. La réflexivité ergative en français moderne. *Le Français moderne* 55, 23-54.

Zubizarreta, M.-L. 1982. *On the Relationship of the Lexicon to Syntax.* Unpublished Ph.D. dissertation, MIT.

# Evidence from the Italian dialects
# for the internal structure of prosodic domains

## Martin Maiden
### *University of Cambridge*

This paper is concerned with the internal structure of prosodic constituents in phonology, and is intended to complement and refine the general framework established by Nespor & Vogel (1986). They claim that the range of prosodic domains to which phonological rules may make reference is represented by a hierarchy of at least seven types of universally available prosodic constituent, ranging from the syllable to the 'phonological utterance' (1).

> (1)     Nespor & Vogel's constituent hierarchy
>
> syllable
> foot
> phonological word
> clitic group
> phonological phrase
> intonational phrase
> phonological utterance

By the 'Strict Layer Hypothesis' (SLH), constituents are exhaustively dominated by the immediately superordinate constituent; conversely, constituents dominate only whole subordinate constituents: there are no 'stray' elements. The prosodic constituents are n-ary branching (imposition of binary branching creates elements of structures not required by any phonological rule), and lack internal prosodic structure (for example, postulation

of onset and rhyme, or other syllable-internal subdomains, is rejected because all prosodic rules apparently referring to such domains are purportedly reformulable in terms of domain-limit rules). While favourable to Nespor & Vogel's proposals, I wish to challenge the view that constituents
have no internal prosodic structure. I suggest that some, perhaps all, constituents contain what I shall label a nucleus (the maximal stressed vowel,
or designated terminal element), a pretonic prosodic domain (all material to
the left of the stressed vowel) and a posttonic prosodic domain (all material
to the right of the stressed vowel). The suggested innovation is not a radical one: I shall show that it in fact follows quite naturally from Nespor &
Vogel's existing theoretical apparatus.

Virtually every rule purportedly making reference to the internal content of constituents (the so-called domain-span rules) is arguably a kind of
domain-limit rule: quite simply, rules specified as operating only inside
constituents, and not at or across domain limits, are actually negative domain-limit rules. There remains, however, one class of rule examined by
Nespor & Vogel which is irrefutably domain-internal, the so-called DTE
rules, referring either to positive values of the DTE (the Italian rule length-
ening the DTE vowel of the phonological word), or to minus values (the
Italian rule raising ɛ and ɔ to e and o[1] in unstressed syllables at word level)
(2).

    (2)    Italian [–DTE] vowel raising at phonological word level

|   |   |   |
|---|---|---|
| a. | 'tɔlgo | toʎ'ʎevo |
|    | 'I remove.' | 'I removed.' |
| b. | 'lɛggo | led'dʒevo |
|    | 'I read.' | 'I was reading.' |
|    | (present) | (past) |

The bulk of the constituent-internal rules I shall be concerned with are
[–DTE] rules akin to those identified for Italian by Nespor & Vogel, except
that they distinguish between pretonic and posttonic domains.

Over a very wide area of southern Italy, the five atonic vowels of Vul-
gar Latin have been subject to extensive subsequent neutralization, generally involving merger as schwa. However, one observes repeatedly that the
range of possible atonic vowel contrasts to the left of the DTE of the word
is greater than that occurring to its right. A typical example appears in
Lausberg's account of southern Lucanian (Lausberg 1939), where posttonic

vowels generally merge as schwa, while we find **a, u** and **ə** in pretonic position (3). Note that henceforth the forms marked with an asterisk are the postulated historically underlying forms.

(3)    Lucanian posttonic vowel reduction at word level

Pretonic

    a.    na'ta < *na'tare
        'to swim'

    b.    məsu'ra < *mesu'rare
        'to measure'

    c.    suɲɲ'a < *soɲɲ'are
        'to dream'

    d.    βə'de < *ve'dere
        'to see'

Posttonic

    e.    'fikətə < *'fikatu
        'liver'

    f.    'fumə < *'fuma
        'he smokes'

    g.    'prɛβətə < *'prɛbete
        'priest'

    h.    'partənə < *'partono
        'they leave'

A similar conservatism in respect of the pretonic section is observable in dialects with less radical atonic vowel neutralization. Thus in the Lazio dialect of Sant' Oreste (Elwert 1958:147), posttonic non-final **o, e, u, i**, and a either merge (as **e** or as **i**) or are subject to assimilation to a following vowel where the intervening consonant is a liquid. In pretonic position they generally remain intact (4).

(4)    Posttonic vowel neutralization in Sant' Oreste (Lazio)

Pretonic

    a.    lavan'nara < *lavan'dara
        'washerwoman'

    b.    utu'mɔbbile < *auto'mɔbile
        'automobile'

    c.    affila'rati < *affila'rati
          'in a row'
    d.    peku'raru < *peko'raru
          'shepherd'

Posttonic

    e.    'trapinu < *'trapanu
          'drill'
    f.    'ʃtɛfine < *stɛfanu
          'Stephen'
    g.    'dʒakimu < *'dʒakomo
          'James'
    h.    biʃ'ʃɔkala  biʃ'ʃɔkele  < *be'stjɔkkola -e
          'lizard'    'lizards'
    i.    'arbulu    'arbili    < *'arberu -i
          'tree'    'trees'

Similarly, a rule raising unstressed **o** to **u** in the history of Tuscan dialects (cf. Rohlfs 1966:165) is limited to the pretonic position. The distinction between pretonic and posttonic sections is not restricted to processes neutralizing and assimilating vowels. A number of central dialects have a rule of apocope of personal names and professional titles, especially in vocative forms. This rule deletes all material to the right of the primary stressed vowel, including the coda of the stressed syllable — that is to say that it deletes the whole posttonic section (5).

(5)    Deletion of the posttonic section in central Italian vocatives

    a.    avvo'ka < avvo'katu
          'lawyer!'
    b.    mi'ke < mi'kele
          'Michele!'
    c.    ma < 'marko
          'Marco!'
    d.    do'me < do'meniko
          'Domenico!'

Undoubtedly the most striking example of differentation at phonological word level between the posttonic and the pretonic domains is central Italian vowel harmony (cf. Maiden 1988). A group of dialects (in Tuscany, the Marche, Umbria and Lazio), displays regressive harmony, of which there are two main subvarieties, each operating across adjacent syllables: *raising harmony* (RH), and *complete harmony* (CH). I focus here on the dialect of Servigliano (Camilli 1929), where both varieties coexist.

In RH, high mid vowels (**e** and **o**) become [–mid] (i.e., **i** and **u**) in the environment of a following high non-mid vowel **i** or **u** (6).

(6)     Raising harmony in pretonic domain (Marche)

       a.     pu'timo < *po'timo
              'We can.'

       b.     fjuril'litti < *fjorel'litti
              'little flowers'

       c.     viri'ta < *veri'tate
              'truth'

       d.     kuntsu'ma < *konsu'mare
              'to consume'

       e.     furmi'ketta < *formi'ketta
              'ant'

       f.     bbiʃʃi'ka < *vessi'kare
              'to remove the bladder'

       g.     dilibbe'ra < *delibe'rare
              'to set free'

       h.     suspi'ra < *sospi'rare
              'to sigh'

In Servigliano the domain in which RH appears is the pretonic section of the phonological word (as it is in certain other dialects). It is important to note that RH is not necessarily triggered by the primary stressed vowel. A lexically specified **i** or **u** occurring at any point in the pretonic section triggers raising in mid vowels immediately to the left. RH is firmly bounded to the left by the phonological word boundary; the rule does not operate, for example, on preceding words (including clitic pronouns) (7). Henceforward, clitic boundaries are marked by a '+'.

(7)     Absence of raising harmony in proclitics

       a.     lo+di'tʃia
              it I-said
              'I said it.'

b.    se+puti'ria
itself could
'One could.'

CH (8) involves complete assimilation in all features to the vowel of a following syllable. Stressed vowels (i.e., those carrying primary word stress)
do not participate in the relevant forms of harmony.

(8)    Complete harmony to the right of the clitic group

a.    'prɛdoko 'prediki 'prɛdaka < *'prɛdiko -i -a
'I preach.' 'You preach.' 'He/she preaches.'

b.    do'mennaka do'menneke < *do'menika -e
'Sunday' 'Sundays'

c.    'stommuku 'stommiki < *'stomaku -i
'stomach' 'stomachs'

d.    'alama 'aleme < *'anima -e
'soul' 'souls'

e.    'metto+lo 'mettu+lu < 'mette+lo, -+lu
he-puts it  he-puts him
'he puts it/him'

f.    'mettu+tʃu+lu 'metta+tʃa+la < 'mette+tʃe+lu,+la
puts-there-him  puts-there-her
'He puts him/her there.'

g.    'ɛjju+lu 'ɛjja+la < 'ɛjjo+lu,-+la
behold-him  behold-her
'Here he/she is.'

The domain of CH (in those dialects where it is present) is bounded both to
the left and to the right by the clitic group limit (9).

(9)    Complete harmony among proclitics

a.    to+lo+di'tʃia < *te+lo+di'tʃia
to-you it I-said
'I said it to you.'

b.    ti+li+'diko < *te+li+'diko
to-you them I-say
'I say them to you.'

    c.    tʃa+la+'metto < *tʃe+la+'metto
           there her I-put
           'I put her there.'

    d.    matre ssu+lu+'pijja < *matre+se+lu+'pijja
           mother to-herself him takes
           'Mother picks him up.'

    e.    ma+tʃa+la+'ditʃe < *me+tʃe+la+'ditʃe
           to-me there it (FEM.) he-says
           'He says it to me there.'

What is striking, however, is that CH is *absent* from the pretonic section of the host phonological word (10). That is to say that CH is absent precisely where RH is present: the pretonic domain of the host word.

  (10)  Absence of complete harmony in the pretonic section

    a.    ɲenok'kjo
           'kneeling'

    b.    brani'ma
           (proper name)

    c.    kolat'tsjo
           'breakfast'

    d.    mari'ta
           'marry'

CH interacts in interesting ways with clitic particles (among them unstressed object pronouns; enclitic possessive adjectives; some prepositions). The examples in table 8 show that CH not only operatesbetween consecutive enclitic particles, but also penetrates the host word. In contrast, proclitic particles harmonize with proclitics to their right (9), but neither receive harmony from the host word, nor trigger harmony in any preceding word.

The asymmetry between the right and left hand sides of the DTE is replicated in constituents above the level of the phonological word. In many southern dialects there is a rule centralizing atonic **a** as schwa. This process, which I label **a**-reduction, has as its domain not the phonological word (11) but a superordinate constituent, and is wholly restricted to the right-hand side of the DTE.[2]

(11)   **a**-reduction to right of word DTE

 Agnone

  a. marga'rojtə < *marga'rita
   'daisy'
  b. 'prehənə < *'prɛgano
   'they pray'
  c. ka'rɔfənə < *ka'rɔfanʊ
   'carnation'
  d. kata'fworkjə < *kata'fɔrkjʊ
   'caterpillar'

In fact, there are two varieties of **a**-reduction, one operating on non-final **a** to the right of the DTE of the clitic group (12), and another applying to **a** to the right of the DTE of the phonological phrase (13). The examples in (13) show that **a**-reduction does *not* apply to final **a** in the clitic group. Such reduction is, rather, a function of the phonological phrase.

(12)   **a**-reduction to the right of the clitic group DTE

 Montefalcone

  a. la+'kandə < *la+'kanta
   it he-sings
   'He sings it.'
  b. a'ʃpɛttə+m < *as'pɛtta+me
   await me
   'Wait for me.'
  c. kaj'natə+mə < *kog'nata+ma
   sister-in-law-my
   'my sister-in-law'
  d. as'siukə+tə+lə < *as'suka+te+le
   dry to-yourself them
   'Dry them (to) yourself.'

 Agnone

  e. la+'vajdə < *la+'vede
   her he-sees
   'He sees her.'

      f.     'mamə+tə < *'mama+ta
            mother-your
            'your mother'

      g.     'kandə+lə < *'kanta+la
            sing it
            'Sing it.'

      h.     maɲa+t+'illə < *'mandʒa+te+·illu
            eat-to-yourself it
            'Eat it up.'

(13)   Conservation of clitic-group final **a** to left of phonological phrase DTE.

    Henceforth, phrasal (as opposed to clitic group) stress will be marked ".

      Agnone

      a.     fa'tija sprə"keatə < *fa'tika spre"kata
            effort wasted
            'wasted effort'

      b.     la 'tɛrra "sandə < *la 'tɛrra "santa
            the land holy
            'the Holy Land'

      c.     lə 'fikəra "frɛskə < *le 'fikora "freske
            the figs fresh
            'the fresh figs'

      d.     'kella "femmənə < *'kwella "femina
            'that woman'

      e.     na 'brutta "vojtə < *una 'brutta "vita
            'a nasty life'

      f.     n 'tsanda "peatʃə < *in 'santa "patʃe
            'in holy peace'

The following examples, from other southern Italian dialects, involve a clitic possessive adjective:

      g.     Lucera           'sɔrə+ma ku"tʃinə
                            sister-my cousin
                            'my cousin'

> h.    Palagiano              ku'dʒinə+ma "fɛmmənə
>                              cousin-my woman
>                              'my cousin'
>
> i.    Monte di Procida       'sɔrə+ma kunsu"rinə
>                              sister-my cousin
>                              'my cousin'

Indeed, there is an inversion of phonological phrase level **a**-reduction such that **a** is introduced counteretymologically to the left of the DTE. This rule has the interesting property of occurring only in environments which are characteristically pretonic (14), for example, before possessives and demonstrative adjectives, which, in the relevant dialects, are always phrase-final and always carry phrasal stress. Before other adjectives, which are not inherently phrase-final, such introduction of **a** does not occur.

(14)   Inversion of **a**-reduction in intrinsically pretonic environments:

Casalincontrada

> a.    'tanda "vakkə < *'tante "vakke
>       'many cows'
>
> b.    li 'vuva "mi < *li 'bɔvi "mɛi
>       the oxen my
>       'my oxen'
>
> c.    l 'wɔmməna "si < *li 'ɔmini "sɛi
>       the men his
>       'his men'
>
> d.    ʃti 'vuva "kiʃtə < *esti 'bɔvi "kwesti
>       these oxen these
>       'these oxen'
>
> e.    kəli 'tjemba "killə < *kwelli 'tɛmpi "kwelli
>       those times those
>       'those times'
>
> BUT   f.    li 'vuvə "nirə < *li 'bɔvi "neri
>             the oxen black
>             'the black oxen'

g.   lǝ 'vakkǝ "nirǝ < *le 'vakke "nere
     the cows black
     'the black cows'

h.   l 'wɔmmǝnǝ "bunǝ < *li 'ɔmini "bɔni
     the men good
     'the good men'

We have seen a series of rules which uncontroversially refer to segments lying either to the left or to the right of the DTE. Of course these
observations do not, by themselves, justify postulation of pretonic and
posttonic domains. I shall seek now to account for these phenomena, remaining within the theoretical framework postulated by Nespor & Vogel.
One possibility is that the right- or left-hand sides of the DTE are actually
familiar constituents from Nespor & Vogel's hierarchy. While CH is
bounded by the clitic group, the exemption of the pretonic section of the
host remains to be explained. The same problem arises if we propose an n-
ary branching foot as its domain: the pretonic domain is analysable as a
foot in its own right, yet does not undergo CH. Moreover, under the strict
layer hypothesis, each word boundary is also a foot boundary: operation of
the rule across the word boundary therefore disqualifies the foot as the domain of the rule. As for RH, restricted to the pretonic section of the phonological word, its domain cannot be a foot, both for the reasons just outlined,
and because the rule may be triggered by the principal stressed vowel,
which belongs in the adjoining foot.

Another possible approach, consistent with the Nespor & Vogel model,
is to postulate directional spreading rules which have whole constituents as
their domains, but are either blocked or triggered by the DTE. A leftward
spreading rule blocked by the DTE would not operate to the left of the
DTE (i.e., the pretonic domain); the same rule triggered by the DTE would
scan leftwards from the domain limit, but only be triggered by the DTE,
thereby applying only in the pretonic domain. This approach creates the
following problems. Firstly, we lose the insight that such rules are part of a
general class of neutralization phenomena pertaining to unstressed vowels
(cf. the [–DTE] analysis of Italian unstressed mid vowel raising). The loss
of generalization is particularly apparent when we consider that in closely
cognate dialects of the Lazio region (cf. Lindsström 1907; Merlo 1922), we
find RH identical to that observed in Servigliano with the sole exception

that it is 'symmetrical', operating both to the right and to the left of the stressed vowel. While symmetrical RH can be stated as a [–DTE] rule, its asymmetrical counterpart, which quite possibly conserves a historically earlier stage in the evolution of the rule, apparently has to be presented from a completely different perspective: it is viewed as applying across whole constituents and happens, incidentally, to be blocked or triggered by the DTE. Moreover, in the case of 'paradigmatic' segmental neutralizing rules like **a**-reduction, attribution of direction to the rule, and correspondingly of a blocking or triggering function to the DTE, is arbitrary.

However, some of the rules we have seen appear to be statable in terms of the domain limit. It seems at first glance that **a**-reduction applies to the penultimate syllable of the clitic group. But examples like (12d) suggest that the rule actually applies to any non-final posttonic **a**. As for reduction of **a** at phonological phrase level, its restriction to the final vowel is a consequence of the fact that in all the relevant dialects the DTE of the phonological phrase always falls on the final clitic group constituent. In other words, there is never more than one clitic-group final **a** to the right of the DTE of the phonological phrase, so nothing guarantees that this rule is intrinsically restricted to constituent-final position. A further problem is that formulation of **a**-reduction within the clitic group as a penultimate syllable rule, and **a**-reduction within the phonological phrase as a final syllable rule, obscures a generalization: the rule applies in both cases to posttonic vowels. If it is specified as applying to the posttonic domain, with subordinate differentiation between final and non-final vowels, then the insight that **a**-reduction is essentially the same rule wherever it occurs cannot be captured.

For the sake of argument, let us assume however that apparent final-syllable and penultimate-syllable rules should in fact be formulated as simple domain-limit rules. (15) shows that formulation in terms of a posttonic domain requires reference to exactly the same categories and labels as a domain-limit formulation, but is less cumbersome in that it requires no reference to the (possibly variable) distance of **a** from the domain limit.

(15)   Specifications required for 'domain limit' vs. 'posttonic domain' formulations

Domain limit formulation:
(i) Constituent
(ii) [–DTE]
(iii) Domain limit
(iv) Right-hand
(v) Zero or more segments away from limit

Posttonic domain formulation
(i) Constituent
(ii) [–DTE]
(iii) Right-hand

The superiority of the posttonic domain approach is apparent when we consider the rule deleting all syllables to the right of the DTE. I propose that this rule be specified simply as deleting the posttonic domain. In a domain-limit approach we have to assume, with no independent justification, that the deletion rule is cyclic, and we can only *guess* at what exactly is being deleted: it deletes the final syllable (or the final segment?) remaining after each cycle of the rule, until it encounters the DTE. If this were the case, we might expect to find historically intermediate stages in cognate central Italian dialects, where only the 'first' final syllable (or final segment?) was deleted. No such systematic stages are observable, however, and nothing tells us the nature of the deletion on each cycle.

Complete harmony offers a case of sensitivity to the pretonic domain which cannot be captured in terms of domain limits. The rule spreads leftwards from the right-hand limit, and has as its domain the entire clitic group, operating both to the right of the DTE and in proclitics. But it 'skips over' the pretonic domain of the host phonological word: this domain is of varied or indeterminate distance from the clitic-group limit, and its exemption from CH can be captured only if we specify this domain directly as immune to the rule. The analysis is, of course, corroborated by the many other cases we have seen in which specification of a pretonic/posttonic distinction has provided the least arbitrary and most plausible account of prosodic data.

We have seen evidence for constituent-internal prosodic structure at at least three levels of the constituent hierarchy. I tentatively propose that

similar internal structure defined in relation to the maximally sonorous element of the constituent may be replicated at every level. I have at present
no evidence from the foot or from constituents higher than the phonological phrase. However, the syllable has been frequently claimed (e.g., Fudge
1969; also Hulst & Smith 1987:41f.) to consist of an onset (pretonic domain), a nucleus, and a coda (posttonic domain). This structure has been
postulated primarily to account for the interaction between syllable structure and stress placement. Material to the left of the nucleus is widely
found to be irrelevant to such phenomena, whence the onset-rhyme distinction. Analysis of the rhyme into a nucleus and a coda has been postulated
by some linguists to account for the distinction between light and heavy
syllables (others claim that this distinction can be captured merely in terms
of a branching vs. non-branching rhyme structure). But do these constituents constitute *prosodic domains*? The problem is intrinsically refrac-
tory, since the syllable is a very small constituent, and 'onsets' and 'codas'
are usually too short (being frequently monosegmental) to provide clear
answers. Rules referring to them are easily formulable as domain-limit
rules. Indeed, I know of no evidence for onset *prosodies*. However, certain facts indicate the desirability of recognizing syllable-internal constituents. Harris (1983) claims that certain consonantal rules in Spanish
have the rhyme as their domain. It is actually a moot point whether the
correct analysis is in terms of a rhyme or a coda: the rule operates to the
right of the nucleus, but the typical syllabic structure of a vocalic nucleus
flanked by consonants means that the rule can equally be formulated as
applying to the consonantal content of the rhyme. Be this as it may,
Nespor & Vogel (1986:73-77) claim that this and all other internal-constituent based analyses can be reformulated as a syllable domain-limit rule.
Examples (16a) and (16b) present Harris's and Nespor & Vogel's respec-
tive analyses of a rule velarizing **n** in varieties of Spanish.

(16)   Internal prosodic structure of the syllable: Spanish **n → ŋ**

a.      Rhyme (coda?) formulation

**n → ŋ** _____

b.      Domain limit formulation

**n → ŋ** ___$C_0$].
rhyme

It is evident that (b) involves a cumbersome disjunction and loss of generalization.  Formulation (a) says that the rule operates on any **n** in the rhyme, while (b) redundantly specifies that the rule applies to any **n** *either* at the syllable boundary, *or* separated from the syllable boundary by one or more consonants.  In contrast, 16a elegantly captures the fact that the rule operates anywhere in the rhyme (or coda?).  On grounds of superior generalizing power, I suggest that the internal-constituent (rhyme or coda) based account is preferable.

The claims I make for internal prosodic structure are neither radical nor surprising.  The notions 'left' (initial) and 'right' (final), are part of the established descriptive apparatus of prosodic phonology, and indeed play a far more important role in it than is usually recognized.  Not only must 'left' and 'right' be specified in directional spreading rules, but the distinction between initial and final limits is crucial to many domain-limit rules.  Pretonic and posttonic domains are simply prosodic projections of 'right' and 'left', delimited within the constituent by another independently required element, the DTE or vocalic nucleus.  It is often observed that the 'ends' of constituents (e.g., the syllable, the word) are 'weaker' than the corresponding 'beginnings', in that the former are especially subject to deletion or general weakening along the phonological strength hierarchy, while the latter are more resistant to deletion and neutralization processes, and are frequently subject to 'strengthening'.  The Italo-Romance phenomena I have investigated are simply suprasegmental manifestations of such behaviour: the posttonic domain is variously subject to deletion or more extreme forms of neutralization (complete harmony; reduction to schwa); the pretonic domain resists neutralization, or is susceptible to less radical forms of harmony.  Further investigation of Italo-Romance and other languages may reveal that the internal prosodic structure of constituents is more complex than I have indicated; what I hope to have established at least is that recognition of such structure is motivated, and by no means inconsistent with the overall theoretical framework constructed by Nespor & Vogel.

# Notes

1. Phonetic symbols are given in the text in bold characters. Since the phonemic status of the sounds affected is not relevant, I dispense with the traditional apparatus of slashes and square brackets.
2. The following dialect examples are taken from: Ziccardi (1910), for Agnone; the unpublished materials of the Atlante linguistico italiano for Montefalcone (survey point 674); the AIS for Lucera (point 707), Monte di Procida (point 720) and Palagiano (point 737); De Lollis (1901) for Casalincontrada.

# References

AIS — see Jaberg & Jud.

Camilli A. 1929. Il dialetto di Servigliano (Ascoli Piceno). *Archivum Romanicum* 13, 220-251.

De Lollis C. 1901. Dell'-A in qualche dialetto abruzzese. *Miscellanea Ascoli*, 275-293.

Elwert W. T. 1958. Die Mundart von S. Oreste. *Romanica. Festschrift für Gerhard Rohlfs*, 121-158. Halle: Niemeyer.

Fudge E. 1969. Syllables. *Journal of Linguistics* 5, 253-286.

Harris J. 1983. *Syllable Structure and Stress in Spanish*. Cambridge, Mass.: MIT Press.

van der Hulst H. & Smith N. 1987. *Advances in Non-Linear Phonology*. Dordrecht: Foris.

Jaberg, Karl & Jakob Jud. 1928-1940. *Sprach- und Sachatlas Italiens und der Südschweiz*. Zofingen: Ringier.

Lausberg H. 1939. *Die Mundarten Südlukaniens*. Halle: Niemeyer.

Lindsström A. 1907. Il vernacolo di Subiaco. *Studi romanzi* 5, 237-300.

Maiden M. 1988. Armonia regressiva di vocali atone nell'Italia meridionale. *L'Italia dialettale* 51, 111-139.

Merlo C. 1922. *Fonologia del dialetto di Cervara in provincia di Roma*. Rome: Società filologica romana.

Nespor, M. & Vogel, I. 1986. *Prosodic Phonology*. Dordrecht: Foris.

Rohlfs G. 1966. *Grammatica storica della lingua italiana e dei suoi dialetti. Fonetica*. Turin: Einaudi.

Venturelli G. 1979. Varietà di armonizzazioni vocaliche nella Garfagnana centro-meridionale. *Atti del XIV Congresso internazionale di linguistica e filologia romanza, Napoli, 1974*, ed. A. Varvaro, 3, 101-104. Napoli: Macchiaroli; Amsterdam: Benjamins.

Ziccardi G. 1910. Il dialetto di Agnone. *Zeitschrift für romanische Philologie* 34:405-436.

# Some observations on the syntax of clitic pronouns in Piedmontese*

## M. Mair Parry
### *University of Wales, Aberystwyth*

**1.1.**    Contemporary standard Piedmontese,[1] like Italian, French, and other Romance varieties, is basically a SVO language; but, like them, it displays a different order in the case of unstressed pronoun objects[2] — these normally precede the finite verb:

> (1)   *Ël parco a-j fa'n pò d prédica.*
>       The parish-priest 3SC[3] to-her makes a little of sermon.
>       'The parish-priest gives her a little sermon.'
>       (*Il parroco le fa un po' di predica.*)
>             (Brero 1977:47)

However, as in Italian, unstressed pronouns are attached enclitically to non-finite verb forms: infinitive, imperative, gerund and past participle used in the absolute sense:

> (2)   *Ël padron a l'era vnù 'd corsa ... a feje festa.*
>       The master 3SC had come quickly... to make-to-her congratulations.
>       'The master had come quickly to congratulate her.'
>       (*Il padrone era venuto di corsa ... a farle festa.*)
>             (*ibid.*:25)
> (3)   *Scuseme, monsù.*
>       Excuse-me, sir.
>       'Excuse me, sir.'
>       (*Scusatemi, signore.*)
>             (*ibid.*:51)

(4)    *E dimne 'n pò doe.*
       And tell-me-of-them a little two.
       'And just tell me two of them.'
       (*E dimmene un po' due.*)
                         (*ibid.*:52)

(5)    *Guardandse d'antorn...*
       Looking-himself around...
       'Looking around...'
       (*Guardandosi attorno...*)
                         (*ibid.*:25)

(6)    *Trovalo setà davant a l'uss...*
       Found-him seated in front of the door...
       'Having found him seated in front of the door...'
       (*Trovatolo seduto davanti all'uscio...*)
                         (*loc. cit.*)

**1.2.**    Piedmontese varieties (but not Canavese) differ from Italian and most Romance varieties, however, in that the rule of pronominal enclisis to non-finite verb forms also applies to compound tenses (i.e., sequences of 'auxiliary + past participle').

(7)    *A l'avia scotalo.*
       3SC had listened to him.
       'he/she had listened to him.'
       (*Lo aveva ascoltato.*)
                         (*ibid.*:50)

(8)    *A l'ha mandane.*
       3SC has sent-us.
       'He/she has sent us.'
       (*Ci ha mandato.*)
                         (*Piemontèis ancheuj* 1989, 76:7)

(9)    *E l'àngel che am parlava a l'ha dime.*
       And the angel that 3SC-me was speaking 3SC has told-me.
       'And the angel that was speaking to me told me.'
       (*E l'angelo che mi parlava mi ha detto.*)
                         (*Musicalbrandé* 1988, 118:2)

(10)  [a la mɑj par'lɑnne][4]
      3SC has never spoken-to-us-of-it.
      'He/she has never spoken to us of it.'
      (*Non ce ne ha mai parlato.*)
(11)  *Balin a l' é partisne.*
      Balin  3SC has left-himself-from-there.
      'Balin has left.'
      (*Balin se n' è partito.*)
                  (Brero 1977:16)
(12)  *L' ultim goblòt a l' é 'ndaje pèr travers.*
      The last glass  3SC has gone-to-him crosswise.
      'The last glass went down the wrong way.'
      (*L' ultimo bicchiere gli è andato di traverso.*)
                  (*ibid.*:117)

This enclitic positioning of object clitics on the past participle of the perfect periphrasis is unusual in the context of the Romance languages. Although various theories have been proposed regarding its origin, this has not been established with any certainty. The construction does not feature in medieval and Renaissance Piedmontese texts — compare (13).

(13)  *E sì l' àn spolià tut nu*
      *e durament l' an ferù e batù.*
      And thus him-they-have stripped all bare
      and harshly him-they-have wounded and beaten.
      'And thus they have stripped him bare
      and they they have wounded and beaten him harshly.'
      (*E così l' hanno spogliato tutto nudo*
      *e duramente l' hanno ferito e battuto.*)
                  (Brero & Gandolfo 1967:125, ll. 3-4)

It cannot therefore be attributed to a simple continuation and generalization of early enclitic positioning of unstressed pronouns, barred from occurring sentence initially (Law of Tobler and Mussafia) (see Simon 1967:34). One is tempted to postulate the emergence of a morphosyntactic constraint that requires object clitics within clauses containing non-finite verb forms to be attached enclitically to the latter. The progressive periphrasis also normally requires enclitic positioning of object clitics:

(14)  *A stasìa mangiandlo.*
      3SC was eating-it.
      'He/she was eating it.'
      (*Stava mangiandolo./Lo stava mangiando.*)

Structures of the *A lo stasìa mangiand* type were judged to be Italianisms
by my informants. As we shall see below, in Piedmontese complex verb
structures involving a modal verb followed by an infinitival complement,
object clitics are again attached to the non-finite form — that is, to the infinitive. The passive construction with auxiliary *esse*, however, shows no
such requirement — in fact, enclisis is not allowed:

(15)  a.  *La litra a t sarà mandà stasera.*
          The letter 3SC to-you will-be sent this evening.
          'The letter will be sent to you this evening.'
          (*La lettera ti sara mandata stasera.*)
      b.  *\*La litra a sarà mandàte.*
          The letter 3SC will-be sent-to-you.

Meyer-Lübke (1900:III, 439-440) suggested that enclitic positioning of
the object pronouns on the past participle of the perfect periphrasis was a
response to the need to resolve an ambiguity arising in third-person singular expressions. Since the third-person singular subject clitic was *a* before
consonants, *al* before vowels, and since third-person object clitics *lo* and *la*
were reduced to *l* in pre-vocalic contexts, *Al ha mangià*, 'He/she has eaten'
and *A l'ha mangià*, 'He/she has eaten it' sounded identical. The problem,
presumably, became more acute when, as a result of the morphological reanalysis of *al ha* as *a l'ha*, the *l* was generalized in Turinese to all the other
persons of the verb *avèj* in order to avoid the hiatus which would otherwise
occur between all subject clitics (except the second person singular) and the
verb forms.[5] Other potential sources of ambiguity are not lacking — for
example, the generalization of *j* to finite forms of *esse* beginning with a
vowel (except third person singular) (see Brero 1988:90) would presumably have erased the difference between the forms corresponding to Italian
*Ero stato* 'I had been' and *C'ero stato* 'I had been there' or *Gli ero stato* 'I
had been to him', all rendered as *I j'era stait*. Repetition of the clitic, attached enclitically to the past participle, according to the already existing
pattern of the absolute construction, would have served to disambiguate
these structures: *A l'ha mangialo*, Italian *L'ha mangiato*, 'He/she has eaten

it'; *A l' ha mangià*, Italian *Ha mangiato*, 'He/she has eaten'. According to this hypothesis, clitic copying in the perfect periphrasis then spread to involve all the other clitics.[6]

**1.3.**    The conservative, basically Piedmontese, dialect of Cairo Montenotte, on the Piedmontese-Ligurian border, displays the clitic-copying stage in the development: the preverbal object clitic occurs in front of the auxiliary verb and is also attached to the past participle:[7]

(16)  [a tlø 'ditle]
        1SC to-you-it-I have (SING.)  said-to-you-it.
        'I have said it to you.'
        (*Te l' ho detto.*)

(17)  [u mna 'dɔmne duj]
        3sSC to-me of-them-has  given-to-me-of-them two.
        'He has given me two of them.'
        (*Me ne ha dati due.*)

(18)  [u snɛ aŋ'dɔsnɛ]
        3msSC himself-from-there-is gone-himself-from-there.
        'He has gone away.'
        (*Se n' è andato.*)

(19)  [a ɹø var'dɔɹa]
        1SC her-have (SING.) looked-at-her.
        'I have looked at her.'
        (*L' ho guardata.*)

Evidence of this earlier stage is to be found in Turinese seventeenth- and eighteenth-century texts:

(20)  *aij a mostraje nôstra vigna e 'l pra.*
        3SC-to-him has shown-to-him our vineyard and the meadow.
        'She has shown him our vineyard and the meadow.'
        (*Gli ha mostrato la nostra vigna e il prato.*)
                    (Tana [1649-1713] *'L Cont Piolet* II, 728.)

(21)  *Ch'i t' m' as robame 'l cheur.*
        That 2sSC from-me have stolen-from me the heart.
        'That you have stolen my heart.'
        (*Che mi hai rubato il cuore.*)
                    (Isler [1702-1788] in Brero & Gandolfo 1967:278)

The situation is still fluid in the nineteenth century, with the same writer using expressions containing preverbal clitic only, preverbal clitic plus enclitic copy as in Cairese, as well as enclitic pronoun only (for instance, Angelo Brofferio — see Brero & Gandolfo 1967:540-601; also Parry 1994b).

**1.4.**    Occasionally in the modern language (taking as representative the relatively standardized Turinese variety, found in a number of Piedmontese language magazines) residual instances of the clitic copying construction may be found, for example:

> (22)   *Ëd bot an blan a l'é voltasse e a s'é trovasse ant na leja.*
>           Suddenly 3SC has turned-himself and 3SC himself-has found-
>                 himself in an avenue.
>           'Suddenly he turned round and found himself in an avenue.'
>           *(Di botto si è voltato e si è trovato in un viale.)*
>                          (*Musicalbrandé* 1988, 117:16)

However, it seems that the only clitic involved is the third-person reflexive form *se* (in all its various meanings — less frequently in its reflexive than in its passive, middle and impersonal senses). The repetition of all other pronoun clitics (as found in the Val Bormida and a few other Piedmontese dialects[8]) has been eliminated in Turinese and in standard Piedmontese (see (7-12)).

**2.1.**    Interestingly, a rather similar pattern of object clitic positioning to that described above for Piedmontese and Cairese is to be found in another area of verb syntax: complex verb structures involving modal, aspectual or motion verbs. This is the one area of Italian syntax that allows a measure of optionality in the positioning of clitic pronouns, e.g.

> (23)   *Posso/devo/voglio farlo.// Lo posso/devo/voglio fare.*
>           'I can/must/want (to) do it.'
> (24)   *Comincio a scriverlo./Lo comincio a scrivere.*
>           'I start to write it.'
> (25)   *Vengo a vederti./Ti vengo a vedere.*
>           'I am coming to see you.'

The configurational change involved in the extraction of clitics from an embedded infinitival clause has been described in the generative framework in terms of a 'Restructuring' rule: the main verb and its infinitival complement are replaced by a single complex-verb structure, with the result that any clitics must then attach to the leftmost constituent of the new complex verb.[9] Recent, pragmatically orientated, research has shown that clitic climbing in Italian is not purely optional, but is governed by various syntactic, semantic, and especially pragmatic factors.[10] It is more frequent in spoken than in written Italian (Berretta 1986; Skytte 1983:93-94), a fact almost certainly related to the high topicality of clitic pronouns.[11] The more topical a constituent is, the earlier it will be introduced into the discourse — hence movement to the left.

**2.2.** Clitic climbing is not common in written Piedmontese; in the majority of cases the object pronoun clitics are found attached enclitically to the embedded infinitive:

> (26) *La cassiëtta un a peul catela.*[12]
>      The cassette one 3SC can buy-it-FEM.
>      'The cassette can be bought.'
>      (*La cassetta, uno può comprarla.*)
>                (*Musicalbrandé* 1988, 118:25)
> (27) *Mach la musica a peul ofrine...*
>      Only the music 3SC can offer-us...
>      'Only music can offer us...'
>      (*Solo la musica può offrirci...*)
>                (*Piemontèis ancheuj* 1989, 77:5)
> (28) *A l'ha dovu pieghesse.*
>      3SC has had to bend-himself.
>      'He had to bend.'
>      (*Ha dovuto piegarsi.*)
>                (*ibid.*:4)

Spoken Turinese also affords few examples of the phenomenon. Informants asked to provide Turinese equivalents of Italian sentences containing complement clitics almost invariably produced constructions with pronouns enclitic on the infinitive:

(29)    a.  [t it 'pøle de**mlu** 'sybit]
            You 2sSC can give-me-it immediately.

and     b.  [t 'pøle de**mlu** 'sybit]
            2sSC can give-me-it immediately.

for Italian  *Me lo puoi dare subito.*
            'You can give it to me immediately.'

(30)        [ɑ vu'ria mus'tre**mlu**]
            3SC wanted to show-me-it.

for Italian  *Me lo voleva mostrare.*
            'He/she wanted to show it to me.'

(31)        [ɑ duv'ria 'deme le seŋt lire]
            3SC should  give-me the hundred lire.

for Italian  *Mi dovrebbe dare le cento lire.*
            'You (POLITE) should give me the hundred lire.'

They considered versions containing preverbal clitics as far less common, and tended to ascribe them to the influence of Italian.

**2.3.**    Clitic climbing is acceptable, however, in the following contexts:

a.  when the modal, aspectual, or motion verb has a compound form, see (32-34)

b.  when the modal, aspectual, or motion verb is itself an infinitive, see (35)

c.  when the modal, aspectual, or motion verb is an imperative, see (36)

d.  when the clitic involved is the reflexive third-person form *se* (Italian *si*) used in the passive or impersonal sense, see (37) and (38).

(32)  *A sarà-lo[13] che un diavlot a l' ha vorsuje buté la coa?*
      3SC will-be-3msSC that a little devil 3SC has wanted-there
          to-put the tail
      'Is it possible that a little devil has had a hand in this?'
      (*Sarà che un diavoletto ci ha voluto mettere la coda?*)
      (*Musicalbrandé* 1988, 120:9)

(33)           a. [i lav'riu vur'syla duver'te]
                  1SC would have (PLURAL) wanted-it to-open.
as well as     b. [i lav'riu vur'sy duver'tela]
                  1SC would have (PLURAL) wanted to-open-it.
for Italian       *Avremmo voluto aprirla.*
                  'We would have wanted to open it.'
(34)           [a la vur'syte de tyt loŋ k a la'via]
               3SC has wanted-to-you give all that which 3SC had.
for Italian    *Ti ha voluto dare tutto ciò che aveva.*
               'He/she wanted to give you all he/she had.'
(35)  *Pèr podej-je vive 'ndrinta*
      'To be able-there to live inside'
      'So as to be able to live there'
      (*Per poterci vivere dentro*)
               (*Musicalbrandé* 1989, 125:11)
(36)  *Andelo a vëdde.*
      Go-it to see.
      'Go and see it.'
      (*Andatelo a vedere.*)
               (*Piemontèis ancheuj* 1989, 74:6)
(37)  *A piasi as peul butesse 'l parmigian gratà.*
      At pleasure 3SC-SI can throw-SI the parmesan grated.
      'Grated parmesan may be sprinkled on top.'
      (*Si può cospargere con parmigiano grattugiato a piacere.*)
               (*Musicalbrandé* 1989, 121:31)
(38)  *As dovrìo nen dovresse ... le forme dialetaj.*
      3SC-SI should NEG use-SI ... the forms dialectal.
      'Dialectal forms should not be used.'
      (*Non si dovrebbero adoperare ... le forme dialettali.*)
               (*Piemontèis ancheuj* 1988, 71:2)

**2.4.**  Furthermore, diachronic study shows that a resistance to clitic climbing has not always been a feature of Piedmontese. Earlier periods of Piedmontese, like French, place the complement clitics in front of the modal verb, with seventeenth-century texts revealing a gradual change towards the enclitic positioning on the infinitive. The possibility of two different orders of elements in these structures would seem to correspond to

two opposing linguistic tendencies: on the one hand, a discourse-orien-
tated, pragmatic tendency to introduce topical elements as early as possible,
and, on the other, a tendency for greater transparency of sentence surface
structure. The former tendency is given formal support by the basic ordering in simple sentences of clitics before the finite verb. The fact that popular registers of Italian, as well as Tuscan and Southern Italian dialects, have
maintained this ordering[14] suggests that the change to attachment to the infinitive cannot be due to an overwhelming, popular desire for a more trans-
parent grammatical structure. In French certain ambiguities were also
avoided by the new order,[15] and Galet (1971) sees this as crucial in bring-
ing about the change. However, de Kok (1985:453-519) rejects Galet's arguments:

> Tous les arguments que Galet a avancés pour soutenir cette conclusion reviennent
> en fait à un seul point: la clarté. C'est-à-dire que Galet adopte le point de vue
> d'un grammairien classique. Mais ce manque de clarté s'il y en a, n'a jamais pro-
> duit de problème avant le XVIIe siècle, et avec certains verbes ce manque de
> clarté existe encore de nos jours (*ibid.*:505)

and attributes the change to

> l'interaction de trois causes: 1) l'affaiblissement de la valeur nominale des verbes
> non finis en faveur de leur valeur verbale, 2) l'homogénéisation de la nature dif-
> férente, selon le contexte, du verbe non fini dépendant d'un seul et même verbe et
> 3) l'instauration d'un ordre fonctionnel où le constituant ayant la fonction de sujet
> précède le constituant ayant la fonction de verbe (*ibid.*:514).

Wanner (1987:283-375) provides an extremely detailed investigation of the
origins of Romance clitic movement (CM) seen as

> a natural outgrowth of Latin infinitival subordination patterns. The gradual post-
> medieval reduction in clitic movement is linked to the dissolution of the syntacti-
> cally productive Romance principle of Tobler-Mussafia's law (TM).
>     At the point where clitic placement and linearization cease to be actively
> derived in the syntactic domain, they become morphological principles of fixed
> clitic collocation. This is visible in the abandonment of the venerable Wacker-
> nagel's law = second position condition prohibiting clause initial clitics. The TM-
> determined corollary called clitic movement thus becomes a phenomenon of its
> own. It leads to important reanalyses which must then postulate variable princi-
> ples of restructuring and/or clitic movement operating independently of place-
> ment/ linearization. (*ibid.*:359)

**2.5.** However, the almost complete disappearance of clitic climbing from
French and Northern Italian dialects — in contrast, for example, to Italian,
Spanish (Harmer & Norton 1961:89) and Catalan (Badía Margarit

1962:210-211) — suggests the possibility that in varieties with mandatory subject clitics, a contributory factor was a reluctance to interrupt *unnecessarily* (that is, with clitics not dependent on the finite verb) the close sequence of subject clitic and verb. Kayne (1980) proposed a relationship between clitic climbing and the null subject parameter, which was taken up by Rizzi (1982):

> Kayne (1980b) has noticed that the restructuring process discussed in chapter I appears to be typologically related to the 'Null Subject' Parameter. This is suggested by the distribution of the two properties in the Romance area (e.g., Italian, Spanish, Portuguese have both, French lacks both), and, more significantly, by the history of French: Old French had both properties, which were lost in the course of the evolution of the language. Kayne has put forth the conjecture that these typological and diachronic facts are not accidental. (Rizzi 1982:172).

Rejecting Kayne's explanation of the correlation between the 'null subject' property and restructuring, Rizzi tentatively offers an alternative hypothesis to account for the fact that clitic climbing does not occur in non 'null subject' languages such as French. Kayne (1987) has subsequently explored 'the possibility of expressing a relation between clitic climbing and null subjects within an approach to the former that makes no use of a restructuring rule'.[16] That clitic climbing is dependent on the 'null subject' property of a language but not a necessary corollary of it is demonstrated by Northern Italian dialects. These are generally analysed as 'null subject' languages (Rizzi 1986:414) but, on the whole, show resistance to clitic climbing, as we have seen for Piedmontese. Kayne (1987:254 note 9) briefly mentions the resistance to clitic climbing in Northern Italian dialects, but queries its extent.

The suggestion that the change in the position of clitics in modal structures in French and Northern Italian dialects could have been influenced by a reluctance to interrupt unnecessarily the sequence 'subject clitic + verb' needs detailed investigation beyond the scope of this paper. Compulsory clitic climbing involving the subject of the infinitive with causatives and verbs of perception does not invalidate this hypothesis, since these are quite different structures, involving a separate subject for each verb. According to Wanner (1987:356) it is this 'functionally distinct nature of the subject$_2$ pronouns' in Causative and Perception situations that allows them to remain unaffected by reduction in clitic movement in the post-medieval Romance period, whereas 'object$_2$ pronouns in the same Causative and Perception strings followed the lead of the other object by acquiring a certain degree of CM freedom[17]' (*loc. cit.*).

Support for the hypothesis may be found in the fact that modern Piedmontese allows clitic climbing in modal structures when the modal has a compound form (see (32-34)) and when the modal itself is an infinitive (35) or imperative (36). The extracted pronoun (attached enclitically to the past participle in the first case, to the infinitive in the second, and to the imperative in the third) does not in these structures interrupt a 'subject clitic + verb' sequence; therefore clitic climbing is not discouraged. Compare (33a) (repeated here for convenience as (39)):

(39)  [i lav'riu vur'sy**la** duver'te]
      1SC would have (PLURAL) wanted-it to-open.
      'We would have wanted to open it.'
      (*Avremmo voluto aprirla.*)

**2.6.**    What could be viewed as a transitional phase of the development from the earlier proclitic positioning of pronouns before the finite verb to enclitic positioning on the infinitive is to be found in the conservative dialect of Cairo Montenotte. Here, as with the perfect periphrasis, we have two instances of the same clitic: if we assume that the complement clitic originates to the right of the verb with which it is semantically associated, then movement to the left leaves a copy in the original position:

(40)  [u tiŋ pø neŋ perdu'nɛtɛ]
      3msSC you-NEG can NEG forgive-you.
      'He cannot forgive you.'
      (*Non ti può perdonare./Non può perdonarti.*)

(41)  [ɛt lɛ pøj 'fɛlɛ a to 'adʒi]
      2sSC it can do-it at your leisure.
      'You can do it at your leisure.'
      (*Lo puoi fare a tuo agio./Puoi farlo a tuo agio.*)

(42)  [i t 'venu a saly'tɛtɛ]
      3pSC you come to greet-you.
      'They are coming to greet you.'
      (*Ti vengono a salutare.[18]/Vengono a salutarti.*)

Similar structures are found in the popular registers of other Romance varieties and are often castigated by grammarians — see, for example, Badía

Margarit (1962:210-211). They have been recorded in informal spoken Italian and ascribed to uncertainty on the part of the speaker with regard to the organization of the sentence's constituents:

(43)  (Cultured speaker)
      *Spero, presto di poterLa leggerLa con tutto l'apparato.*
      I-hope soon to be-able-you (POLITE) to read-you (POLITE) with all the apparatus.
      'I hope to be able to read your work soon with all the associated documentation.'

(44)  (Cashier to customer)
      *Lei mi potrebbe darmi le trecento lire?*
      You (POLITE) me could give-me the three hundred lire?
      'Could you give me the three hundred lire?'
                  (both examples from Berretta (1986:73); see also Berretta (1985:194)).

The tension between the two linguistic tendencies: on the one hand, towards introducing topical elements as early as possible in the discourse and, on the other, towards greater transparency of surface structure, is resolved in the popular language by the overt repetition of the pronoun.

   Piedmontese may well have passed through a stage of generalized clitic copying in modal and aspectual periphrases. As in the case of the perfect periphrasis, seventeenth- and eighteenth-century texts provide evidence of clitic copying:

(45)  *mi ij veui dìe la côsa franch e net.*
      I 1SC-to-her want to say-to-her the thing frankly and clearly.
      'I want to tell it to her quite plainly.'
      (*Io le voglio dire/voglio dirle la cosa francamente.*)
                  (Tana, *'L' Cont Piolet* III, 253).

(46)  *a ij debia feje part d' soa gioventù.*
      3SC to-him should make-to-him a gift of her youth..
      '(That) she should make him a gift of her youth.'
      (*Gli debba donare la sua giovinezza.*)
                  (*ibid.*:III,1.543.)

(47) '*S quaicadun a-i veul andeje.*
If someone 3SC-there wishes to go-there.
'If someone wishes to go there.'
(*Se qualcuno ci vuol andare/vuol andarci.*)
(Isler, in Brero & Gandolfo 1967:276)

The written language, however, more selfconscious and subject to norma-
tive pressures, would as a rule have eliminated the pronominal repetition
characteristic of popular speech. Eventually the redundant preverbal clitic
would have been dropped — not only for reasons of economy and in-
creased syntactic transparency, but also to avoid interrupting unnecessarily
the 'subject clitic + finite verb' sequence. Interestingly, this process coin-
cides with the loss of the proclitic negative particle from the Piedmontese
discontinuous negative construction, *n ... nen*, leaving post-verbal *nen* only.
Both the demise of clitic climbing and the elimination of the preverbal
negative marker thus appear to be symptoms of an increasing resistance to
the unnecessary interruption of the nexus 'subject clitic + verb'.[19]

**3.1.** As has already been mentioned, clitic climbing and copying has
nevertheless remained the norm in the case of one Piedmontese clitic. The
clitic concerned is, probably not fortuitously, the same one that constituted
an exception in the case of the perfect periphrasis — Piedmontese *se*, the
equivalent of Italian *si*, in its non-reflexive uses. (37) and (38) are repeated
here for convenience as (48) and (49):

(48) *A piasi as peul butesse 'l parmigian gratà.*
At pleasure 3SC-SI can throw-SI the parmesan grated.
'Grated parmesan may be sprinkled on top.'
(*Si può cospargere con parmigiano grattugiato a piacere.*)
(*Musicalbrandé* 1989, 121:31)

(49) *As dovrìo nen dovresse ... le forme dialetaj.*
3SC-SI should NEG use-SI ... the forms dialectal.
'Dialectal forms should not be used.'
(*Non si dovrebbero adoperare ... le forme dialettali.*)
(*Piemontèis ancheuj* 1988, 71:2)

(50)  *As podìa disse.*
       3SC-SI could say-SI.
       'One could say'/'It could be said.'
       (*Si poteva dire.*)
                  (*Musicalbrandé* 1988, 117:13)

(51)  ['si as duv'ria maŋ'dʒese biŋ]
       Here 3SC-SI should eat-SI well.
       'Here one ought to eat well.'
       (*Qui si dovrebbe mangiare bene.*)

(52)  [a s pøl aŋ'dese 'li]
       3SC-SI can go-SI there.
       'One can go there.'
       (*Ci si può andare.*)

(53)  [ɑ s pøl telefu'ŋese]
       3SC-SI can telephone-SI.
       'One can telephone.'
       (*Si può telefonare.*)

(54)  [i fa'zøj as 'pølu maŋ'dʒese aŋ taŋte ma'njɛre]
       The beans 3SC-SI can eat-SI in many ways.
       'Beans can be eaten in many ways.'
       (*I fagioli si possono mangiare in tante maniere.*)

**3.2.**  Examples where clitic climbing has not occurred, as well as instances of clitic climbing in which no copy is left in the original position,
are to be found, though far less frequently:

(55)  *A peul desse.*
       3SC can  give-SI.
       'Maybe.'
       (*Può darsi.*)
                  (*Musicalbrandé* 1988, 120:18)

(56)  *La litra — come as peul vëdde...*[20]
       The letter  — as  3SC-SI  can see...
       'The letter — as can be seen...'
       (*La lettera — come si può vedere.*)
                  (*Piemontèis ancheuj* 1989, 76:5)

One passage by Camillo Brero,[21] the editor of *Piemontèis ancheuj* (*ibid.*,
75:1), displays a range of variations:

(57) a. *Se anche as pronunsio 'aut, quat, mèist, nòst'*
       if even  3SC-SI pronounce (PLURAL)
       *a devo scriv-se anter.*
       3SC must (PLURAL) write-SI whole.
       'Even if they are pronounced "aut, quat, mèist, nòst", they
       must be written in full'
       (*Anche se si pronunciano 'aut, quat, mèist, nòst', si
       devono scrivere interi.*)

   b. *L'istess as peul disse dla 't' ... andoa la 't'*
       The same 3SC-SI can say-SI of-the 't' ... where the 't'
       *a l'é nen pronunsià, ma che as dev ëscrive.*
       3SC is  NEG pronounced, but that 3SC-SI must write.
       'The same can be said of the "t" ... where the "t" is not
       pronounced, but it must be written.'
       (*La stessa cosa si può dire della 't' ... ove la 't' non è
       pronunciata, ma la si deve scrivere.*)

   c. *As dev scriv-se: Quand e Question.*
       3SC-SI must write-SI: *Quand* and *Question.*
       'One must write: *Quand* and *Question.*'
       (*Si deve scrivere: Quand e Question.*)

**3.3.**    If we consider the behaviour of reflexive *se*, we find that it behaves
just like other reflexive pronouns, i.e., it is not normally affected by clitic
climbing:[22]

   (58) a. [dʒua'ɲiŋ a pøl la'vese]
           Giovanni 3SC can wash-himself.
           'Giovanni can wash/get washed.'
           (*Giovanni può lavarsi.*)

      b. *[dʒua'ɲiŋ a s pøl la'vese]  was rejected.[23]

This difference in syntactic behaviour between reflexive *se* that behaves in
the same way as other complement clitics and non-reflexive *se* may be attributed to the fact that non-reflexive *se* is not a complement argument of
the infinitive but a marker of voice (passive or middle) or of the impersonal
construction.

**3.4.**    The Romance impersonal *si/se* construction has developed historically from reflexive forms of the verb used in a passive sense.  Whereas the

reflexive clitic in Piedmontese retains its full argument status and is not allowed to interrupt unnecessarily the 'subject clitic + verb' nexus in modal verb constructions, the grammaticalized particle has not been ousted from this context. The difference could be due to a number of reasons — for instance, as a grammatical morpheme of voice, *se* has no closer semantic link with the embedded infinitive than with the sentence as a whole, so that it remains attached to the modal verb, just as the grammatical morphemes of tense and mood.

In the Italian impersonal construction, *si* has acquired the sort of meaning conveyed by French *on*, German *man*.[24] Structurally also it may be analysed as a subject argument in a transitive construction: *lo si vede* 'one sees it'; *li si vede* 'one sees them'. If it were to be the case that Piedmontese *se* had combined with the dummy subject clitic *a* in a form *as*, perceived as representing an indefinite active human participant, similar to that represented by Italian *si*, there would be no need to explain the non-elimination of *se* from the impersonal modal structures: it would now be part of the subject clitic. The complex question of the status of *se* in Piedmontese will be more amply treated elsewhere, but a brief consideration of a few points will clarify the present discussion.

**3.5.**    The behaviour of the *se* morpheme in Piedmontese has interesting theoretical implications in the context of wider discussions relating to standard Italian and Northern Italian dialects in general (see Cinque 1988, Battye 1989). Cinque (1988) proposes two distinct uses of impersonal *si* in Italian, as an argument and as a nonargument; whereas Battye (1989) raises doubts about the existence of the full syntactic paradigm that one would expect to be associated with an impersonal *si* argument in Genoese. Burzio (1986) assumes that impersonal *se* does exist in Piedmontese, but he does not enter into a detailed discussion of the point. Battye's argument hinges on the lack in Genoese of constructions equivalent to Italian *lo si vede, li si vede*, in which direct object clitics co-occur with *si*. Such constructions are also impossible in Piedmontese and Cairese, and it is clear from the data that the syntactic status of *se* is different from that of Italian *si* in a number of respects — for instance, it does not seem to have acquired subject argument status.

Frequent examples of the impersonal construction type '*se* + singular verb + plural NP' occur in Piedmontese:

(59) [a z 'lɑva i 'pjɑti]
3SC-SI washes the plates.
'One washes the dishes./The dishes are washed.'
(*Si lava*[25] *i piatti.*)

(60) [as pøl ʃtʃai'rese le muŋ'taɲe]
3SC-SI can see-SI the mountains.
'One can see the mountains./The mountains can be seen.'
(*Si può vedere le montagne.*)

as well as the structurally 'passive' expressions showing agreement of the
verb with the NP:

(61) [a z 'lɑvu i 'pjɑti]
3SC-SI washes (PLURAL) the plates.
'One washes the dishes./The dishes are washed.'
(*Si lavano i piatti.*)

(62) [a s 'pølu ʃtʃai'rese le muŋ'taɲe]
3SC-SI can (PLURAL) see-SI the mountains.
'One can see the mountains./The mountains can be seen.'
(*Si possono vedere le montagne.*)

The first construction type, (59) and (60), however, was considered more
authentically Piedmontese by my informants. Neither construction allows
object pronominalization of the NP. When the NP is pronominalized, it
appears as the third person **subject** clitic *a* with the appropriate singular or
plural agreement on the verb: (59), for example, would become (63):

(63) [az 'lɑvu]
3SC-SI wash.
'They are washed.'
(*Si lavano.*)

Contrast with the Italian impersonal construction *li si lava* 'one washes
them', also Venetian *se la vede*, Italian *la si vede* 'one can see her'
(Lepschy 1986:146), all of which contain **direct object** clitics.

Battye (1990) argued for Ligurian, where similar constraints exist, that
the impersonal *se* (+ singular verb) construction is related to the rather formal or archaic French construction found for example in (64):

(64) *Il s'exporte annuellement un nombre croissant de voitures*
    *automobiles.*
    3SC-SI exports annually a number increasing of cars
    automobiles.
    'An increasing number of cars is exported each year.'
        (Stéfanini 1962:127)

Both constructions are related to the *Il est venu 300 personnes* '300 people came' type in French and similar structures in Ligurian. Battye noted that these impersonal structures involving a singular verb followed by a plural NP are found in unaccusative configurations only.[26] A major difference between the French structures on the one hand and the Ligurian and Piedmontese structures on the other is that in the latter there is no definiteness effect — definite nouns occur freely in the dialect constructions (see (59)).

According to this interpretation, *se* is merely the marker of an impersonal passive construction: the use of the *se* passive marker in structures such as (52) ([a s pøl aŋ'dese 'li ...] 'One can go there') corresponds to the impersonal use of passives in Latin, CURRITUR; Old Italian, *Fu andato*;[27] Old French, *Il fut dansé*, etc.

**3.6.**    In modern Italian, as Lepschy (1986:147) has convincingly argued, a typically 'passive' form of the Italian *si* construction (plural verb followed by plural NP) does not rule out an impersonal interpretation that involves the idea of an indefinite human agent experiencer.[28] *Si comprano due penne* means not only 'Two pens are bought' but also 'Someone (indefinite) buys two pens'. The association of the clitic *si* with the idea of an indefinite human agent or experiencer may be behind the tendency noted by Berretta (1986:81) to avoid verb structures involving modal verbs and embedded passive infinitives. These are relatively frequent in the written language but rare in spoken Italian — for instance, *Devono applicarsi* becomes in the spoken register, *Si devono applicare* (*ibid.*:74 & 81, n.8; see also Berretta 1985:211). The extraction of *si* from the embedded clause is attributed to semantic and pragmatic factors: 'È probabile che questo comportamento del parlato sia dovuto al fatto che *si* è trattato, anche nelle frasi formalmente passive, come soggetto'. The topical primacy of the agent or experiencer is well-documented in the world's languages (Givón 1984:140-141), while the semantic saliency of the feature Human has been shown by Manoliu-Manea (1987) to reveal itself clearly in the syntax of the Romance

group: 'Though the syntax of the voices and even of the cases may be sub-
ordinated to the most active participant, the communicative dynamism
shows a higher preference for subjects marked by the feature Human'
(Manoliu-Manea, 1987:240).

In the Piedmontese modal constructions also, as we have seen in (37),
(38) and (50-54), the *se* occurs before the finite verb, as a rule enclitically
attached to the dummy subject clitic.[29] However, the passive infinitive remains as well, even in intransitive constructions (compare (52-53)), a
structure not found in Italian impersonal constructions: **Può andarsi*
'One may go', **Qui può telefonarsi* 'Here one may telephone'.

**3.7.**     Thus, in conclusion, one may seek to explain the non-elimination of
the first *se* in the 'modal verb + infinitive' constructions in Piedmontese not
only by the grammaticalization of the clitic (as described in 3.5), but also
by the fact that in Piedmontese, too, *se* has come to be associated with an
indefinite active human participant. Although structurally unable to function as a subject argument, the combined form *as* could be interpreted semantically as an indefinite subject pronoun. Further support for this hypothesis is given by instances in spoken Turinese of impersonal perfect
constructions containing preverbal as well as postparticipial *se*, — see
(65a) and (66a). The written norm allows only enclitic positioning of *se* on
the past participle, as in the case of object clitics — compare (65b) and
(66b):

> (65)  a.  [a sɛ maŋ'dʒɑse taŋt]
>            3SC SI-has eaten-SI much.
>        b.  [a lɛ maŋ'dʒɑse taŋt]
>            3SC has eaten-SI much.
>            'A lot has been eaten.'
>            (*Si è mangiato molto.*)
> (66)  a.  [a sɛ telefu'ŋɑse]
>            3SC SI-has telephoned-SI.
>        b.  [a lɛ telefu'ŋɑse]
>            3SC has telephoned-SI.
>            (Someone telephoned.)
>            (*Si è telefonato.*)

It seems likely that this context also shows semantic and pragmatic pressures contributing to the early introduction of *se* in the discourse. A final

factor that cannot be discounted, as far as today's dialects are concerned, is the influence of Italian. The process of convergence can be identified at all linguistic levels and may well reinforce the association of Piedmontese *as* with an indefinite human agent/experiencer.

**4.** The above observations on the syntax of clitic pronouns in Piedmontese have focused on two constructions — the perfect periphrasis and modal structures — both of which provide interesting points for comparison with equivalent structures in the major Romance varieties. It has been suggested that varieties of Romance that developed compulsory subject clitics witnessed a growing tendency not to interrupt the 'subject clitic + finite verb' sequence in those structures that allowed an alternative positioning for complement clitics, namely, attachment to non-finite verb forms (following the model of pronominal cliticization to non-finite forms occurring independently). The discussion has also provided further evidence of the idiosyncratic behaviour of Romance reflexes of the Latin reflexive pronoun, SE. In this last case, in particular, much more remains to be investigated, but it is hoped that the data presented here will at least have revealed the importance of the study of non-standard varieties for testing the predictions and for the development of contemporary linguistic theory.

# Notes

* I should like to dedicate this paper to the memory of Adrian Battye, whose tragic death has meant an end to our frequent discussions, especially about the Romance clitic *si/se*. I am very grateful to him, as well as to Winifred Davies, Giulio Lepschy, Glanville Price, and Nigel Vincent, for their valuable criticism of an early version of this paper. All responsibility for remaining errors and misinterpretations is naturally mine. My sincere thanks also go to the British Academy for a Small Personal Research Grant which funded a visit to Italy in August 1989.

1. This, mainly written, variety is frequently referred to by its supporters as *la lenga piemontèisa*, 'the Piedmontese language'; it is based on the dialect of Turin (see Parry (1994a) for historical and sociolinguistic details).

2. This is not simply a relic of Latin SOV word order illustrating Givón's pithy phrase, 'Today's morphology is yesterday's syntax' (Givón 1979:238), but, as Wanner (1987:238) makes clear:

   'Proclisis of the Latin ex-NP = Romance object clitic is archaic only as a survival item of SOV typology: yet in Romance terms, the pre-determination pattern *determinans* > *determinatum* or *operator* > *operand*, or *modifier* > *head*) is the innovative type associated typologically with SVO. A hold-over condition acquires status as a forward looking reinterpretation through the independently changed conditions, SOV having developed into SVO, and unstressed object pronouns now being cliticized and having lost NP status (*cf* Bossong 1982:42).'

3.   3SC = 3rd person subject clitic, identical in Piedmontese for masculine, feminine, singular and plural. The data from the dialect of Cairo Montenotte (see below) distinguishes between singular and plural and, in the singular, between masculine and feminine: 3msSC, therefore stands for the masculine singular. Morpheme-by-morpheme glosses as well as free glosses are provided in English. Italian free glosses are also given (in parentheses), so as to allow useful comparisons to be made.

4.   The spoken data from Turinese derive from the responses of native speakers, asked in August 1989 to provide Piedmontese versions of Italian sentences. The Cairese data below derive from extensive recordings of free discourse and responses to questionnaires, from 1973-1989 (see Parry 1985).

5.   'Si usa *l'* immediatamente dinanzi a tutte le voci del verbo *avèj* (eccetto la seconda persona singolare e la prima e la seconda plurale dell'imperativo, l'infinito, i gerundi, i participi) e dinanzi alla terza persona singolare indicativo presente e imperfetto del verbo *ése*' (Aly-Belfadel 1933:167); see also Brero (1988:75). See Aly-Belfadel (*loc. cit.* and *ibid.*:155) for some interesting remarks concerning the analysis of third-person singular forms of *avèj* and *esse* (vowel initial), preceded by the object pronouns *lu* (modern Piedmontese orthography *lo*) and *la*. Further investigation and a detailed examination of Piedmontese texts are needed to clarify the exact evolution of expressions involving preverbal *l*.

6.   Other explanations are proposed by Benucci (1989; 1990) and Tuttle (1993). Benucci argues that, through a process of 'destructuring' (the reverse of 'restructuring' — see Rizzi (1982) and below, §2.1), the complex verb of periphrastic constructions (compound tenses, as well as modal/aspectual structures with the infinitive) is broken down into its two components, with the result that the object clitics attach to the (nonfinite) verb of which they are the arguments. Reduplication is a transitional stage, during which the object clitics still climb to the higher verb, but their deep structure link with the embedded infinitive, instead of featuring as a phonologically null trace, is represented in surface structure by an overt 'copy'. Tuttle (1993) attributes clitic reduplication to the topicality of personal pronouns, which encourages overuse in popular and colloquial registers (see below, §2.6). The phenomenon may be the result of multiple causation; but the whole question awaits further investigation.

7.   In the modern dialect, however, examples of non-repetition of the object clitics may be heard (due presumably to the combined influence of neighbouring Ligurian dialects and standard Italian) — for example, (i) instead of (ii):

(i)   [ki u tla ditʃ]                     (ii)   [ki u tla 'ditle]
      Who 3msSC you-it-has told?                Who 3msSC you-it-has told-you-it?
      'Who told you?'
      (*Chi te l' ha detto?*)

8.   See AIS maps IV 834; VI 1111; VIII 1617, 1618.

9.   See Rizzi (1982); but Kayne (1987): 'we now also doubt the correctness of a restructuring approach to (16) [*Gianni li vuole vedere*]'.

10.  See Berretta (1986).

11.  See Givón (1984:364): 'By "highly topical" we mean here, informally, "highly continuous", "predictable" or "recurrent" in the discourse'.

12.  The context immediately following a topicalized NP is particularly favourable to clitic climbing. See Berretta (1986:76): 'La posizione che sembra invece preferita è quella

immediatamente successiva ad un elemento tonico: il "fuoco" di una interrogativa, un soggetto tonico (pronominale ...) o *un nominale coreferenziale col clitico stesso, dislocato a sinistra ...*' (italics mine).

13. This is the expletive enclitic interrogative subject pronoun, which is morphologically identical to the masculine third-person singular pronoun.

14. See Rohlfs (1966-1969:172-174).

15. For Vaugelas's comments regarding the choice of construction facing seventeenth-century French speakers, see Ayres-Bennett (1987:118-119).

16. 'There are two necessary conditions for clitic climbing up to a higher V: First, the infinitival I must be able to L-mark VP, and second, the matrix must be compatible with I to (C to) I movement. Crucially neither of these two conditions is by itself sufficient' (Kayne 1987:251).

17. subject$_2$ = subject of V$_2$, i.e. the embedded infinitive
    object$_2$ = object of V$_2$, i.e. the embedded infinitive.

18. The occurrence of clitic pronouns in a complex verb structure involving a compound form of the auxiliary followed by the infinitive can occasionally result in a double repetition, i.e., three instances of the pronoun:

    (i)  [i **m** a'vɛjsi pu'ʃymæ dʒi'tɛmɛ]
         2pSC me-would-have been able-me to help-me.
         'You could have helped me.'
         (*Mi avreste potuto aiutare./Avreste potuto aiutarmi.*)

19. Cairo's conservative dialect maintains, as we have seen, optional clitic climbing, (39-41), clitic copying in the perfect periphrasis, as well as the preverbal negative marker:

    (i)  [a **ŋ** lø **neŋ**t 'viʃtle]
         1SC NEG him-have NEG seen him.
         'I have not seen him.'
         (*Non l' ho visto.*)

Among the factors suggested as having contributed towards the elimination of the preverbal negative particle in French is the reluctance to interrupt the array of preverbal clitics (see Harris (1978:118), Ashby (1981:680-681), Posner (1985:188-189)). For a brief study of Piedmontese negation, see Parry (1989).

20. The lack of a copy may be phonetically motivated — [a **z** vøl 'parte] was preferred by an informant to [a **z** vøl 'partse] for euphonic reasons.

21. Camillo Brero is an ardent promoter of Piedmontese. His prolific publications include edited volumes of Piedmontese literature, a history of Piedmontese literary development, several volumes of folk tales and poetry, and a number of Piedmontese grammars.

22. Compare Torinese:

    (i)  [i 'devu aw'seme]          (ii)  ?[i **m** 'devu aw'se]
         1SC must rise-myself              1SC myself must rise
         'I must get up.'
         (*Devo alzarmi./Mi devo alzare.*)

23. [a s pøl la'vese] means 'It can be washed' or 'One can wash', compare Italian *Si può lavare*; or it can sometimes be used as the reflexive of an *impersonal* construction 'One can wash (oneself)', Italian *Ci si può lavare*; it cannot however be the reflexive of a personal construction. For the reflexive of an impersonal expression recourse is often made to impersonal [yŋ], Italian *uno*: [yŋ a pøl la'vese], see Brero (1988:110).

24. See Stefanini (1983:105-106) and Lepschy (1986:143): 'There is a similar construction, usually called impersonal *si* construction, in which *si* appears to mark not a passive verb, but an indefinite subject. Apparently, this must be human: neither *si cade* (one falls), speaking of leaves, nor *si miagola* (one miaows), speaking of cats is possible.'

25. In Italian, according to Lepschy (1986:146), the use of a singular verb with plural object 'although [...] not actually impossible, [...] sounds rather awkward'.

26. Battye pointed out, however, that in French a locative clitic allows 'a broadening of the possibilities of this structure with the imperfect tense', for instance, \*\**Il mange quelques étudiants*, but *Il y mangeait quelques étudiants*. Recent investigations of mine in Liguria and Piedmont (see Parry forthcoming) suggest that, at least in some varieties, the non-agreement between the verb and a postposed subject NP also occurs with some unergative verbs in the context of a thematic locative phrase (not necessarily overt) and imperfective verbal aspect. The Genoese examples offered by Vattuone (1975:346) with transitive verbs (as in Trentino, for example — see Brandi & Cordin 1989:121-122) were not acceptable to my informants.

27. Compare Bertuccelli Papi (1980:6): 'L'altra mattina seguente *fu andato* allo campana di casa Tornaquinci ... e appena che *si vedesse* lo lume, *fu bussato* (Sacchetti, *Trecento Novelle*, LXXVIII).

28. Lepschy (1986:143-146) contains a valuable discussion of the distinction between Italian passive and impersonal constructions involving *si* — a distinction which is not accepted by everyone.

29. Before verbs with initial *s* + consonant, *se* is realized not as [s] but as [sə]; dummy pronoun and *se* are then orthographically represented thus: *a së sbrincia*, 'it is sprinkled'.

# References

AIS — see Jaberg & Jud.

Aly-Belfadel, Arturo. 1933. *Grammatica piemontese.* Noale: Guin

Ashby, William. 1981. The loss of the negative morpheme in French: a syntactic change in progress. *Language* 57, 674-687.

Ayres-Bennett, Wendy. 1987. *Vaugelas and the Development of the French Language.* London: The Modern Humanities Research Association.

Badía Margarit, Antonio M. 1962. *Gramatica catalana.* Madrid: Gredos.

Battye, Adrian. 1989. Genovese middle *se*. Unpublished paper given at the XVII Romance Linguistics Seminar, Cambridge, January 1989.

————. 1990. Quirky agreement in Genoese. Unpublished paper presented at the First Workshop on the Syntax of Central Romance Languages, Geneva, 6-7 July 1990.

Benucci, F. 1989. 'Ristrutturazione', 'destrutturazione' e classificazione delle lingue romanze. *Medioevo romanzo* 14, 305-337.

————. 1990. *Destrutturazione: classi verbali e costruzioni perifrastiche nelle lingue romanze antiche e moderne.* Padova: Unipress.

Berretta, Monica. 1985. I pronomi clitici nell'italiano parlato. *Gesprochenes Italienisch in Geschichte und Gegenwart*, ed. G. Holtus & E. Radtke, 185-224. Tübingen: Narr.

————. 1986. Struttura informativa e sintassi dei pronomi atoni: condizioni che favoriscono la 'risalita'. *Tema-Rema in italiano*, ed. H. Stammerjohann, 71-83. Tübingen: Narr.

Bertuccelli Papi, Marcella. 1980. *Studi sulla diatesi passiva in testi italiani antichi.* Pisa: Pacini (Quaderni della Cattedra di Linguistica dell'Università di Pisa, Serie Monografica 2).

Bossong, Georg. 1982. Historische Sprachwissenschaft und empirische Universalienforschung. *Romanistisches Jahrbuch* 33, 17-51.

Brandi, Luciana & P. Cordin. 1989. Two Italian dialects and the Null Subject Parameter. *The Null Subject Parameter*, ed. O. Jaeggli & K. J. Safir, 111-142. Dordrecht: Kluwer.

Brero, Camillo. 1977. *Conte, faule, e legende piemontèise.* Turin: Piemonte in Bancarella.

————. & Remo Bertodatti. 1988. *Grammatica della lingua piemontese. Parola – vita – letteratura.* Turin: 'Piemont/Europa'.

————. & R. Gandolfo. 1967. *La letteratura in piemontese. Dalle Origini al Risorgimento.* Turin: Casanova.

Burzio, Luigi. 1986. *Italian Syntax: a Government-Binding approach.* Dordrecht: Reidel.

Cinque, Guglielmo. 1988. On *Si* constructions and the theory of *Arb*. *Linguistic Inquiry* 19, 521-581.

Galet, Yvette. 1971. *L'Évolution de l'ordre des mots dans la phrase française de 1600 à 1700: la place du pronom personnel complément d'un infinitif régime.* Paris: Presses Universitaires de France.

Gallina, Mario & Camillo Brero. 1987. *La Génesi, le Litre Canoniche 'd San Gioann, l'Apocalisse.* Turin: Marigros.

Givón, Talmy. 1979. *On Understanding Grammar.* New York: Academic Press.

————. 1984. *Syntax: a functional, typological introduction.* Vol. 1. Amsterdam & Philadelphia: Benjamins.

Harmer, L. C. & F. J. Norton. 1961. *A Manual of Modern Spanish.* London: University Tutorial Press (reprint of 2nd edition 1957).

Harris, Martin. 1978. *The Evolution of French Syntax: a comparative approach.* London & New York: Longman.

Jaberg, Karl & Jakob Jud, ed. 1928-1940. *Sprach- und Sachatlas Italiens und der Südschweiz.* Zofingen: Ringier.

Kayne, Richard S. 1980. Vers une solution d'un problème grammatical: *Je l'ai voulu lire, j'ai tout voulu lire. Langue Française* 46, 32-40.

————. 1987. Null subjects and clitic climbing. *The Null Subject Parameter,* ed. O. Jaeggli & K. J. Safir, 239-261. Dordrecht: Kluwer.

Kok, Ans de. 1985. *La place du pronom personnel régime conjoint en français. Une étude diachronique.* Amsterdam: Rodopi.

Lepschy, Giulio. 1986. Aspects of Italian constructions with *si. The Italianist,* 6, 139-151.

Manoliu-Manea, Maria. 1987. The myth of the agent: roles and communicative dynamism in Romance. *Alphonse Juilland. D'une passion l'autre,* ed. Brigitte Cazelles & René Girard, 261-275. Saratoga, California: Anma Libri.

Meyer-Lübke, W. 1900. *Grammaire des langues romanes.* [Translation of *Grammatik der Romanischen Sprachen* by A. & G. Doutrepont.] Paris: H. Welter.

*Musicalbrandé, arvista piemontèisa.* Suplement ëd la Colon-a Musical dij Brandé. Turin.

Parry, M. Mair. 1985. *The Dialect of Cairo Montenotte.* Unpublished PhD thesis, University of Wales.

————. 1989. Strutture negative nei dialetti piemontesi. *At dël V Rëscontr antërnassional dë studi an sla lenga e la literatura piemontèisa,* 169-177. Alba: Famija Albèisa.

————. 1994a. Ël piemontèis, lenga d'Euròpa. *The Changing Voices of Europe: political and social changes and their linguistic repercussions,* ed. M. M. Parry, W. V. Davies & R. A. M. Temple, 173-192. Cardiff: University of Wales Press.

————. 1994b. Posizione dei clitici complemento nelle costruzioni verbali perifrastiche del piemontese. *At dël VIII Rëscontr antërnassional dë studi an sla lenga e la literatura piemontèisa, Alba, 4-5 magg 1991*, ed. G. P. Clivio & C. Pich, 247-259. Alba: Famija Albèisa.

————. Forthcoming. *Il dialetto di Cairo Montenotte*. Alessandria: Edizioni dell'Orso.

Posner, Rebecca. 1985. Post-verbal negation in non-standard French: a historical and comparative view. *Romance Philology*. 39, 2. 170-197.

*Piemontèis ancheuj*. Turin: Centro Studi 'Don Minzoni'.

Rizzi, Luigi. 1982. *Issues in Italian Syntax*. Dordrecht: Foris.

————. 1986. On the status of subject clitics in Romance. *Studies in Romance Linguistics*, ed. O. Jaeggli & C. Silva-Corvalán, 391-419. Dordrecht: Foris.

Rohlfs, Gerhard. 1966-1969. *Grammatica storica della lingua italiana e dei suoi dialetti*. Turin: Einaudi.

Sacchetti, Franco. 1946. *Il Trecentonovelle*, ed. V. Pernicone. Firenze: Sansoni.

Schiaffini, Alfredo. 1954. *Testi fiorentini del Dugento e dei primi del Trecento*. Firenze: Sansoni.

Schwegler, Armin. 1983. Predicate negation and word-order change: a problem of multiple causation. *Lingua* 61, 297-334.

————. 1988. Word-order changes in predicate negation: strategies in Romance languages. *Diachronica* 5, 21-58.

Simon, Hans Joachim. 1967. *Beobachtungen an Mundarten Piemonts*. Heidelberg: Winter.

Skytte, Gunver. 1983. *La sintassi dell'infinito in italiano moderno*. København: Munksgaard.

Stéfanini, Jean. 1962. *La voix pronominale en ancien et en moyen français*. Aix-en-Provence: Ophrys (Publications des *Annales de la Faculté des Lettres* 30).

Stefanini, Ruggero. 1983. Riflessivo, impersonale e passivo in italiano e in fiorentino. *Quaderni dell'Atlante lessicale toscano* 1, 103-114.

Tana, Carlo Giambattista. 1956. 'L Cont Piolet. *Teatro del Seicento*, ed. Luigi Fassò. Milano: Ricciardi.

Tuttle, E. F.  1993.  Dal pronome d'oggetto suffiso al sintagma verbale: in calce ad una nota salvioniana del 1903. *L'Italia dialettale* 55, 13-63.

Vattuone, B.  1975.  Notes on Genoese syntax.  Kernel 'VOS' strings and theme-rheme structures. *Studi italiani di linguistica teorica ed applicata* 2/3, 335-378.

Wanner, Dieter.  1987. *The Development of Romance Clitic Pronouns from Latin to Old Romance*.  Berlin: Mouton de Gruyter.

# Perceptual factors and the disappearance of agreement between past participle and direct object in Romance*

## John Charles Smith
*University of Manchester*

Latin exhibits a construction in which the verb HABERE ('to have') occurs together with a direct object and a past participle modifying this direct object and agreeing with it. The construction in question undergoes a progressive semantic shift; thus, for instance, HABEO SCRIPTUM LIBRUM — literally, 'I possess the book which is written' — comes to signify 'I have got the book written', and is ultimately grammaticalized to yield a compound past tense form in the Romance languages (compare French *J'ai écrit le livre*, Italian *Ho scritto il libro*, Spanish *He escrito el libro* — all meaning (with various degrees of aspectual nuance) 'I have written the book'). This development is an example of the process referred to by Timberlake (1977:141) as 'reanalysis' — 'the formulation of a novel set of underlying relationships and rules'.

One of the results of this grammaticalization is that the noun which in the original construction was the direct object of the verb 'to have' becomes the direct object of the past participle, with the consequence that the adjectival link between participle and noun is lost (see Vincent 1982; Ramat 1987:141-164). This development is reflected on the surface in the fate of the agreement between the two items, which, in the majority of the modern Romance languages, has been either curtailed or completely lost (compare Latin HABEO SCRIPTOS LIBROS with French *J'ai écrit les livres*, Italian *Ho scritto i libri*, Spanish *He escrito los libros* — 'I have written the books'). The loss of agreement between the past participle and the direct object is intuitively fairly easy to understand; it is an example of what Timberlake (1977:141) calls 'actualization' — 'the gradual mapping out of the consequences of the reanalysis', which takes the form of 'concrete changes in norms and output' (Timberlake 1977:143).

In the modern Romance languages, we find a variety of 'concrete changes in norms and output'. In western Languedocien dialects of Occitan, in many varieties of Friulan, and in some southern Italian dialects, the process of actualization has hardly begun, and agreement is still normal with any direct object; whilst the actualization is complete in languages such as Portuguese, Spanish, and Rumanian, and in many northern and eastern dialects of French, from which object-participle agreement in the compound past tenses has vanished completely. Diachronic and comparative synchronic data appear to show that the disappearance of object-participle agreement has been progressive, and has not taken place randomly. Whilst it is not possible in this paper to examine in detail the pattern of object-participle agreement to be found in every Romance dialect (fuller discussion can be found in Smith (1987; 1989; 1991a; 1991b; 1993a; forthcoming)), certain tendencies can be isolated. The resilience of agreement appears to be a function of two attributes of the direct object. The first is its position — the prescriptive *règle de position* of French, which states that the participle agrees with a preceding direct object, but not with one which follows (see, for instance, Grevisse (1986:§907)), although it represents a gross simplification of the facts, is a well-known attempt to state this criterion, which appears to be valid for many French dialects (especially western dialects; see Lepelley (1974:31); Tomlinson (1981:98-99); Liddicoat (1988:241); Chauveau (1984:214)), as well as for the prescribed standard language. The second is its categorial and morphological identity. Agreement takes place only with clitic-pronoun direct objects in Provençal and Auvergnat dialects of Occitan (Jouveau 1907:17-18, 38; Bonnaud 1972:47). This pattern of agreement is also normal for many speakers of Italian; whilst for many other Italian-speakers, agreement is limited to third-person clitic-pronoun direct objects (Hall 1958; Brinker 1984), a phenomenon also encountered in some dialects of Occitan (see, for the Limousin dialect of Cellefrouin, Rousselot (1892:52-53)). Finally, in some languages and dialects in which the participle agrees only with third-person clitic-pronoun direct objects, agreement appears to be less frequent when the clitic pronoun is masculine plural. In standard Catalan and many Catalan dialects, absence of agreement in these circumstances is the norm (Fabra 1912:§105; 1954-1956:§593; Badía Margarit 1962:§227); it is well-entrenched as a tendency in the Dolomite Ladin dialects of the Val Badia (Gautron 1963:50-52), and, to a lesser extent, in certain Engadinish

dialects (Arquint 1979:227-228), and is sporadically present in some local-
ities of southern Sardinia (as can be seen from a comparison of the data
presented on maps 834 and 913 of the *AIS* (Jaberg & Jud 1928-1940)).

The data enable us to establish a number of implicational hierarchies (in
the sense of Greenberg (1963)), of the form: 'if, in a given language or
dialect, the past participle agrees with a direct object of type X, then it will
also agree with a direct object of type Y'. I have established four such
implicational hierarchies, as follows (where the notation X>Y is to be interpreted to mean that agreement with X implies agreement with Y):

**a. Position of Direct Object:**
Following > Preceding

**b. Identity of Preceding Direct Object:**

$$\left\{ \begin{array}{l} \text{Topics} \\ \text{Interrogatives} \\ \text{Exclamatives} \end{array} \right\} > \text{Relatives} > \text{Clitic Pronouns}$$

**c. Person of Clitic Pronoun:**
First and Second Persons > Third Person

**d. Number and Gender of Third-Person Clitic Pronouns:**
Masculine Plural > Other Forms

No varieties of Romance appear to exhibit a pattern of object-participle
agreement which is at variance with these implicational hierarchies.

Perhaps the most frequently encountered traditional explanation for the
participle being invariable when the direct object follows and variable
when the direct object precedes (implicational hierarchy a.) is that agreement cannot take place with an item which has not yet been expressed,
since its identity is not known. As early as the eighteenth century, Olivet
(1767:217) put forward this explanation for the specific phenomenon of
participial agreement:

> Au reste, si l'on demande, comme ont fait quelques Grammairiens, pourquoi le
> Participe se décline, lorsqu'il vient après son régime; & qu'au contraire, lorsqu'il
> le précède, il ne se décline pas: je m'imagine qu'en cela nos François, sans y en-
> tendre finesse, n'ont songé qu'à leur plus grande commodité. On commence une
> phrase, quelquefois sans bien savoir quel substantif viendra ensuite. Il est donc
> plus commode, pour ne pas s'enferrer par trop de précipitation, de laisser indé-
> clinable un Participe, dont le substantif n'est point encore annoncé, & peut-être
> n'est point encore prévû.

Similar attempts at an explanation of the *règle de position* are made by a host of nineteenth- and twentieth-century French grammarians (see, for instance, Bescher (1810:115), Obry (1851:57), Bourciez (1900:258), and Brunot (1926:xxii), and, for a summary, Smith (1993b:111-112)), and by Lucchesi (1963:213) for Old Italian and Macpherson (1967:250) for Old Spanish, in both of which a similar pattern is found. Such accounts are surely based on a false premiss — namely, that the linear order of surface syntactic structure corresponds to a linear order of conceptualization on the part of the speaker. Moreover, studies of slips of the tongue involving the transposition of words and phrases provide some evidence for the simultaneous presence of quite widely separated constituents at a 'planning level' of language processing (see, for instance, Garman (1990:172-173)). In any case, 'explanations' of the type quoted tackle only one of the implicational hierarchies with which we are dealing.

There are a number of generative accounts of certain patterns of object-participle agreement in Romance. Casagrande (1970) offered an interpretation of the French data based on global rules, whilst Fauconnier (1971, 1974) sought to explain the *règle de position* in terms of the Ross-Langacker constraint on pronominalization. Several attempts have been made to account for object-participle agreement in terms of Government and Binding theory — Hyams (1980) and Burzio (1986:53-63) analyse some of the Italian data, Lefebvre (1986; 1988) offers an account of the phenomenon in French, and Kayne (1985; 1989) examines some of the differences between French and Italian, working in the same theoretical framework. Other accounts which adopt a Government and Binding approach are Taraldsen (1986), Bouchard (1987), Brown (1988), and Lois (1990). More recently, Parodi (1993) and Cortés (1994) have addressed the problem of agreement in Spanish and Catalan, respectively, from the perspective of Minimalism. Non-Chomskyan approaches include those of Frank (1991) (Lexical-Functional Grammar) and La Fauci (1988) (Relational Grammar).

However, at a pan-Romance level, none of the accounts of object-participle agreement proposed by successive generations of generative grammarians achieves even the level of observational adequacy, let alone provides an accurate description or explanation of the phenomenon. In general, they fail to take sufficient account of comparative factors (the situation obtaining across several languages and dialects) which would yield a fuller picture of agreement patterns, and enable a less fragmentary, and hence more generally valid, interpretation to be made. This criticism can be levelled even at the influential and well-documented study by Kayne (1989), some of whose data (culled for the most part from secondary sources) are insufficient or inaccurate. As Posner (1976:75) points out, 'sometimes descriptions of known facts about a language fail to be explanatory in a satisfying way, because they ignore parallelisms in related languages'.

It strikes me that a unified, pan-Romance, account of the data may be possible and that all the implicational hierarchies I have proposed may be amenable to a functional explanation based on perceptual factors. I suggest, for instance, that one motivation for the *règle de position* may be sought in sentence-processing strategies and the concept of 'parsability'. In a sentence which exhibits unmarked word order in a modern Romance language, the direct object follows the verb; I take this to be the underlying order for all sentences. When the direct object precedes the verb, I therefore assume that it forms part of a chain (in the sense of Chomsky (1981:45)) together with a phonologically null element in the postverbal object position. Two cases are to be envisaged: first, that the direct object has been moved to preverbal position by the rule Move-$\alpha$, leaving behind a trace (this is the case with relatives, for instance); secondly, that the direct object is base-generated in preverbal position and is coindexed with a base-generated phonologically null NP (I assume this to be the case with clitic pronouns — see Chomsky (1982:64-65, 88)). Notational variants are available in other theories.

In these circumstances, it is clearly necessary for the binding between the elements of the chain to be established in order for the sentence to be interpreted. In this sense, a sentence in which the direct object precedes the verb is more difficult to parse than one in which the direct object appears in its unmarked postverbal position. In this case, restriction of agreement of the past participle to sentences in which the direct object precedes the verb will serve to 'flag' both the presence of a phonologically null NP in direct object position and the identity of the item elsewhere in the sentence to which it is bound.

This claim may seem tenuous. Sentences in which a direct object precedes the verb in a simple tense do not, of course, exhibit such 'flagging'; and yet this type of sentence appears to present no insurmountable parsing problems. It could therefore be objected that the functionality of participial agreement in the cases under discussion is highly marginal. Whilst this is undoubtedly the case, I am not, of course, claiming that agreement with a preceding direct object was **introduced** in order to facilitate the recovery of the binding between a preceding direct object and a phonologically null NP in postverbal position, but rather that the marginal functionality of such agreement has none the less been a factor in the differential disappearance of participial agreement — that is, given a tendency for this type of agreement to disappear, agreement with a following direct object will be lost first because it has less functional value than agreement with a direct object which precedes the verb.

There is a clear parallel between this explanation and the traditional 'speakers do not know what they are going to say next' view discussed at the beginning of this paper. The crucial difference between the two accounts, however, is that, whereas the traditional version (the 'production' hypothesis) is formulated from the point of view of the speaker, the present account (the 'processing' hypothesis) is defined with reference to the hearer. Explanations of syntactic phenomena based on speakers' uncertainty as to how they will develop the conceptual content of their sentences seem inherently unsound; but in relating syntactic constraints to problems of processing and perception we are on firmer ground. The present hypothesis can be related to work by Fodor (1981) on the relationship between 'performance' and 'competence'. The focus of her argument is the relationship between overt surface elements ('fillers') and phonologically null elements which form part of the same chain ('gaps'). She claims that parsing routines play a role in determining syntactic constraints, but that this role is relatively unspecific — 'They call for *some* restrictions on filler and gap positions, but not for any *particular* restrictions' (Fodor 1981:285). Indeed, their role is so imprecise that

> The only useful point that emerges is that sentence parsing would be assisted by the existence of *some* fairly stringent limits on where gaps can appear. Clearly the ideal situation would be one in which the parser, having detected a filler constituent, could tell immediately where its gap must be, without having to search for it at all. This would be so if each filler were associated by the grammar with a unique gap position. (Fodor 1981:289)

The role of participial agreement in sentence processing is clearly far from the ideal outlined by Fodor; in particular, the position of the gap is not indicated (by the inflection on the participle) until immediately before it is reached. However, I argue that such agreement is sufficiently functional to account for the slower disappearance of agreement when the direct object precedes the verb.

Processing strategies may also be invoked to account for the greater likelihood of agreement when the preceding direct object is a relative, and for its much greater prevalence when the direct object is a clitic pronoun. In the case of topics and interrogative and exclamative NPs, all the information required in order to determine the referent of the direct object is present in the same sentence as the participle. Participial agreement is therefore of minimal use in recovering the identity of this referent. Similar arguments could be advanced in the case of relatives — they require an antecedent, which is normally found in the same matrix sentence; although here the risk of ambiguity is greater, as there may be more than one plausible antecedent. *That woman down the road with the dog you can't stand* would be an example from English — is it the woman or the dog that the addressee detests? Often, but not always, context or intonation will resolve any ambiguity; none the less, the fact that such sentences are potentially more difficult to process gives the agreement of the participle a functional value which is absent from sentences involving topics and interrogative and exclamative NPs. Clitic pronouns, however, are arguably more ambiguous still — they may be exophoric to the sentence which contains them, referring to an item in a preceding or following sentence; they may even be exophoric to the discourse, with a referent which is not linguistically present, and so require pragmatic resolution. Even when 'endophoric' (i.e., anaphoric or cataphoric), third-person pronouns are often notoriously difficult to resolve. Some examples from English are discussed by Sampson (1983:88-89); his conclusion — that it is frequently difficult and sometimes impossible to resolve the pronoun *it* in English — can be carried over, *mutatis mutandis*, to other languages. Moreover, in the Romance languages, when a clitic ends in a vowel, this is often elided before the initial vowel of the auxiliary 'have', giving rise to identical surface forms for clitics with referents of different numbers and genders. In these circumstances, it will often be valuable to have some additional indication of the referent of the clitic pronoun, and participial agreement, by indicating the number and gender of this referent, will fulfil this role. It can therefore be argued that the functionality of agreement is greater when the direct object is a clitic pronoun than when it is some other item.

At first sight, such a theory might seem to entail that agreement would be most functional with first- and second-person clitics, which are **always** exophoric to the discourse; whereas, as we have noted, it is precisely in these cases that there is a greater tendency for the participle to remain invariable. However, I argue that this is in fact a logical consequence of the theory, for, although the first- and second-person clitics are exophoric, they are unambiguously so, the first-person form always denoting the speaker and the second-person form the addressee. It is clear that in these cases, the referent is automatically recoverable from the pragmatic context, and the functionality of participial agreement is minimal. It is with third-person clitics that agreement will be most functional, and it is therefore not surprising that we find it maintained longest in these contexts.

A similar point is made by Parisi (1976:103-104). Comparing Italian sentences such as (1-2) and the more colloquial (3-4):

(1)  *L'ho preso.*
     'I have taken it (m.).'
(2)  *L'ho presa.*
     'I have taken it (f.).'
(3)  *L'ho presi.*
     'I have taken them (m.).'
(4)  *L'ho prese.*
     'I have taken them (f.).'

he comments:

> It is obvious that what is dropped in these sentences is the very element that would help the hearer retrace the semantic material that the pronoun carries in surface form, that is to say, the omission of the terminal vowel of the pronoun does not allow him to detect whether the nominal is masculine or feminine, singular or plural. [...] We therefore find it quite reasonable in these cases that the P[ast] P[articiple] be made to agree with the direct object, so that the information the hearer loses through the omission of the terminal vowel of the pronoun is still provided to him through the varying terminal vowel of the P[ast] P[articiple].[1]

However, in the case of first- and second-person pronouns, the extralinguistic context makes the reference of the pronoun clear; and, since the number is in addition evident from the surface form of the pronoun, participial agreement is optional. The same view is put forward by Lucchesi

(1963:221-222), in his discussion of the identical pattern of agreement in Old Italian and in the modern language.

There are none the less some significant gaps in the arguments of Parisi and Lucchesi as they stand. According to their reasoning, which is purely synchronic, we might expect agreement with first- and second-person forms to be optional or non-existent in other cases, too, such as subject-predicate agreement and agreement of the participle with the subject when the auxiliary is 'be'; but, on the contrary, we find that agreement is obligatory in these cases — it is not possible for a woman to state *Sono stanco ('I am tired') or to be asked *Sei andato? ('Did you go?'). The fact that the referent of first- and second-person forms can be recovered from the pragmatic context does not obviate the requirement that agreement should take place. It is only in circumstances in which the agreement is unstable and disappearing from the language that we may expect the lesser functionality of agreement with first- and second-person clitics to create a differential agreement pattern in which agreement takes place less frequently with this type of clitic than with third-person forms, as part of a transition to complete invariability. In other words, the principle of 'recoverability' does not constrain the **synchronic** phenomenon of agreement; it constrains the **diachronic** process of the disappearance of (certain types of) agreement. The differential agreement patterns observed are synchronic reflexes of this constraint on a diachronic process.

It may also be observed that, in languages and dialects in which agreement is rare or impossible with a first- or second-person clitic-pronoun direct object, and in which pronominal verbs form their compound past tenses with the auxiliary 'have', the past participle also fails to agree with a third-person reflexive clitic-pronoun direct object. This pattern of agreement is found in most varieties of Catalan, and in some dialects of Italian and Friulan (see Benincà & Vanelli 1984:189). I suggest that a similar principle is at work here, inasmuch as the referent of a reflexive pronoun is by definition identical with the subject of the verb, and is therefore automatically recoverable from the context.

The present analysis can be further extended, albeit in a tentative way, with some interesting consequences. It may, for instance, offer an explanation for the earlier disappearance of object-participle agreement in Spanish, Portuguese, and Rumanian. For observe that, in these languages, the four 'accusative' clitic pronouns are always distinguished from one another when they occur as the direct object of a compound past tense. In Spanish, the vowel of the masculine singular *lo* and the feminine singular *la* is never elided (although there may be synalepha or synæresis with a following vowel, the forms will remain distinct), and in the plural, the vowels of the distinct forms *los* (masculine) and *las* (feminine) are 'protected' from elision by the presence of a following *s*. The same arguments apply *a fortiori* to the monophonemic singular forms *o* (masculine) and *a* (feminine) of Portuguese, and to the plural forms *os* (masculine) and *as* (feminine), with some additional provisos: the auxiliary in Portuguese is normally *ter*, rather than *haver*, precluding elision of a preceding vowel; and, in affirmative main clauses when no adverb precedes the verb, the pronouns in question are in any case usually enclitic to the auxiliary in the compound past tenses. In Rumanian, the masculine singular 'accusative' clitic and the corresponding masculine and feminine plural forms are proclitic to the auxiliary in a compound past tense, and each exhibits a distinct form — masculine singular *l*, masculine plural *i*, feminine plural *le*. The feminine singular form *o* is distinguished from the other pronouns not only phonetically, but also syntactically, since it is enclitic to the participle. By way of example, I append the translation of the sentences 'I have taken it (m. & f.)/them (m. & f.)', corresponding to the Italian sentences (1-4) above:

| | | |
|---|---|---|
| Spanish: | (5) | *Lo he tomado.* |
| | (6) | *La he tomado.* |
| | (7) | *Los he tomado.* |
| | (8) | *Las he tomado.* |
| Portuguese: | (9) | *Tenho-o tomado.* |
| | (10) | *Tenho-a tomado.* |
| | (11) | *Tenho-os tomado.* |
| | (12) | *Tenho-as tomado.* |
| Rumanian: | (13) | *L-am luat.* |
| | (14) | *Am luat-o.* |
| | (15) | *I-am luat.* |
| | (16) | *Le-am luat.* |

In all three languages, then, the third-person 'accusative' clitic pronouns have distinct forms for each number and gender when they occur as the direct object of a compound past tense. In these circumstances, object-participle agreement is redundant, as it conveys no information which cannot be obtained from other items in the sentence; given its lack of functionality, it is not surprising that it should disappear from these languages earlier than from languages in which it does enable hearers to retrieve information which would not otherwise be available to them.

In French, there is always an audible distinction between singular and plural clitics; however, in the compound past tenses formed with *avoir*, there is syncretism between the masculine and feminine forms in both numbers, the singular pronoun always sounding as [l], and the plural form as [lez]. Gender agreement, but not number agreement, will therefore be functional in French. As audible number agreement has in any case virtually disappeared from the language (for independent phonetic reasons), whilst a gender distinction remains audible for what is admittedly a small minority of past participles, we might expect, under the present hypothesis, to find agreement maintained longer in French than in the languages discussed above. This is indeed the case for the standard language, as shown by the French translations of (1-4), given below:

(17)  *Je l'ai pris.* [pʀi]
(18)  *Je l'ai prise.* [pʀiz]
(19)  *Je les ai pris.* [pʀi]
(20)  *Je les ai prises.* [pʀiz]

— although there are many dialects to which the analysis does not extend.

It was also noted above that, in some varieties of Catalan, Rhæto-Romance, and Sardinian, agreement appeared to be less frequent with a third-person clitic-pronoun direct object when this was masculine plural. I suggest that, here, too, perceptual factors may play a role in determining the pattern of agreement. In all these varieties of Romance, final-vowel elision leads to the masculine and feminine third-person clitics' having identical phonetic forms in the singular when followed by the auxiliary 'have'; whilst, in the plural, the two genders are always distinguished, in any phonetic environment.

| Catalan: | singular (both genders) | *l'* |
|---|---|---|
| | masculine plural | *els* |
| | feminine plural | *les* |
| | (see Yates (1975:131); Gili (1943:45)) | |

| Engadinish: | singular (both genders) | *l'* |
| | masculine plural | *ils, als* |
| | feminine plural | *las* |
| | (see Ganzoni (1977:61); Scheitlin (1962:77)) | |

| Badiot: | singular (both genders) | *l'* |
| | masculine plural | *i* |
| | feminine plural | *les* |
| | (see Gautron (1963:50-52)) | |

| Sardinian: | singular (both genders) | *l'* |
| | masculine plural | *los* |
| | feminine plural | *las* |
| | (see Pittau (1972:139)). | |

In all these languages and dialects, then, whilst the gender of the singular pronoun can be retrieved only through the inflection of the participle, the gender in the plural is evident from the surface form of the pronoun itself. In these circumstances, agreement with the object pronoun is functional in the singular, but redundant in the plural; it is therefore not surprising that it should be more prevalent in the former case. It is less easy to account for the apparently differential disappearance of agreement from the plural; it may be that the feminine agreement is more resilient under the influence of agreement with the feminine singular. However, we should note that, in several of the dialects under discussion, agreement is less likely to take place with a feminine plural clitic than with a feminine singular one. Despite the written Catalan norm, Fabra's formulation (Fabra 1956:§73) is that agreement should take place with a preceding clitic pronoun direct object when this is a feminine singular form; and Wheeler (1988:194) observes that agreement between the participle and a third-person clitic-pronoun direct object is most likely with a feminine singular, next most likely with a feminine plural, and least likely with a masculine plural. Of the seven examples of non-agreement with a third-person clitic preceding direct object in Engadinish given by Arquint (1979:226-227), one involves a feminine singular, with three apiece of masculine plural and feminine plural. Similarly, Gautron (1963:50-52) notes that in the Val Badia agreement regularly takes place with feminine singular clitic-pronoun direct objects, but that there is hesitation regarding agreement with plural clitic-pronoun direct objects of either gender, although the hesitation is greater when the clitic is masculine plural. These data suggest that the disappearance of agreement is most advanced when the direct object is a plural 'accusative' clitic of either gender, and that agreement is most resilient with the feminine singular form. Once again, an approach based on perceptual factors and processing strategies makes correct predictions and provides a plausible explanation of the data.

The role of 'perceptual strategies' in language change is discussed by Vincent (1976). In one sense, the role which I am suggesting for the 'perceptual strategy' is quite distinct from that considered by Vincent — he maintains that the 'perceptual strategy' plays a part in initiating or catalysing a change, whilst I am claiming that considerations of processing may block or retard an independently motivated change once it is under way. However, Vincent's discussion is relevant to the present argument. He notes (Vincent 1976:55):

> Perceptual factors are of necessity 'fuzzy', since the degree to which they obtrude on the successful performance of any act of linguistic communication varies with the amount of context non-linguistically recoverable, or more generally with the amount of redundancy. Hence any constraints on languages deriving from limitations on the perceptual system would only make themselves felt gradually over a period of time, thereby allowing for the existence of intermediate stages and mixed types.

My own findings concerning the differential disappearance of agreement between past participle and direct object are consistent with this view — although the overall tendency is clear, the progression is gradual, and the pattern of agreement often 'fuzzy', exhibiting substantial variation and apparent 'optionality' at any given moment.

I think the data concerning the decline of object-participle agreement in Romance show that the functional load of the agreement may have been significant in determining its survival in a given context. If this is the case, then the problem I have attempted to outline runs somewhat counter to a widely-held view of agreement, which is summed up by Martinet (1962:55) in the words 'Concord is redundancy'. I also argue that, although agreement between a past participle and a direct object is clearly a synchronic fact in those varieties of Romance in which it occurs, and can be described as such, any explanation of the phenomenon which ignores the diachronic dimension will be incomplete. In this sense, object-participle agreement must be viewed as a synchronic residue of a con-

tinuing process of language change, along the lines suggested for other
phenomena by Gross (1975; 1979). Gross (1975:227) observes that 'dans
de nombreuses descriptions synchroniques, il s'introduit des formes qui ont
souvent une interprétation diachronique naturelle' and also that 'Un état de
langue comporte simultanément des niveaux diachroniques et dialectaux
variés' (Gross 1975:228). More extensively, he claims (Gross 1979:868)

> that the bulk of linguistic phenomena exhibits great irregularity, and that in many
> cases the source of the irregularity lies in historical and cultural accidents. When
> a property is studied, one should attempt to evaluate whether it is general, or
> whether it is an accident inherited from special circumstances. Diachronic dis-
> cussions are then fundamental.

I would not use Gross's term 'accident', with its implications of random-
ness, to describe the pattern of object-participle agreement observed in the
Romance languages, which I claim to be the result of a logical process.
However, his basic insight (echoing that of Posner (1976:75), quoted
above, and more recently reiterated by Labov (1994:583)) — that synchronic data may not be amenable to simple synchronic explanation, but
may require diachronic factors to be taken into account — is borne out by
an analysis of the differential patterns of agreement between past participle
and direct object in Romance. I also claim that the data and analysis which
I have presented provide evidence for the view that syntactic change is a
gradual process, that actualization can lag spectacularly behind reanalysis,
and that perceptual factors can play an important role in constraining this
type of change.

## Notes

*   I am grateful to William Croft, Martin Maiden, Nigel Vincent, and Jean-Philippe
    Watbled for their comments on this paper. Any errors of fact or interpretation are, of
    course, my own.
1.  In fact, sentences such as (3) and (4), in which the final vowel of *li* and *le* is elided,
    are rather rare in Italian, according to most of my informants. However, in the speech
    of many Italians, it is normal for the vowel of the plural clitic to become a glide in this
    position (see Lichem 1969:132). This synæresis makes the distinction between the
    two forms extremely difficult, if not impossible, to perceive (for an autosegmental
    treatment of i-glides and e-glides which sheds some light on this issue, see Harris
    (1994:104-105)); so that the agreement of the participle still provides information
    which is not readily available from the surface form of the pronoun.

# References

Arquint, J. C.  1979.  *Zur Syntax des Partizipiums der Vergangenheit im Bündnerromanischen mit Ausblicken auf die Romania.*  Chur: Arquint (Romanica Rætica 3).

Badía Margarit, A. M.  1962.  *Gramática catalana.*  Madrid: Gredos.

Benincà, P. & Vanelli, L.  1984.  Italiano, veneto, friulano: fenomeni sintattici a confronto.  *Rivista italiana di dialettologia* 8, 165-194.

Bescher, [R.-F.]  1810.  *Théorie nouvelle et raisonnée du participe français.*  Paris: chez l'auteur, au Lycée Impérial.

Bonnaud, P.  1972.  *Abrégé de grammaire auvergnate.*  Clermont-Ferrand: Cercle occitan d'Auvergne — Auvernha terra d'oc.

Bouchard, D.  1987.  A few remarks on past participle agreement.  *Linguistics and Philosophy* 10, 449-474.

Bourciez, E.  1900.  La simplification de la syntaxe française.  *Revue des lettres françaises et étrangères* 2, 237-267.

Brinker, J. H.  1984.  *Problemi dell'accordo del participio passato nell'italiano moderno.*  Groningen: Regenboog.

Brown, B.  1988.  Problems with past participles [*sic*] agreement in French and Italian dialects.  *Advances in Romance Linguistics*, ed. D. Birdsong & J.-P. Montreuil, 51-66.  Dordrecht: Foris.

Brunot, F.  1926.  *La Pensée et la langue: méthode, principes et plan d'une théorie nouvelle du langage appliquée au français.*  Paris: Masson.

Burzio, L.  1986.  *Italian Syntax: a Government-Binding approach.*  Dordrecht: Reidel (Studies in Natural Language and Linguistic Theory).

Casagrande, J.  1970.  A case for global derivational constraints.  *Papers in Linguistics* 2, 449-459.

Chauveau, J.-P.  1984.  *Le Gallo: une présentation.*  Brest: Université de Bretagne Occidentale (*Studi* 26-27).

Chomsky, N.  1981.  *Lectures on Government and Binding.*  Dordrecht: Foris (Studies in Generative Grammar 9).

———.  1982.  *Some Concepts and Consequences of the Theory of Government and Binding.*  Cambridge, Mass.: MIT Press (*Linguistic Inquiry* Monographs 6).

Cortés, C. 1994. Participle Agreement, Auxiliary Selection, and the GTC. Unpublished paper given to Twenty-Fourth Linguistic Symposium on Romance Languages, Los Angeles, March 1994.

Fabra, P. 1912. *Gramática de la lengua catalana*. Barcelona: L'Avenc.

———. 1954-1956. *Converses filològiques*. Barcelona: Barcino.

———. 1956. *Gramàtica catalana*. Barcelona: Teide.

Fauconnier, G. R. 1971. *Theoretical Implications of some Global Phenomena in Syntax*. Ph.D. dissertation, University of California, San Diego (published in mimeo by Indiana University Linguistics Club).

———. 1974. *La Coréférence: syntaxe ou sémantique?* Paris: Seuil (collection 'Travaux linguistiques').

Fodor, J. D. 1981. Does performance shape competence? *Philosophical Transactions of the Royal Society of London*, series B, volume 295 (no. 1077), 285-295.

Frank, A. (1991) Argumentstruktur, grammatische Relationen und lexicalische Regeln: ein LFG-Fragment zu Partizipialkongruenz, Auxiliarselektion und Clitic-Climbing im Französischen. *Romanistische Computerlinguistik: Theorien und Implementationen*, ed. J. Rolshoven & D. Seelbach, 19-75. Tübingen: Niemeyer (Linguistische Arbeiten 266).

Ganzoni, G. P. 1977. *Grammatica ladina: grammatica sistematica dal rumauntsch d'Engiadin'Ota per scolars e creschieus da lingua rumauntscha e tudas-cha*. Cuira [Chur]: Lia Rumauntscha & Uniun dals Grischs.

Garman, M. 1990. *Psycholinguistics*. Cambridge: Cambridge University Press.

Gautron, R. 1963. *Die Hilfs- und Modalverben im Ladinischen des Gadertals: eine syntaktische Untersuchung*. Dissertation, Leopold-Franzens-Universität, Innsbruck.

Gili, J. 1943. *Introductory Catalan Grammar*. Oxford: Dolphin.

Greenberg, J. H. 1963. Some universals of grammar with particular reference to the order of meaningful elements. *Universals of Language (report of a conference held at Dobbs Ferry, New York, April 13-15, 1961)*, ed. J. H. Greenberg, 58-90. Cambridge, Mass.: MIT Press.

Grevisse, M. 1986. *Le Bon Usage: grammaire française* (12e édition refondue par André Goosse). Paris & Gembloux: Duculot.

Gross, M. 1975. *Méthodes en syntaxe: régime des constructions complétives*. Paris: Hermann.

———. 1979. On the failure of generative grammar. *Language* 55, 859-885.

Hall, R. A. jr. 1958. Statistica sintattica: l'accordo del participio passato coniugato con *avere*. *Lingua nostra* 19, 95-100.

Harris, J. 1994. *English Sound Structure*. Oxford: Blackwell.

Harris, M. B. 1978. *The Evolution of French Syntax: a comparative approach*. London: Longman (Longman Linguistics Library 22).

Hyams, N. 1980. The Θ-criterion in Italian syntax. *Studi di grammatica italiana a cura dell'Accademia della Crusca* 9, 359-370.

Jaberg, K. & Jud, J. 1928-1940. *Sprach- und Sachatlas Italiens und der Südschweiz*. Zofingen: Ringier.

Jouveau, M. 1907. *Eléments de grammaire provençale et petit manuel de l'instituteur provençal pour la correction des provençalismes*. Marseille: Ruat.

Kayne, R. S. 1985. L'accord du participe passé en français et en italien. *Modèles linguistiques* 7, 73-89.

———. 1989. Facets of Romance past participle agreement. *Dialect Variation and the Theory of Grammar*, ed. P. Benincà, 85-103. Dordrecht: Foris.

Labov, W. 1994. *Principles of Linguistic Change: Volume 1, Internal Factors*. Oxford: Blackwell.

La Fauci, N. 1988. *Oggetti e soggetti nella formazione della morfosintassi romanza*. Pisa: Giardini.

Lefebvre, C. 1986. L'accord du participe passé en français: accord = cas. *Revue québécoise de linguistique* 15, 121-134.

———. 1988. Past participle agreement in French: agreement = Case. *Advances in Romance Linguistics*, ed. D. Birdsong, & J.-P. Montreuil, 234-249. Dordrecht: Foris.

Lepelley, R. 1974. *Le Parler normand du Val de Saire (Manche): phonétique, morphologie, syntaxe, vocabulaire de la vie rurale*. Caen: Musée de Normandie (Cahiers des *Annales de Normandie* 7).

Lichem, K. 1969. *Phonetik und Phonologie des heutigen Italienisch.* München: Hueber.

Liddicoat, A. J. 1988. *The Dialects of Jersey and Sark.* Unpublished Ph.D. thesis, University of Melbourne.

Lois, X. 1990. Auxiliary selection and past participle agreement in Romance. *Probus* 2, 233-255

Lucchesi, V. 1963. L'accordo fra participio passato e oggetto nei tempi perifrastici retti da 'avere' nel volgare antico (secc. XIII-XIV). *Atti e memorie dell'Accademia toscana di scienze e lettere* 27, 191-278.

Macpherson, I. R. 1967. Past participle agreement in Old Spanish: transitive verbs. *Bulletin of Hispanic Studies* 44, 241-254.

Martinet, A. 1962. *A Functional View of Language.* Oxford: Clarendon Press.

Obry, J.-B. F. 1851. *Etude historique et philologique sur le participe passé français et sur ses verbes auxiliaires.* Amiens: Duval & Herment.

Olivet [= P.-J. Thoulier] 1767. *Remarques sur la langue françoise.* Paris: Barbou.

Parisi, D. 1976. The past participle. *Italian Linguistics* 1, 77-106.

Parodi. C. 1993. Participle agreement and Object Shift in Old Spanish: a Minimalist Theory approach. Unpublished paper given to Eleventh International Conference on Historical Linguistics, Los Angeles, August 1993.

Pittau, M. 1972. *Grammatica del sardo-nuorese, il più conservativo dei parlari neolatini.* Bologna: Pàtron.

Posner, R. R. 1976. The relevance of comparative and historical data for the description and definition of a language. *York Papers in Linguistics* 6, 75-87.

Ramat, P. 1987. *Linguistic Typology.* Berlin: Mouton de Gruyter.

Rousselot, P. J. 1892. *De vocabulorum congruentia in rustico Cellæ-Fruini sermone.* Paris: Welter.

Sampson, G. R. 1983. Fallible rationalism and machine translation. *Proceedings of the First Conference of the European Chapter of the Association for Computational Linguistics, Pisa, 1-2 September 1983,* 86-89.

Scheitlin, W. 1962. *Il pled puter: grammatica ladina d'Engiadin'ota.* Samedan: Uniun dals Grischs.

Smith, J. C. 1987. Perceptual factors and the disappearance of object-participle agreement in Romance. Unpublished paper given to Eighth International Conference on Historical Linguistics, Lille, September 1987

———. 1989. Actualization reanalyzed: evidence from the Romance compound past tenses. *Synchronic and Diachronic Approaches to Linguistic Variation and Change (Georgetown University Round Table on Languages and Linguistics, 1988)*, ed. T. J. Walsh, 310-325. Washington, D.C.: Georgetown University Press.

———. 1991a. Problemi dell'accordo del participio passato coll'oggetto diretto nei tempi composti coniugati con *avere* in italiano, con speciale riferimento ai dialetti. *Tra Rinascimento e strutture attuali: saggi di linguistica italiana (Atti del Primo Convegno della Società Internazionale di Linguistica e Filologia Italiana, Siena, 28-31 marzo 1989, volume 1 °)*, ed. L. Giannelli, N. Maraschio, T. Poggi Salani & M. Vedovelli, 365-371. Torino: Rosenberg & Sellier.

———. 1991b. Thematicity and 'object'-participle agreement in Romance. *New Analyses in Romance Linguistics: selected papers from the Eighteenth Linguistic Symposium on Romance Languages, April 7-9, 1988*, ed. D. Wanner & D. A. Kibbee, 335-352. Amsterdam: Benjamins (Current Issues in Linguistic Theory 69).

———. 1992. Circumstantial complements and direct objects in the Romance languages: configuration, Case, and thematic structure. *Thematic Structure: its role in grammar*, ed. I. M. Roca, 293-316. Berlin: Foris.

———. 1993a. La desaparición de la concordancia entre participio de pasado y objeto directo en castellano y catalán: aspectos geográficos e históricos. *Actas del Primer Congreso Anglo-Hispano: tomo I, Lingüística*, ed. R. Penny, 275-285. Madrid: Castalia.

———. 1993b. The agreement of the past participle conjugated with *avoir* and a preceding direct object: a brief history of prescriptive attitudes. *Authority and the French Language: papers from a conference at the University of Bristol*, ed. R. Sampson, 87-125. Münster: Nodus.

————. Forthcoming. Agreement between past participle and direct object in Catalan: the hypothesis of Castilian influence revisited. To appear in *Language Contact and Linguistic Change*, ed. J. Fisiak. Berlin: Mouton de Gruyter.

Taraldsen, T. 1986. Clitic/Particle [*sic*] agreement and auxiliary alternation in Romance. *Studies in Romance Languages*, ed. C. Neidle & R. Nuñez Cedeño, 263-281. Dordrecht: Foris.

Timberlake, A. 1977. Reanalysis and actualization in syntactic change. *Mechanisms of Syntactic Change*, ed. C. N. Li, 141-177. Austin & London: University of Texas Press.

Tomlinson, H. 1981. *Le Guernesiais: étude grammaticale et lexicale du parler normand de l'île de Guernesey*. Unpublished Ph.D. thesis, University of Edinburgh.

Vincent, N. 1976. Perceptual factors and word order change in Latin. *Romance Syntax: synchronic and diachronic perspectives*, ed. M. Harris, 54-68. Salford: University of Salford.

————. 1982. The development of the auxiliaries HABERE and ESSE in Romance. *Studies in the Romance Verb: essays offered to Joe Cremona on the occasion of his 60th birthday*, ed. M. Harris & N. Vincent. London: Croom Helm

Wheeler, M. W. 1988. Catalan. *The Romance Languages*, ed. M. Harris & N. Vincent, 170-208. London: Routledge.

Yates, A. 1975. *Catalan*. London: Hodder & Stoughton ('Teach Yourself' Series).

# Segmental and Suprasegmental Structure
# in Southern French

Jean-Philippe Watbled
*Université de Provence*

## 1. Introduction

In the present work, I am concerned with the interaction between syllable structure and the phonetic realizations of vowels in the Provence variety of Southern French as spoken in Marseille.

Most phonologists now agree that phonological representations do not consist of linear strings of segments and boundaries. However, despite widespread agreement on the basic tenets of non-linear phonology, several issues have given rise to considerable theoretical discussion. Opinions diverge on the following questions, among others:

- the number and the nature of prosodic units
- binary branching vs. n-ary branching.

Moreover, linguists who adopt exactly the same theoretical principles are liable to disagree on the proper interpretation of the same set of data.

In the present work, following Nespor & Vogel (1986), who give convincing evidence against binary branching, I assume that prosodic constituents are n-ary branching; furthermore, I postulate only one prosodic category: S. The symbol S stands for 'syllable', and prosodic units above the level of the syllable are regarded as projections of S (S', S'', etc.). This extension of some of the principles of X-bar syntax (see Jackendoff 1977) to the field of prosodic phonology allows us to dispense with such labels as 'foot', 'superfoot', 'group', 'phrase' etc. (some of which are obviously *ad hoc*: see Anderson & Ewen (1987:100-101)). In the same spirit, I propose a set of multi-valued features. The application of this non-binary and multi-linear model to the treatment of three fundamental problems in Provence French reveals some interesting properties of suprasegmental structures. These problems are:

- the phonological status of mid vowels
- the phonological status of schwa
- the correct interpretation of nasalized vowels.

## 2. Theoretical principles

### 2.1. Segmental and prosodic units

The 'skeleton' consists of a sequence of 'x's. Each occurrence of this symbol represents a phoneme, as in the following example (*paradis* 'paradise':

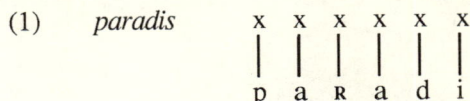

(1)    *paradis*         x  x  x  x  x  x
                         |  |  |  |  |  |
                         p  a  ʀ  a  d  i

'x' is therefore a segmental unit. The basic suprasegmental unit is S (= syllable).

In the following structures, which illustrate my notational conventions, B is the 'head' or 'governor':

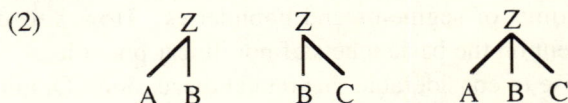

(2)           Z           Z            Z

            A  B        B  C        A  B  C

A vertical line links the head of the structure to the higher node, while oblique lines link the subordinate elements to this node. Dependency relations are thus expressed in the simplest manner, without recourse to such labels as 'strong' and 'weak' (see Anderson & Ewen 1987:101).

In the word *paradis*, each syllable consists of a consonant plus vowel sequence, and the vowel is the head of the syllable:

(3)         S      S      S

          x  x   x  x   x  x
          |  |   |  |   |  |
          p  a   ʀ  a   d  i

For the moment I shall assume that every S' dominates only one S, except in the case of polysyllabic words with a final schwa (*galette* 'flat cake'):

(4)
```
    S'  S'  S'
    |   |   |
    S   S   S
    |   |   |
    pa  ra  dis
```

(5)
```
     S'  S'
     |   /\
     S   S   S
     |   |   |
     ga  le  tte
```

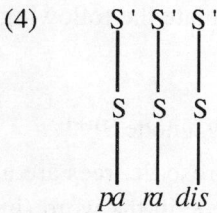

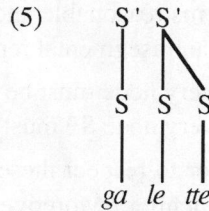

The final syllable in (5) forms a constituent with the preceding syllable. The word *tête* 'head', for example, will therefore consist of only one S':

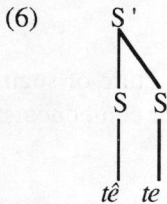

(6)
```
      S'
     /\
    S   S
    |   |
    tê  te
```

The structure of S' is always:

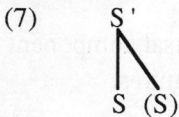

(7)
```
      S'
     /\
    S  (S)
```

where (S) is an optional constituent, and the first S is the head.

As in the French of other regions, the last syllable of the citation form of a word is stressed, except if its nucleus is schwa (in which case it is the penultimate syllable which is stressed). In my framework, the word-stress rule (for lexical stress) is very simple:

(8)    Stress the rightmost S'.

According to my notational conventions, a vertical line links the rightmost S' to a node S":

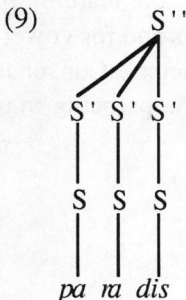

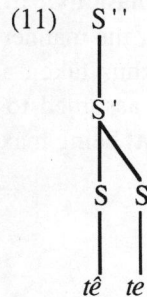

(9)
```
         S''
        /|\
     S' S' S'
     |  |  |
     S  S  S
     |  |  |
     pa ra dis
```

(10)
```
         S''
         /|
      S' S'
      |  /\
      S S  S
      |  |  |
      ga le tte
```

(11)
```
        S''
         |
         S'
         /\
        S  S
        |  |
        tê te
```

Note that it seems reasonable and natural to postulate the following formal constraints on suprasegmental representations:

    (12)  Every node must be labelled.

    (13)  Every node $S^n$ must be dominated by a node $S^{n+1}$.

It is much easier to respect these constraints if prosodic trees are assumed to be n-ary branching. Moreover, the highest node in the word (in lexical representations) is always labelled S"; if trees were binary branching, there would be no limit to the value of the exponent of the highest node .

## 2.2. Components and features

I shall now sketch my conception of the internal structure of segments. I posit submatrices, called 'components'. There are four components:

    (14)  a.  initiatory component
           b.  phonatory component
           c.  nasal component
           d.  articulatory component

In the present work, I am concerned only with the nasal component and the articulatory component. I postulate the following features:

    (15)  a.  aperture
           b.  place

The feature 'place' will not concern me here (for a full discussion, the reader is referred to Watbled & Autesserre 1989). The feature 'aperture' is a multi-valued parameter and plays a role both in the nasal component and in the articulatory component. In the nasal component, two underlying values are possible: '0' and '2'. '0' means that the velum is raised (the degree of opening being null), and '2' means that it is lowered (the degree of opening being maximal). The value '1', which means 'narrowing', is not relevant to nasality. In the articulatory component, the feature 'aperture' accounts for the manner of articulation of consonants and for vowel height, which are thus taken as values of a single parameter. Consonants and vowels are assumed to form a continuous series, stops being maximally close, and [a] being maximally open:

(16)  a.  stops: 0
      b.  fricatives: 1
      c.  approximants, high vowels: 2
      d.  mid-high vowels: 3
      e.  mid-low vowels: 4
      f.  low vowels: 5

Affricates have the value '0→1', where '→' indicates sequentiality, and [l], a lateral approximant with mid-closure, is characterized by the value '0+2', where '+' indicates simultaneity.

    This feature system allows us to describe and formalize natural processes more adequately. It also accounts for the hierarchical relations between segments within the syllable: for example [i], with the value of '2', is higher on the Sonority Scale than [l], with the value of '0+2'; similarly [l] is higher than [p] ('0'). The most open segment in a French syllable is always the head of the syllable (compare (17) *pli* 'fold'):

(17)

$$
\begin{array}{c}
S \\
\diagup\diagup\vert \\
x \quad x \quad x \\
\vert \quad \vert \quad \vert \\
p \quad l \quad i
\end{array}
$$

articulatory
aperture                   0  0+2  2

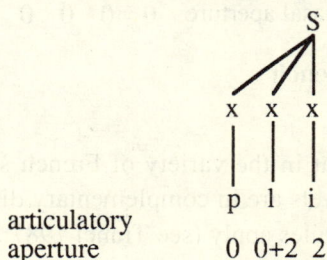

The degree of articulatory aperture takes priority over velic opening. Thus, the lateral consonant [l] ('0+2') is higher on the Sonority Scale than both [p] and [m] ('0'); but [m] is higher than [p], because of its greater degree of aperture in the nasal component ('2', as opposed to '0'). Note that the degree of aperture in this approach plays the same role as the labels 'strong' and 'weak' in the binary branching structures. We are therefore able to dispense with these labels at all structural levels (compare (18) *pastis* 'pastis'):

(18)

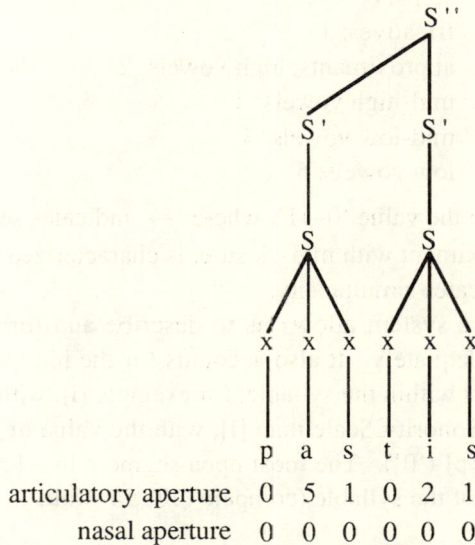

| | | | | | | |
|---|---|---|---|---|---|---|
| | p | a | s | t | i | s |
| articulatory aperture | 0 | 5 | 1 | 0 | 2 | 1 |
| nasal aperture | 0 | 0 | 0 | 0 | 0 | 0 |

## 3. Vowels in Southern French

### 3.1. Mid vowels

It is a well known fact that in the variety of French spoken in Marseille mid-high and mid-low vowels are in complementary distribution. In Standard French the following rules apply (see Tranel 1987:51-62):

(19) mid unrounded vowels are mid-low in closed syllables:
*sept*: 'seven' [sɛt], not *[set]

(20) mid rounded vowels are mid-high in word-final position:
*sot*: 'silly' [so], not *[sɔ].

However, the following contrasts are possible in Standard French:

(21) mid-high and mid-low unrounded vowels contrast in word-final position:
*thé* 'tea' [te]; *taie* 'pillow case' [tɛ]

(22) mid-high and mid-low rounded vowels contrast in word-final closed syllables:
*rauque* 'hoarse' [ʀok]; *roc* 'rock' [ʀɔk].

In Southern French, one rule accounts for the distribution of all mid vowels, whether they are rounded or not:

(23)   mid vowels are mid-high in open syllables, and mid-low in
          closed syllables.

Rules (21) and (22) do not apply in Southern French. The consequence is
that it is not legitimate to postulate an underlying opposition between the
following triplets:

(24)   a.   /e   ø   o/
          b.   /ɛ   œ   ɔ/

This opposition characterizes varieties other than Southern French. In the
dialect of Marseille, we find only three mid vowels in underlying representations: /E, Œ, O/; these underlying vowels are partially specified, inasmuch as it would be arbitrary to regard them as mid-high, or mid-low: they
simply constitute the set of mid vowels (their degree of articulatory aperture is neither '2' nor '5'). Rule (23) accounts for their realizations:

(25)   a.   *thé* [te]; *sot* [so]; *peu* 'little' [pø]
          b.   *sept* [sɛt]; *roc* [ʀɔk]; *peur* 'fear' [pœʀ]

The underlying representations of these words are:

(26)   /tE, sO, pŒ, sEt, ʀOk, pŒʀ/

The underlying degree of articulatory aperture of these vowels can be defined as 3/4 (/ = 'or'). Rule (23) can then be reinterpreted in a more formal
manner:

(27)   articulatory aperture 3/4   →   3   (= 'elsewhere context')
                                       →   4   if the vowel governs a
                                              segment on its right within
                                              the same constituent
                                              (S or S')

In (25a), the vowel governs nothing on its right; in (25b), it governs the
final consonant, since the vowel is the head of the syllable (its degree of
aperture is greater).

## 3.2.  Schwa in Southern French

### 3.2.1.  A stable phoneme

I follow Durand, Slater & Wise (1988:74) in defining schwa as the segment
corresponding to any graphic 'E' which is not liable to be interpreted as [e]
or [ɛ]. A similar definition is given by Walter (1990:27). This graphic

criterion is of course provisional, and we are concerned with the phonological status of the segment in question in the Provence variety of French.

Schwa is not a stable phoneme in Standard French:

(28)  *Tu redemandes.* 'You are asking for more.'
      [ʁødømãːd]/[ʁødmãd]/[ʁdømãd]

But in the French of Provence graphic 'E' corresponds to a stable vowel in most cases:

(29)  *Tu redemandes.*  [ʁødø'mãdə]

and is pronounced even in prepausal context; my transcription shows that schwa is realized as [ø], like graphic 'EU', except when it ends a polysyllabic word; in this case it is more centralized, less labialized, and shorter (see Durand, Slater & Wise (1988:82-83)). Moreover, in polysyllabic words, final schwa is never stressed, and it is regularly 'weaker' than the preceding nucleus; it is also elided before a vowel:

(30)  *Cette fill(e) est belle.* 'This girl is beautiful.'  [sɛtəfije'bɛlə]

### 3.2.2. Word-final schwa

The suprasegmental structure accounts for the dependency relations (*semaine* 'week'):

(31)

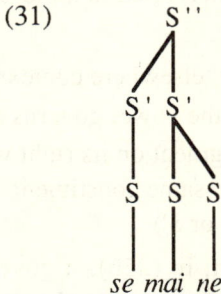

In this configuration, the word-final schwa is governed by the preceding nucleus, as discussed above. It is interesting to note that, whenever the penultimate syllabic nucleus is a mid vowel governing a final schwa, its degree of aperture in the phonetic representation is '4' (= mid-low), although it stands in an open syllable:

(32)  *semaine* 'week' [ɛ]; *faute* 'fault' [ɔ]; *meute* 'pack' [œ].

Rule (27) accounts for this fact, since the penultimate nucleus governs a segment on its right within the same constituent; in *semaine*, for example, the stressed vowel /E/ governs the final schwa, because the S node which dominates /E/ governs the S node which dominates schwa in the constituent S'. Compare:

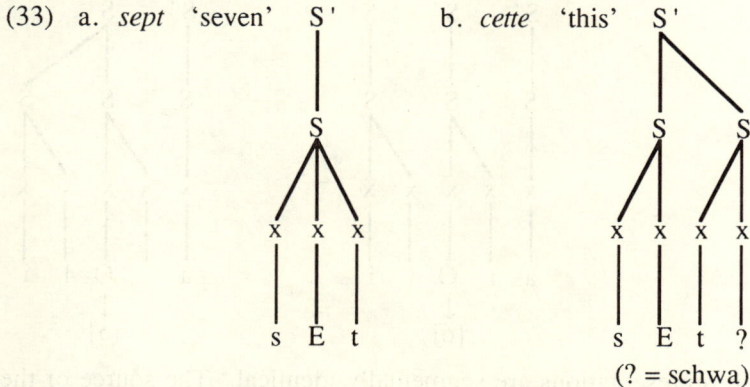

(33)   a.  *sept*  'seven'     S'              b.  *cette*  'this'     S'

```
(33)  a. sept 'seven'    S'            b. cette 'this'     S'
                         |                                / \
                         |                               /   \
                         S                              S     S
                        /|\                            /|    /|
                       / | \                          / |   / |
                      x  x  x                        x  x  x  x
                      |  |  |                        |  |  |  |
                      |  |  |                        |  |  |  |
                      s  E  t                        s  E  t  ?
                                                     (? = schwa)
```

In *sept*, /E/ governs /t/ within the constituent S; in *cette*, /E/ governs schwa within the constituent S'. More precisely, in *sept* the x node which dominates /E/ governs the x node which dominates /t/, and in *cette* the S node which dominates /E/ governs the S node which dominates schwa. In both cases rule (27) yields '3'; we therefore need only one rule for two apparently different contexts.

The validity of rule (27) is confirmed by the two variants of a word like *aïoli* 'garlic mayonnaise':

(34)   *aïoli*:   a.  [ajo'li]
                  b.  [a'jɔli]

*Aïoli* is one of a small number of paroxytones (other examples are *raspi* 'stingy', *garri* 'rat') which have been borrowed into Provence French from the Provençal dialect of Occitan with their stress-pattern intact. (34a) represents a 'standard' French pronunciation, with stress on the final syllable (the result of analogical restructuring), which is adopted by some Southern speakers; (34b) represents the 'original' pronunciation, which is still in widespread use. I assume that this small number of items have the same structure as the other paroxytones of Southern French, all of which end in schwa; that is, that their final syllable forms a constituent with the preceding syllable.

It is noteworthy that the two variants conform to rule (27):

(35)  a.

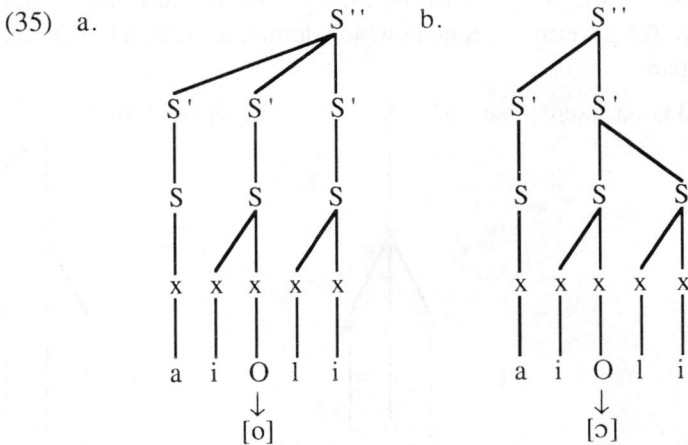

Both representations are segmentally identical. The source of the difference is simply the status of the final vowel: the final nucleus is governed by the penultimate nucleus in (35b), but not in (35a).

### 3.2.3.  Schwa in word-internal position and in monosyllables

It is noticeable that schwa (graphic 'E') in word-internal position is often phonetically identical to the mid-high variant of /Œ/, i.e., [ø] (see below): *melon* 'melon' and *meulon* 'haystack' are strictly homophonous, and so are *médecin* 'doctor' and *mes deux seins* 'my two breasts'. The phonetic representation of *crever* 'to burst' is [kʀøve], as though it were spelt *\*creuver* (the only difference between *crever* and *creuser* 'to dig' is that between the consonants [v] and [z]). Durand, Slater & Wise (1988:84) write that the schwa in *genêts* 'is indistinguishable from the /ø/ which occurs in e.g. *jeune*'. Regarding the phonetic realization of schwa in monosyllables, Durand, Slater & Wise (1988:83) note that 'it is always identical to that of the mid-high vowel [ø]: *je dis* and *jeudi* are homophonous [...]'. If we add that schwa is a stable vowel in Southern French, only one conclusion can be drawn: in such cases graphic 'E' and 'EU' both correspond to the phoneme /Œ/, whose realization is [ø] in open syllables. The underlying representation of *élever* 'to bring up', for example, is:

(36)

```
                              S''
                          ╱  ╱  │
                     S'    S'   S'
                     │     │    │
                     │     │    │
                     S     S    S
                     │    ╱│   ╱│
                     x   x x  x x
                     │   │ │  │ │
                     E   l Œ  v E
```

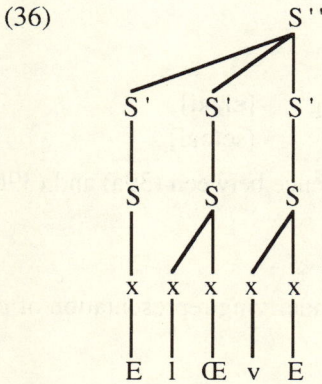

If we apply rule (27) to this representation, we obtain [eløve].

## 3.2.4. Strong and weak internal schwas

This neat pattern is unfortunately marred by the existence of words whose behaviour is different from that outlined above. Compare *élever* with *ennemi* 'enemy':

(37) *élever*   [eløve]          *ennemi*   [εnəmi]

In both items, the first nucleus is a mid vowel, the second nucleus is a word-internal schwa, and all syllables are open. It is true that the realizations of schwa in the two words are slightly different: the schwa of *ennemi* is very similar to a word-final schwa (as in *tête, cette*), hence the symbol [ə]. Moreover, according to my initial hypothesis (see §3.1.), [e] and [ε] are realizations of one phoneme: /E/. The rejection of this hypothesis would produce a paradox: [e] and [ε] would contrast only in unstressed syllables, and only when the following nucleus is schwa; in all other contexts, and more particularly in stressed syllables, the contrast would be neutralized. This view is, of course, highly implausible, and I shall not adopt it. A second solution would consist in postulating the following representations:

(38) *élever*   /ElŒvE/          *ennemi*   /Enəmi/

This solution is adopted by Durand, Slater & Wise (1988). Graphic schwa would correspond to two different phonemes. In this view, only /ə/ would cause lowering of the preceding mid vowel. However, in the next section I put forward some arguments in favour of an alternative analysis.

### 3.2.5. A suprasegmental solution

Let us compare the following examples:

(39)  a.  *elle rit*  'she is laughing'  [ɛləʀi]
      b.  *céleri*    'celery'           [sɛləʀi]

All informants agree that the only difference between (39a) and (39b) is the initial [s] in *céleri*:

(40)  *elle rit = (c)éleri*

If we ignore the segmental aspect, the underlying representation of *elle* is:

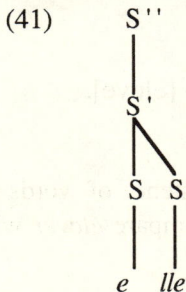

(41)

```
        S''
         |
        S'
        /|
       S  S
       |  |
       e  lle
```

In (41), the first syllable governs the second. My informants unanimously declare that they regard the first syllable as 'stronger' in the citation form of *elle*. Their intuitions therefore accord with the structure postulated in (41). When the same speakers are confronted with (39a), they regularly respond as follows: the strongest syllable is [ʀi], but [ɛ] is still regarded as stronger than [lə]. The underlying representation of *rit* is:

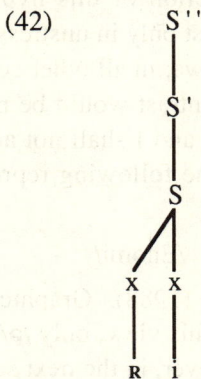

(42)

```
        S''
         |
        S'
         |
         S
        /|
       X  X
       |  |
       ʀ  i
```

When the two words are chained together, only *rit* can keep its stress, and the first S" node must be deleted:

(43)  a.

$$S'' \quad S''$$

$$S' \quad S'$$

$$S \; S \; S$$

$$\rightarrow$$

e *lle* rit

b.

$$S''$$

$$S' \quad S'$$

$$S \; S \; S$$

e *lle* rit

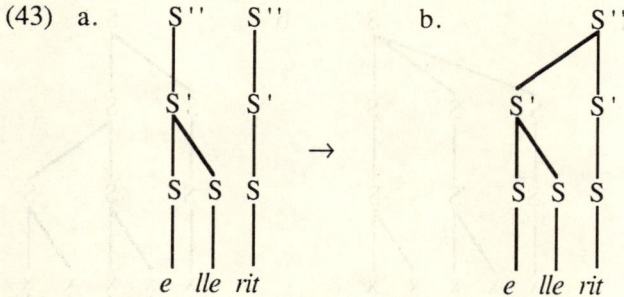

(43b) reflects the prosodic hierarchy corresponding to native speakers' intuitions. It is easy to deduce that the underlying representation of *céleri*, which follows the same prosodic pattern, is:

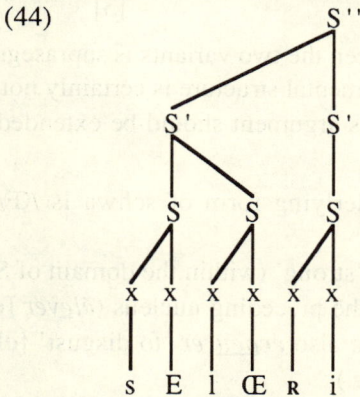

(44)

$$S''$$

$$S' \quad S'$$

$$S \quad S \quad S$$

$$X \; X \quad X \; X \quad X \; X$$

s  E  l  Œ  R  i

It is clear, then, that some internal schwas behave exactly like word-final schwas, and others do not: compare (44) with (36). The internal schwa in (44) is governed by the preceding nucleus, while the internal schwa in (36) is not. The distribution of the two types is unpredictable. In (44), rule (27) yields the mid-low variant of /E/ ([ɛ]), and in (36) it yields the mid-high variant ([e]).

Let us now return to the problem of *aïoli* in (34) and (35), which I repeat here for convenience as (45) and (46):

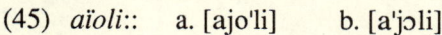

(45)  *aïoli*::  a. [ajo'li]    b. [a'jɔli]

(46)  a.

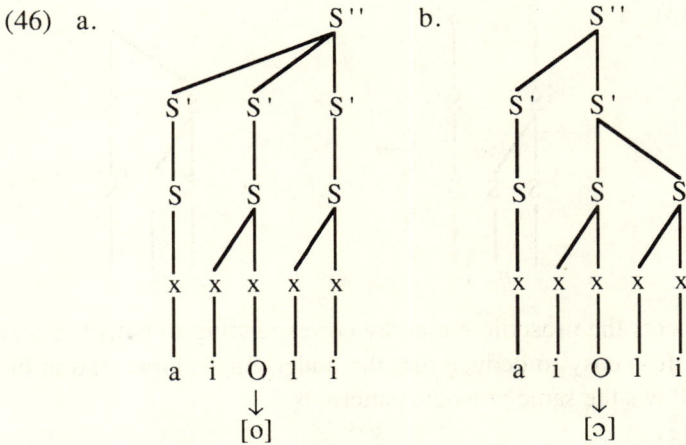

The only underlying difference between the two variants is suprasegmental; moreover, this difference in suprasegmental structure is certainly not conditioned by any segmental factor.  This argument should be extended to the problem of schwa:

- In Southern French, the underlying form of schwa is /Œ/ in all cases.
- Some occurrences of /Œ/ are 'strong' (within the domain of S'); that is, they are not governed by the preceding nucleus (*élever* [eløve], *médecin* [medøsɛ̃], etc..., but also *écoeurer* 'to disgust' [ekøʀe], *esseulé* 'forsaken' [esøle], etc.).
- Other occurrences of /Œ/, in non-initial syllables, are 'weak' — that is, they are governed by the preceding nucleus (*ennemi* [ɛnəmi], *céleri* [sɛləʀi], etc.).  In such cases /Œ/ is always spelt 'E'.  /Œ/ may be weak either in final or in non-final syllables.
- The distribution of strong or weak schwa in internal open syllables is unpredictable.

The consequence of this view is that the only difference between *heureux* 'happy' and *heure* 'hour' is prosodic:

(47) a. *heureux*        b. *heure*

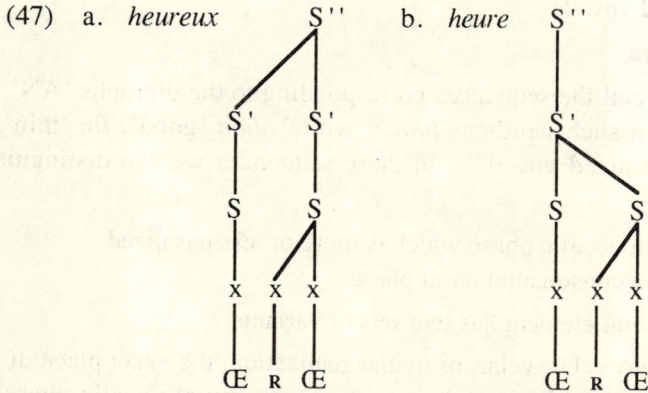

Rule (27) yields the correct outputs: the first vowel of *heureux* is [ø], while the first vowel of *heure* is [œ], in phonetic representations:

(48) *heureux*  [ø'ʀø]
     *heure*    ['œʀə]

Regarding the word-final schwa (as in *heure*), Durand, Slater & Wise (1988:83) note that 'its quality in this context is distinguishable from both (Ø) and (ø): it often has a centralized quality, less labialization than the front rounded vowels [...]'. In my view, these phonetic differences between the strong final /Œ/ of *heureux* and the weak final /Œ/ of *heure* are due to suprasegmental factors, and more precisely to the dependency relations between the vowels; they cannot therefore be taken as arguments against identical segmental representations for *heureux* and *heure* at underlying level.

### 3.2.6. The oral vowel system of Southern French

My analysis reveals that schwa is not a separate phoneme in Southern French, and there is no underlying contrast between mid-high and mid-low vowels. I therefore posit the following system of oral vowels:

(49)      i    y    u
          E    Œ    O
               a

## 4. Nasalized vowels

### 4.1. The data

I tentatively call the sequences corresponding to the digraphs 'AN', 'ON', 'IN', 'UN' in such words as *blanc* 'white', *bon* 'good', *fin* 'thin', *brun* 'brown' 'nasalized vowels'.  In these sequences we can distinguish two phases:

(i)   a vocalic phase which is more or less nasalized
(ii)  a consonantal nasal phase.

The consonantal element has two sets of variants:

* a palato-velar, velar, or uvular realization, the exact place of articulation depending on the quality of the initial vocalic phase; these variants occur in word-final position when no consonant follows: *il est grand* 'he is tall' (see Watbled & Autesserre (1988:218-219) for details).
* a realization where the consonantal element is homorganic with that of the following consonant, both in word-internal position (*encore* 'again') and across word boundaries (*bon pain* 'good bread').

Moreover, the consonantal element is an audible nasal stop when a stop follows, and a practically inaudible nasal fricative before a fricative.  In short, this element shares the manner of articulation with the following segment:

(50) *planter*  'to plant'   [plãnte]
     *penser*   'to think'   [pãs̃se]

Durand (1988) analyses the same sequences in the Languedoc French of Pézenas, which is closely related to the Provence variety, and derives them from underlying sequences of vowel plus underspecified nasal (N).  The nasal element is assumed to undergo velarization and assimilation in the proper contexts; in other cases, the underspecified N is realized as [n] by a default rule.

However, in this approach, we are left with a set of exceptions. Examples of such exceptions are *boum* 'party', *rhum* 'rum', *FEN* (*Fédération Education Nationale* = 'Teachers' Union'):

(51) *une boum* ([bum]) *superbe*      'a superb party'
     *un rhum* ([ʀɔm]) *très corsé*    'strong rum'
     *la FEN* ([fɛn]) *pense que...*    'the FEN thinks that ...'

In the diphonemic analysis these words have to be marked as exceptions to *several* processes:

> (52) a. nasalization of the vocalic element
> b. velarization
> c. place and manner assimilation

Either a word is 'regular', and subject to all processes, or it is 'exceptional', and subject to none. This curious property leads me to suspect that the items in (51) are not exceptions to rules, but to phonotactic constraints.

## 4.2. Complex phonemes

Whatever analysis of nasalized vowels one adopts, the underlying representations of the exceptions referred to above are:

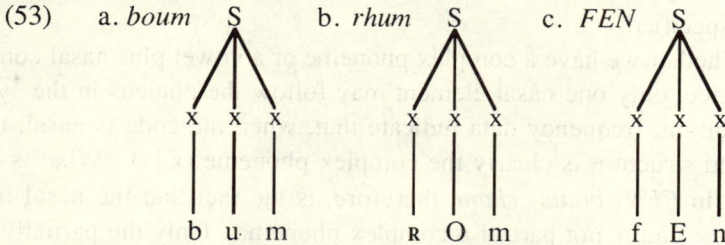

> (53) a. *boum* b. *rhum* c. *FEN*

I shall regard the nasalized vowels of the 'regular' sequences (*bon* 'good' *banc* 'bench' *pain* 'bread' *un* 'one') as complex phonemes. In my view, complex phonemes are similar to diphonemic sequences, except for the fact that — from a functional point of view — they must be interpreted as monophonemic. I adopt the following notational convention:

> (54) x–x = complex (monophonemic) phoneme

The underlying representations of *bon* and *fin* are:

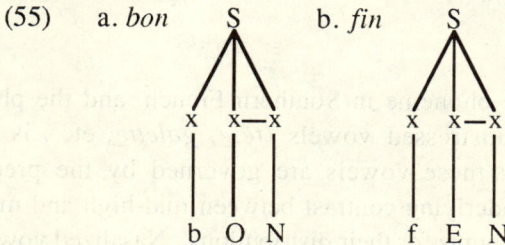

> (55) a. *bon* b. *fin*

Compare *rond* 'round' and *rhum* 'rum':

(56)     a. *rond*    S          b. *rhum*    S

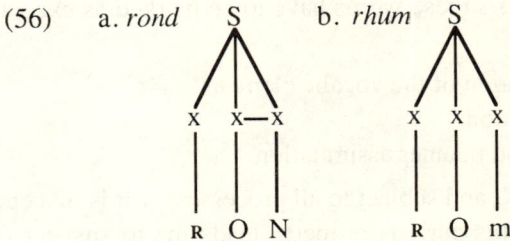

Note that the second part of the complex phoneme is necessarily partially specified (N is simply nasal). More precisely, the degree of aperture (see §2.2 above) is specified in the articulatory component only for the first part of the phoneme ($\underline{x}$–x), and in the nasal component only for the second part (x–$\underline{x}$). On the other hand, 'true' nasal consonants (*FEN rhum boum*) are fully specified.

Whether we have a complex phoneme or a vowel plus nasal consonant sequence, only one nasal element may follow the nucleus in the syllable. In addition, frequency data indicate that, when the coda is nasal, the unmarked structure is clearly the complex phoneme (x–x). What is exceptional in *FEN, boum, rhum*, therefore, is the fact that the nasal is autonomous, and is not part of a complex phoneme. Only the partially specified nasal is subject to velarization and assimilation, and triggers nasalization of the nucleus (see 52). The autonomous nasal consonants in (53) are regularly immune to these processes, which are therefore exceptionless. It is also noteworthy that the only possible complex phonemes are:

(57)

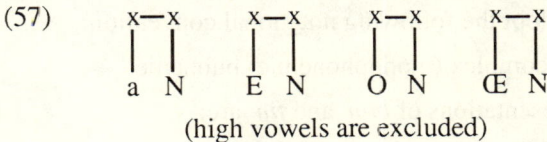

(high vowels are excluded)

## 5. Conclusion

Schwa is not a separate phoneme in Southern French, and the phonetic quality of word-final unstressed vowels (*tête, galette,* etc.) is due to suprasegmental factors: these vowels are governed by the preceding nucleus. There is no underlying contrast between mid-high and mid-low vowels, and rule (27) accounts for their distributions. Nasalized vowels are interpreted as complex monophonemic segments at underlying level, and these segments are distinct from sequences of oral vowel plus nasal consonant. Several rules account for the various realizations of the complex vowels.

The Southern French system includes seven oral vowels and four complex vowels with a partially specified nasal element:

(58) a.  i    y    u
         E    Œ    O
              a
     b.  EN   ŒN   ON
              aN

# References

Anderson, J. M. & C. J. Ewen. 1987. *Principles of Dependency Phonology*. Cambridge: Cambridge University Press

Durand, J. 1988. An exploration of nasality phenomena in Midi French: dependency phonology and underspecification. *French Sound Patterns: Changing Perspectives*, ed. C. Slater, J. Durand & M. Bate. 30-70. Colchester: University of Essex & Association for French Language Studies (Occasional Papers of the University of Essex 32).

————., C. Slater, & H. Wise. 1988. Observations on schwa in Southern French. *French Sound Patterns: Changing Perspectives*, ed. C. Slater, J. Durand & M. Bate, 71-103. Colchester: University of Essex & Association for French Language Studies (Occasional Papers of the University of Essex 32).

Jackendoff, R. 1977. *X-bar Syntax: A Study of Phrase Structure*. Cambridge, Mass.: MIT Press (*Linguistic Inquiry* Monographs 2).

Nespor, M. & I. Vogel . 1986. *Prosodic Phonology* . Dordrecht: Foris (Studies in Generative Grammar 28).

Tranel, B. 1987. *The Sounds of French: an introduction*. Cambridge: Cambridge University Press

Walter, H. 1990. Une voyelle qui ne veut pas mourir. *Variation and Change in French: essays presented to Rebecca Posner on the occasion of her sixtieth birthday*, ed. J. N. Green & W. Ayres-Bennett, 27-36. London: Routledge.

Watbled, J.-Ph. & D. Autesserre. 1988. Application d'un modèle phonologique lexicaliste à l'étude des voyelles oro-nasalisées en français de Marseille. *Travaux de l'Institut de Phonétique d'Aix* 12, 205-227

——. 1989. Positions et oppositions en phonologie multilinéaire. *Sigma* 12-13, 153-178.

# 'Underspecification' and 'misagreement' in Catalan lexical specifiers*

## Max W. Wheeler
### *University of Sussex*

**1.** The context in which the present piece of work arises is the task of trying to give an adequate description of the grammar of those lexical items which normally precede the heads of noun phrases in Romance. Part of the difficulty, and interest, of the matter arises from some apparent mismatches between syntax, semantics, and morphology which are particularly notable in Catalan, though, as will be seen, they can be paralleled in many other languages of the family. The elements I shall be concerned with consist of the so-called determiners, quantifiers, and indefinites, to which is often added a vague 'etcetera' which reflects grammarians' unease at trying to organize the items under the traditional headings. In so far as anyone commits themselves to a 'part-of-speech' classification, such items are generally listed as adjectives, either on account of their syntactic function as modifiers of nouns, or on account of their morphological agreement pattern consisting of inflectional marking for gender and number. (Others appear to treat determiners, quantifiers, numerals, and so on as being themselves syntactic categories, though usually without taking a stand on the matter.) The items in question — those which necessarily or normally precede nominal heads — form a closed class. Open-class modifiers of nouns, of course, typically follow them in Romance. Following Jackendoff (1977), and similarly Bonet & Solà (1986) for Catalan, I am using the term 'specifiers' to refer to all those modifiers which appear to the left of heads in surface order. (Others in the Generative Grammar tradition restrict

'specifiers' to left daughters of maximal projections (Radford 1988:278)
and use terms such as 'pre-head modifiers' (Gazdar 1985:126 after Chomsky 1970) or 'attributes' (Radford 1988:196) for those modifying elements
which are daughters and sisters of X').

**2.** I shall be focussing here on a subset of specifier adjectives, together
with some related items which are not adjectives. The forms in question,
the polyvalent lexical specifiers, are listed in (1).

| (1) | A | Adv | N |
|---|---|---|---|
| *altre* | other | _____ | something else |
| *altre tant* | as much/many (again) | _____ | as much again |
| *bastant* | enough/ sufficient | enough/quite, rather* | enough/ quite a lot |
| *com* | _____ | how/as, the* | (?) how much |
| *força* | much/many/ a lot of | quite/very/ a lot, much* | _____ |
| *gaire* | few/little | (a) little | little |
| *gens* | _____ | at all/any | (not) a bit/any |
| *mica* | _____ | at all/any | (not) a bit/any |
| *igual* | _____ | equally | the same |
| *massa* | too much/many | too, too much* | too much |
| *menys* | less/fewer | less | less |
| *més* | more | more | more |
| *mig* | half | half | half |
| *molt* | much/many | very/a lot, much* | much/a lot |
| *poc* | (a) little/ (a) few | (a) little | (a) little |
| *prou* | enough | enough | enough |
| *quant* | how much/many | how much | how much |
| *que* | how much/many! | how! | _____ |
| *quelcom* | _____ | somewhat | something |
| *qui-sap-lo* | ever so much/ many | ever so | (?) ever so much |
| *tal* | such | (?) so | such a thing |
| *tan(t)* | so much/many | so, so much* | so much |
| *tot* | all/every | all/wholly/ quite | all/everything |

*form before comparative in English

The Catalan items listed in (1) in fact appear, without derivational affixation of any kind, in modifying roles corresponding to several different word classes: not only (i) as A acting as specifier of N (column 1); but also (ii) as Adv(erb) acting as specifier of A, Adv or P(reposition) or modifier ('adjunct') of V(erb) (column 2); (iii) as N acting as specifier of N and other categories, or as pronominal head of NP (column 3).[1] Most of these 'polyvalent' lexical items are semantically quantifiers, though not *altre*, *tal*, or perhaps *tot*. And there are many quantifiers which are not polyvalent, such as *algun* 'some', *cap* 'no', and *nombrosos* 'numerous', which are adjectives only. What the polyvalent quantifier items do share is the potential for semantically quantifying [–count] items, and it is this property which makes them suitable candidates for modifying non-nominals.

**3.** The first curious fact about the list in (1) is that it exists at all, for it is claimed by Emonds (1985) as a universal that polyvalent lexical specifiers are not normally found:

> The central morpheme categories of syntax have deep structure distributions in the languages of the world which appear quite constant...N, V, A... Each of these lexical categories X can be paired with a category of grammatical formatives SP(X) — the specifier of X — which typically appears with it in the same phrase, and not in combination with the other lexical categories (Emonds 1985:156, and compare also 19).

While Emonds may have been led to this view by noting differences such as English *much money*, *very strange*, *greatly disapprove* — though for Emonds the typical specifiers of verbs are Auxiliaries — the glosses given in (1) suggest the claim is not very plausible even for English, as regards the quantifiers, at least. In so far as most lexical specifiers are so restricted, this probably reflects the semantic type differences of the major lexical categories.

**4.** Traditional grammar of Catalan, even when adequately comprehensive (Badía 1962; DE; DM), deals with all the lexical specifiers and associated items in a rather unsatisfactory way. Bonet (in Bonet & Solà 1986) is the first to make a considered attempt to deal systematically with specifier phrases of various kinds, from the perspective of Generative Grammar. His approach is based on that of Jackendoff (1977) and carries over certain of what now appear as Jackendoff's less attractive features, namely, an excess of elementary grammatical categories (which hinders the expression of generalization, for example, about inflectional morphology), and the incorporation into the phrase-structure rules themselves of too much which might better be left to semantic constraints or other principles. Some of the trees and sub-trees, relating to specifiers of N, which are generated by Bonet's PS rules are illustrated in (2). (In Jackendoff's theory the bar levels are X, X', X", and X'", none of which is recursive; unlike Jackendoff, Bonet does not distinguish a Deg from a Q category.)

(2)    a.    Specifiers of NP according to Bonet (1986: 29, 39, 42, 44)

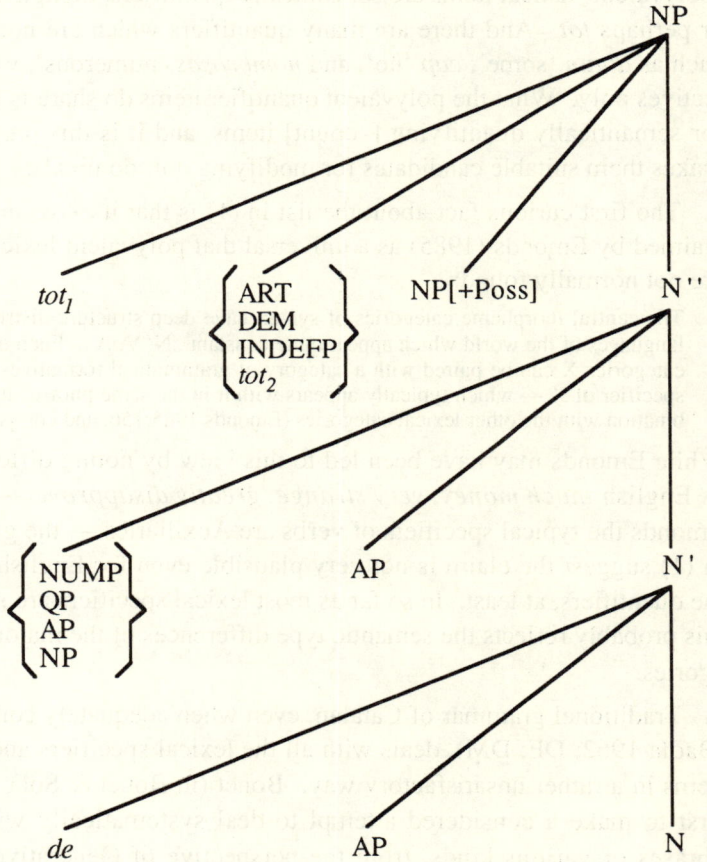

b. Specifiers of QP     c. Specifiers of NUMP
(Bonet 1986:46)      (Bonet 1986:45)
(For Bonet, *poc* is
the only non-null
lexical Q item.)

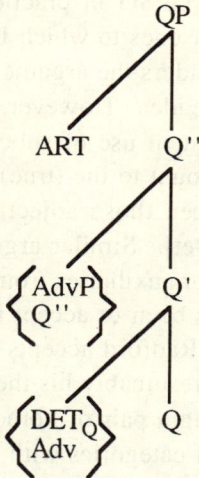

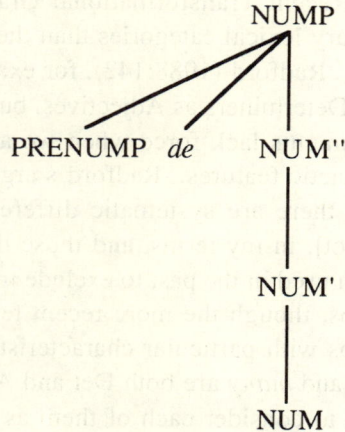

**5.** The phrase-structure framework I shall make use of here for the description of specifier phrases is both more constrained and more general than the proto-X-bar syntax of Jackendoff (1977). It is in outline that proposed in Radford (1988), in which there are two bar levels (above zero), that is, X' and X", both of which may be recursive. The possibility that in addition to X' — the only recursive level in Chomsky (1986) — X" may also be recursive is 'left open' by Radford (1988:255); but the English examples he adduces, and comparable ones from Romance (see below), seem to me to give strong support to this idea. My approach differs from recent Generative Grammar, however, in relying on no more than four basic lexical categories: N, V, A and P (or Adv/P as I shall express it here, to remind the reader that this category contains orthodox Adverbs as well as Prepositions). These categories can be extensively subclassified by features, a procedure developed, though less radically applied, in Generalized Phrase Structure Grammar (Gazdar *et al.* 1985). The four basic categories are themselves taken to be complexes of the features [±N], [±V]. 'Empty' categories can be base-generated in licensed positions. Consequently, many of what are presented as pronouns in traditional descriptions (for instance, *tants* 'so many of them', 'so many men', 'so many people'), or as 'pronominal adjectives', can be regarded as just adjectives followed by empty, anaphoric, N heads. Typically in Romance (unlike English), all adjectives may appear in such constructions (see below §6.3.).

Recent Transformational Grammar and GPSG in practice use more unitary lexical categories than the four major ones to which I restrict myself. Radford (1988:142), for example, considers the arguments for treating Determiners as Adjectives, but rejects the idea. However, his counter-arguments lack force when we admit consistent use of subclassificatory syntactic features. Radford's arguments amount to the (true) observation that there are systematic differences between those adjectives that are [+Det], in my terms, and those that are [–Det]. Similar arguments have been used in the past to exclude modals and/or auxiliaries from the class of verbs, though the more recent tendency has been to accept that they are verbs with particular characteristics. Even Radford accepts that English *few* and *many* are both Det and A, though presumably his theory requires him to consider each of them as representing a pair of homonyms. McCawley (1988:194) discusses the question of categories with considerable subtlety and concludes that, with respect to English, '"Det" does not correspond to a separate lexical category but includes items of the categories A and N'; even so, he does not incorporate this conclusion into the PS rules he formulates for English. In Romance, at any rate, the inflectional argument for treating determiners as adjectives — the fact that determiners inflect for number and gender in agreement with their nominal phrase heads or controllers — is a strong one, stronger, in fact, for this reason, than the argument that numerals are adjectives. In what follows, therefore, Determiners are a subclass of Adjectives. (And 'Quantifier' (Q) is here a semantic characterization only, with no special association with any particular syntactic word class.)

The case for unifying the categories of Adverb and Preposition (along with Conjunction) is made, in part, by Emonds (1985:248-262), who is followed by Radford (1988:133-137), and analogously for Catalan by Bonet & Solà (1986:70-71). Common to all of these is the idea that traditional adverbs (or particles) have no complements (*He took it before*), whereas prepositions have nominal (or PP) complements (*He took it before lunch*), and conjunctions have sentential complements (*He took it before she came in*); that is, prepositions (and conjunctions) are transitive, while adverbs (and particles) are intransitive. The close similarity of the semantic functions of adverb phrases and prepositional phrases has often been remarked upon: in many languages, locative, manner, and degree expressions may be constructed in either way. And, if the unitary class of verbs can be subdivided into transitive and intransitive subclasses, why not the class of Adverbs/Prepositions (Adv/P) likewise? The practice within Generative Grammar has been to exclude from this assimilation of the adverb and preposition categories the derived adverbs (English *-ly*), which are held to be adjectives (Emonds 1985:58,162; Radford 1988:138-141). Radford argues this point explicitly (using curious analogies from chess and morphophonology) on the grounds that derived adverbs and their source adjectives are similar in meaning and are in complementary distribution. But this argument seems to me an inappropriate one in the context. Distributional differences are the basis of syntactic word-class categories in modern linguistics, and the distribution of derived adverbs is, in fact, closely similar to that of non-derived adverbs — hence the traditional terminology. Radford's argument, if applied consistently to cases of relatedness in form and meaning with different distribution, would apparently lead not only to the conclusion that *real* and *really* are of the same syntactic category, but also to the conclusion that *real* and *realize*, or *realize* and *realization* are. So I shall revert to the more traditional view and include derived adverbs together with the non-derived ones within the new proposed class of Adv/P words. Adv/P words and phrases modify words and phrases whose heads are non-nominal; Adv/Ps with appropriate meaning may be complements too.

**6.0.** The following sections (§§6.1-6.3) discuss the grammatical behaviour of lexical specifiers from the Adjective, Adverb/Preposition, and Nominal classes respectively.

**6.1.** Prenominal Adjectives form the most diverse of the lexical specifier classes. This Adjective class includes items called variously articles, demonstratives, determiners, quantifiers, numerals, and indefinites, as well as some qualifying adjectives. With the exception of the majority of numerals, nearly all of these Adjectives share the morphological property of inflectional agreement with a nominal controller (which may be lexically empty). The category of Adjectives is to be subclassified by means of distinctive features, certain of which are complex: they take other features as their values (Gazdar *et al.* 1985). The fact that the lexical items considered here are Adjectives does not debar some of them, in addition to those of (1), from membership of other lexical categories. Such is the case, I would claim, of numerals, which also fulfil Noun roles in some contexts.

PS rules generating positions for A Spec(N) are given in (3); in these rules elements other than heads are, of course, optional. (These 'rules' are strictly sub-tree admissibility conditions; possible complement structures are omitted as being outside our present concern.)

(3)   a.   NP → AP[Det, $\left\{ \begin{matrix} \text{Bar 1} \\ \text{Bar 0} \end{matrix} \right\}$ ] N'

    b.   N' → AP N'

    c.   A'[Det, Bar 1] → AP[Def, Bar 0] A $\left\{ \begin{matrix} \text{[Poss, +Tonic]} \\ \text{[Rel]} \end{matrix} \right\}$

    d.   A[Def, Bar 0] → *el* 'the', *en* (personal article), *quin* 'which', *aquest* 'this', *aqueix* 'that', *aquell* 'that'

    e.   A[Poss, +Tonic] → *meu* 'my', *teu* 'your', etc.

    f.   A[Rel] → *qual* 'which'

These rules generate the familiar phrase types illustrated in (4a); examples such as (4b) will be excluded either for semantic reasons or by means of lexical selection restrictions on *qual*, as in (4c).

(4)   a.   *casa* 'house': (a) head
       *la casa* 'the house': (a), (d)
       *quina casa* 'which house': (a), (d)
       *la teva casa* 'your house': (a), (c), (d), (e)
       *aqueixa teva casa* 'that house of yours': (a), (c), (d), (e)
       *la qual casa* 'which house': (a), (c), (d), (f)
       *la nova* [ø]$_N$ 'the new one': (a), (d), (b)

    b.   *\*quina qual casa*
       *\*aquella qual casa*

    c.   *qual* [Rel, SC[–Dem, –Interr]_____]

Other examples of determiner Adjectives (A[Det]) with some relevant sub-class features are given in (5), where [Bar 0] indicates items that cannot themselves be specified, [Q] denotes semantic quantifiers, and [SC_____] denotes a subcategorization feature.

(5)   a.   A[Det, Q, Bar 0, ...] *ambdós* 'both', *cada* 'each', (*cada un*/*cadascun* [SC____[+Null]] 'each one'), *cap* 'no', *ningun* 'no' (Valencian), *qualsevol* 'any', *sengles* 'one each', *tot* 'every'

   b.   A[Det, Q, Bar 0, +Exiguous, ...] *algun* 'some', *qualque* 'some' (*qualcun* [SC____[+Null]] 'some'), *un* 'a'

   c.   A[Det, Poss, Bar 0, –Tonic, ...] *mon* 'my', etc.

The reason for regarding the quantifier items of (5a, b) as determiners is the fact that they always precede any other type of adjective and that they are not themselves preceded by determiners (though this might be for semantic reasons). The reference in (3a), (3d), and (5) to [Bar 0] is to require that the maximal projection dominate only a lexical category (that is, one that has no modifiers); Gazdar *et al.*'s proposal (1985:25) is that 'minor categories (determiners, complementizers, conjunctions) lack Bar specifications altogether'; but this would rule out complex determiners like Catalan *el qual*, *el meu*, etc.  Wheeler (1991) devotes some attention to the remaining kinds of adjectives which can precede NP heads (3b) and to principles constraining their sequential order in Catalan.  Sequences of prenominal adjectives are generated by recursion of N' in (3b).

**6.2.**   In their Adv/P role, the polyvalent items of (1), together with a few other items, like those in (6), are introduced by the PS rules of (7).  The genuine adverb status of the items in (6) is demonstrated, among other things, by their failure of the noun tests mentioned below (§6.3.).

(6)   a.   *ben* 'well, quite'; *pla* 'quite'; *d'allò* [SC____*més*], e.g., *d'allò més elegant* 'quite the most elegant'

   b.   *plenament* 'fully'; *extremament* 'extremely'; *considerablement* 'considerably'

(7)   PS rules for Adv/PP modifiers:

   a.   AP → Adv/PP A'

   b.   Adv/PP → Adv/PP Adv/P'

   c.   VP → V' Adv/PP ...

I shall shortly claim that the PS rules must also allow quantifier NPs to modify the non-nominal heads as in (7).  Given that I claim that the polyvalent items of (1) are also nouns, it may therefore be wondered whether the PS rules of (7) are not dispensable.  They are required, in fact,

not only for derived adverbs (compare (6b)), but also in the case of other
adverbs whose distribution does not suggest that they are also nouns.

Our first syntax-morphology mismatch arises in the case where the Adverb *tot* 'all', 'wholly', 'completely' modifies an Adjective. Fabra's classic formulation of the phenomenon in Catalan is as (8a), where the behaviour of *tot* is in clear contrast to that of, for instance, *bastant*, *molt*,
*quant*, *mig* (8b).

> (8)   a.   'el mot *tot* usat com adverbi de grau ofereix la particulari-
>            tat que es fa correntment concordar amb l'adjectiu al qual
>            s'adjunta... *l'he trobada tota trista ... on aneu totes soles?*'
>            ['the word *tot* used as a degree adverb is peculiar in that it
>            normally agrees with the adjective it modifies: "I found
>            her all sad" ... "where are you going all alone?"'] (Fabra
>            1956:82)[2]
>
>        b.   *\*bastants tristos* 'quite sad'
>            *\*quantes tristes* 'how sad'
>            *\*molta trista* 'very sad'
>            *\*mitja boja* 'half mad'

This is the only such case that is explicitly remarked on in the Catalan
grammatical tradition. But we shall shortly see that there are indeed other
cases of syntax-morphology mismatch involving false inflectional agreement or 'misagreement'. It is not clear that there is any principled reason
why this phenomenon is restricted to adverbial *tot* in the current context in
Catalan — that is, why items like those of (8b) are ungrammatical.[3]

**6.3.**      The fact that many of the polyvalent items in (1) may fulfil genuinely nominal roles is recognized inconsistently by traditional grammarians and lexicographers, in part because genuine pronouns are not usually
adequately distinguished from 'pronominal adjectives' — that is, adjectives used with anaphoric ellipsis of their NP heads, as in (9). Here, the
lexical content of the 'empty' NP head is contextually derivable; failing
that, it is pragmatically interpreted as referring generically to one or more
humans.

> (9)   a.   *Dels alumnes$_j$, en veia algun* [ø$_j$]$_N$.
>            'Of the students, I saw one or two.'

b. *Entre els coixins$_j$, vaig triar els durs* [ø$_j$]$_N$; *no m'interes-saven els altres* [ø$_j$]$_N$.
'From the pillows I chose the hard ones; I wasn't inter-ested in the others.'
c. *Alguns* [ø]$_N$ *creuen que...*
'Some (*sc.* people) think that...'

The syntactic contexts which identify nominal heads (and thus the categorial status as N of (1) items) include the following: (i) argument positions (subject, direct object, indirect object of verb); (ii) prepositional object; (iii) antecedent of relative clause; (iv) head of a phrase containing a PP complement — or an apparent PP, at least, for I shall want to claim that not all occurrences of the item *de* in fact contain the preposition *de*. In (10a, b) are some phrases illustrating the use of polyvalent items as NP heads ('indefinite pronouns').[4] Nearly all of these are lexically true 'neuter' pronouns, that is, they may not be preceded by determiners, but a few may occur with determiners (10c), resembling simple quantity nouns (10d).

(10) Polyvalent items as NP heads

a. In argument position or as object of P

| | |
|---|---|
| *altre* | *No hi havia altre a fer que rebel·lar-se.* (DE) |
| | 'There was nothing else to be done but to rebel.' |
| *altre tant* | *Nosaltres vam fer altre tant.* (DE) |
| | 'We did likewise.' |
| *bastant* | ?*Ja has fet bastant.* |
| | 'You've already done enough.' |
| *gaire* | *abans de gaire* |
| | 'before long' |
| | *No demanava gaire.* |
| | 'He didn't ask for much.' |
| *gens* | *\*No es va empassar gens.* |
| | 'She didn't swallow at all.' |
| *mica* | ?*No es va empassar mica.* |
| | 'She didn't swallow anything.' |
| *igual* | ?*Costarà igual.* |
| | 'It will cost the same.' |
| *massa* | *En treus massa.* |
| | 'You take too much out of it.' |

*menys*        *Pagaran menys.* (Badía 1962)
               'They will pay less.'

*més*          *per més que* (lit.)
               'by more that' = 'however much'
               *Costarà més.*
               'It will cost more.'

*molt*         *Ha fet molt de no-res.* (DE)
               'He has made a lot from nothing.'
               *No val amb molt tant com tu dius.* (DM)
               'It is not worth by a long way as much as you
                 say.'

*poc*          *20 pessetes és poc.* (DM)
               '20 pesetas is not much.'

*prou*         *Ja has fet prou.*
               'You've already done enough.'

*quant*        *Per quant m' ho vens?*
               'How much will you sell it to me for?'

*quelcom*      *Sentia quelcom a l' estòmac.* (Badía 1962)
               'She felt something in her stomach.'

*qui-sap-lo*   *Enguany han collit qui-sap-lo.* (DCVB)
               'This year they've picked ever such a lot.'

*tal*          *No faré tal.* (DCVB)
               'I won't do such a thing.'

*tant*         *Té tant com tu.*
               'He has as much as you.'
               *per tant*
               'therefore'

*tot*          *Tot li reïx.* (DE)
               'Everything he does is successful.'

*com*          *\*Com costa!*
               'How much it costs!'

*força*        *\*Es va empassar força.*
               'She swallowed a lot'

*mig*          *\*20 pessetes és mig.*
               '20 pesetas is half.'

que          *Que costa!
             'How much it costs!'

b.  Specifier *de* N'

altre tant   ?altre tant d'aigua
             'as much water (again)'
bastant      bastant de sorra  (Badía 1962)
             'quite a lot of sand'
com          Com era de valent.
             'How brave he was.'  [structure unclear]
gaire        gaire de fred  (Badía 1962)
             'not much cold'
             *gaire(s) de nois  (Bonet 1986)
             'not many boys'
gens         No té gens de paciència.  (DE/DM)
             'He hasn't any patience.'
gota/        No té gota de paciència.  (DM)
mica         'He hasn't any patience.'
igual        Són igual d'alts.  (DE)
             'They are the same height.'  [structure unclear]
menys        menys de maletes  (Badía 1962)
             'fewer suitcases'
més          més de neu  (Badía 1962)
             'more snow'
molt         molt de vi  (DM)
             'a lot of wine'
poc          poc de fred
             'little cold'
prou         prou de blat  (Badía 1962)
             'enough wheat'
quant        quant de poder
             'how much power'
qui-sap-lo   ??qui-sap-lo de conyac
             'ever so much brandy'
tant         tant de vent  (DM)
             'so much wind'

|        | tot      | tot d'il·lusions perdudes  (DM)<br>'a great number of lost hopes' |
|--------|----------|------------------------------------------------------------------|
| **N.B.** | cap    | cap de persona coneguda<br>'no person known (to us)'<br>(Valencia, Pallars, Majorca) |
|        | altre    | *altre de paper<br>'(an)other paper' |
|        | força    | *força de pa  (Badía 1962)<br>'a lot of bread' |
|        | massa    | *massa d'ambicions  (Badía 1962)<br>'too many ambitions' |
|        | mig      | *mig de fred<br>'half cold' |
|        | que      | *que de tramvies!  (Badía 1962)<br>'how many trams!' |
|        | quelcom  | *quelcom de blat<br>'some wheat' |
|        | tal      | *tal de paper<br>'such paper' |

c.  *un prou
'an enough'
*un gens
'a no quantity'
*el quelcom de què em parlaves
'the somewhat you spoke to me about'
un poc de fred
'a little cold'
Li envia un tant cada més.
'He sends her so much a month.'

d.  la mica de vi que ens quedava
'the bit of wine we had left'
un nombre de polítics
'a number of politicians'
un quilo de carn
'a kilo of meat'

*una sèrie d'esdeveniments*
'a series of events'
*una mica de bona voluntat*
'a bit of good will'
*Fa un pèl d'aire.* (DM)
'There's a bit of a draught.'
(lit. 'It makes a hair of air.')

The examples in (10b) and (10d) illustrate the so-called pseudo-partitive construction, which is similar to English 'a lot of', 'a bit of', 'heaps of', and so on (Selkirk 1977; Battye, this volume). In this construction, a quantifier NP (NP[Q]) acts as a specifier of N', and the quantified N' is the syntactic and semantic head of the construction, as revealed by number and gender agreement elsewhere in the sentence. Alongside PS rule (3) rewriting NP as A[Det] N', we therefore require a rule of the form (11a):

(11) a. NP → NP[Q] *de* N'
    b. XP → NP[Q] X'

Here I follow Bonet & Solà (1986) in treating *de* as a specified lexical formative. There is considerable evidence elsewhere in Catalan for *de* as a quasi-inflectional element in constructions distinct from prepositional phrases: it is followed by adjectives (*Com era de difícil* 'How difficult it was') and by infinitives (*Cercava de fer-ho* 'She tried to do it'). Comparable arguments have been put forward for some cases of *de* (and *à*) in French, and of *a* in Spanish (Jaeggli 1982, 1986; Battye, this volume). Now, having introduced an alternative PS rule for NP specifiers (11a), X-bar theory would lead us to expect something analogous, that is (11b), as a specifier of the other major categories (or modifier of V'); and this is indeed what we find (compare (12)).

(12) a. *un xic guillat*$_A$ (DE)
    'a bit cracked'
    *un bon xic més*$_{Adv}$ *difícil*
    'a good bit more difficult'
    *un poc abans*$_P$ *de néixer*
    'a little before being born'
    *un gra massa*$_{Adv}$
    'a bit too much'

*No m'agrada$_V$· un pèl.*
'I don't like it a bit.'

b. *No m'agrada$_V$· gens ni mica.*
'I don't like it one little bit.'
*No hi veig$_V$· gota.*
'I can't see at all.'
*una mica menys$_{Adv}$ clar*
'a bit less clear'

c. *\*una mica de rajoles*
'a bit of tiles'
*\*un poc de formigues*
'a little ants'

So PS rules (7a-c) can be expanded as in (13):

(13) a.  AP  →  $\left\{ \begin{array}{l} \text{Adv/PP} \\ \text{NP[Q]} \end{array} \right\}$ A'

b.  Adv/PP  →  $\left\{ \begin{array}{l} \text{Adv/PP} \\ \text{NP[Q]} \end{array} \right\}$ Adv/P'

c.  VP  →  V' $\left\{ \begin{array}{l} \text{Adv/PP} \\ \text{NP[Q]} \end{array} \right\}$ ...

As I mentioned before, most of the polyvalent items may appear indifferently in either of the alternative structures admitted in (13), but a few (*força, que, mig*) are apparently never nouns (in the relevant sense, that is).[5] However, the items illustrated in (12a) are clearly nouns, inasmuch as they take determiners, not adverbs (*pace* Catalan traditional grammarians). Actually, there are very few nouns which may appear in the NP[Q] slots of (13); most of them are illustrated in (12). They all share the feature [+Exiguous] and require (12c) a non-count item following. In (1), I registered *gens* (and associated *mica*) as adverbs in accord with traditional accounts; but it can be argued that they, and also *quelcom*, are always nouns in the constructions in question, and that consequently only the polyvalent items which are adjectives may also be adverbs.

**6.4.** Alongside the familiar pattern of specifier quantifier Adjectives (14a), which all varieties of Catalan accept, some varieties (e.g., Majorcan) allow specifiers of nouns according to the pattern of (14b), in which an Adjective appears to agree with its Nominal head, but is separated from it by the element *de*, as in the pseudo-partitive construction of (10b, d). This was not a problematic construction for traditional grammar, which lacked a theory of phrase structure.

(14) a. *bastants amics*
'quite a few friends'
*molta carn*
'much meat'
*poca gent*
'few people'
*quants llibres*
'how many books'
*tants amics*
'so many friends'
*gaire fred*
'(not) much cold'

b. *bastants d'amics* (DM)
'quite a few friends'
*molta de carn* (DM)
'much meat'
*poca de gent* (Bonet 1986)
'few people'
*quants de llibres* (Badía 1962)
'how many books'
*tants d'amics* (DM)
'so many friends'

c. *tot d'il·lusions* (DM)
'a great number of illusions';
**different from**
*totes il·lusions*
'all illusions'
*\*totes d'il·lusions*
*gaire de fred* (Badía 1962)
'(not) much cold'

*gaires de nois* (Bonet 1986)
'few boys'
??*gaire de nois*

d.   *alguna de carn*
'some meat'
*nombrosos d'amics*
'numerous friends'

(In (14c) it is plausible to argue, along with Bonet & Solà (1986), that the item *tot* involved here is a distinct lexeme from the *tot* 'all', 'every' that we have been considering so far. The N[Q] *gaire*, when used as a specifier (14c), seems to require, as *gens* does, a head which is [–Count], and therefore [–Plural]. Number agreement would be inapplicable for that reason.) Now if we were to try to account for the apparent pattern [A *de* N']$_{NP}$ of (14b) by further elaborating the PS rules, we should run into two difficulties. Firstly, such a pattern would be structurally anomalous and the presence of *de* inexplicable on general grounds. In the pseudo-partitive NP *de* N' pattern, the *de* avoids an otherwise unacceptable NP N' sequence, assimilating it superficially to the acceptable NP PP pattern (where PP is a complement or 'adjunct'); no such surface analogy is appropriate here, however. Secondly, and perhaps more importantly, we would not have accounted for the fact that the few 'adjectives' which can occur in this construction are precisely those which are lexically also nouns. My claim is that the specifier words in (14b) exhibit 'misagreement': although in this context they are syntactically nouns (by PS rule (11a)), they adopt the inflectional morphology which is appropriate for the same lexical items acting as adjective specifiers (14a). To put it another way, the construction of (14b) is a superficial conflation of [N$_j$ *de* N'] and [A$_j$ N'] in those cases where the same lexical item may fill either the N$_j$ or the A$_j$ slot. The borrowed agreement, then, would be a further example of the kind of phenomenon which is recognized to affect adverbial *tot* in (8). Again, unsurprisingly, Catalan is not alone among the Romance languages here. Occitan displays all three surface patterns with quantifier specifiers: (i) [N *de* N'], (ii) [A N'], and (iii) the 'misagreeing' [A *de* N']. Of these, the first is typical of Provençal, and the third is typical of Lengadocian.[6] A superficial model for the agreement of an adjective separated from a noun by *de* is doubtless provided by the true partitive construction with ellipsis,

illustrated in (15a) (Bonet & Solà 1986:52-58). An additional model may
be seen in the pattern of (15b), where the modern standard language requires a comma and treats the full PP as expanding or clarifying the clitic
*en*. The parallel construction in Italian (15c) (Brunet 1981:186), however,
does not demand a comma, and thus resembles the Catalan surface
[A *de* N'] pattern of (14b) more closely. Except in the construction of
(15c), with the clitic *ne*, Italian has no parallel to (14b) of Catalan.

(15) a.  *bastants* $[ø_j]_N$ *d'aquells amics$_j$*
         'many of those friends',
         compare *bastants amics$_j$ d'aquells* $[ø_j]_N$
         'many friends from those (ones)'
         *molta* $[ø_j]_N$ *de la carn$_j$ que hem comprat*
         'much of the meat we bought'
         *poca* $[ø_j]_N$ *de la gent$_j$ coneguda*
         'few of the well-known people'
         *quants* $[ø_j]_N$ *dels seus llibres$_j$*
         'how many of his books'
         *tants* $[ø_j]_N$ *dels antics amics$_j$*
         'so many of the old friends'

     b.  *En tenim tants, de manuscrits.*
         'We have so many manuscripts.'/'We have so many,
         manuscripts, that is.'

     c.  *Ne abbiamo tanti di manoscritti.*
         'We have so many manuscripts.'
         *Ne abbiamo subiti troppi di dibattiti.*
         'We have endured too many debates.'

7.  In Bonet's account (Bonet & Solà 1986) of NP specifiers, there appears
((2) above) a unique specified lexical element '*tot$_1$*' as a possible leftmost
daughter of the maximal NP. For this author, this item is, apparently,
merely homonymous with the word *tot$_2$* which can occur in
(approximately) determiner position (5a), and also with the *tot$_3$* of (14c).
In Bonet's framework *tot$_1$* is not an adjective or an adverb. Something
must be wrong here. Firstly, if *tot$_1$* (16a) is an isolated and non-categorial
formative — a fly in the PS ointment — it is most odd that English should
have exactly the same pattern involving an item with the same meaning
(16c).

(16)  a.  *tota la seva bona fe*
       b.  *tota bona fe*
       c.  all his good faith
       d.  all good faith
       e.  *no totes les sabates*
          'not all the shoes'
          *gairebé totes les sabates*
          'nearly all the shoes'.

Secondly, Bonet's account ignores the fact that $tot_1$, appearing to the left of a determiner, may itself be specified (16e). In fact, there are other items with a similar semantic function which appear in the same position as $tot_1$ (17).

(17)  *Entre els que es troben malament*

hi ha $\left\{\begin{array}{l} \textit{tots} \\ \textit{només} \\ \textit{àdhuc} \\ \textit{almenys} \\ \textit{en general} \\ \textit{just} \end{array}\right\}$ *els alumnes més robustos.*

'Among those who feel ill

there are $\left\{\begin{array}{l} \text{all} \\ \text{only} \\ \text{even} \\ \text{at least} \\ \text{in general} \\ \text{precisely} \end{array}\right\}$ the fittest students.'

The remaining items of (17) are all of the category Adv/P or Adv/PP. There is a substantial paradigm set of such items, whose semantic role is broadly that of limiting or qualifying the applicability or appropriateness of all or part of the phrase within their scope. (In case anyone supposes that these items are not self-evidently sisters of NP, I should point out that, for example, they occur equally well within a PP.) A sample is given in (18).

(18)  Adv/PP[Limit]:
      *àdhuc* 'even', *almenys* 'at least', *amb prou feines* 'hardly', *aparentment* 'apparently', *a penes* 'hardly', *ben bé* 'exactly', *del tot* 'quite', *encara* 'still', *en definitiva* 'definitely', *en*

*principi* 'in principle', *essencialment* 'essentially', *exactament* 'exactly', *fins (i tot)* 'even', *gairebé* 'almost', *just* 'precisely', *més aviat* 'rather', *ni* 'not even', *no* 'not', *només* 'only', *potser* 'perhaps', *probablement* 'probably', *pròpiament* 'strictly', *quasi* 'almost', *sens dubte* 'no doubt', *si fa no fa* 'more or less', *simplement* 'simply', *sinó* 'only', *sobretot* 'especially', *solament* 'only', *sols* 'only', *també* 'also', *tampoc* '(n)either', etc., and perhaps also time adverbials like *sempre* 'always', *sovint* 'often', *de vegades* 'sometimes', *mai* 'never'.

Nor are these elements restricted to positions before NPs — rather they are associated with phrases of all major categories, as can be seen in (19).

(19)  *ben bé iguals*
      'quite the same'
      *del tot net*  (DM)
      'fully clean'
      *sens dubte convincentment*
      'no doubt convincingly'
      *només probablement*
      'only probably'
      *just pel forat*
      'just through the hole'
      *gairebé al mig*
      'almost in the middle'
      *Simplement obeïm.*
      'We simply obey.'
      *Fins i tot ens insulta.*
      'He even insults us.'

In essentially an aside, Radford (1988:255) proposes that X" categories, as well as X' categories (as in Chomsky 1986), are recursive and may be modified with what he calls double-bar Attributes or double-bar Adjuncts. He illustrates this proposal with English *even* (an Adv/P[Limit] item in our terms), which can appear to the left or to the right of any double-bar category. Looking just at the left, specifier, position, for Catalan we would need to add the PS rule schema (20).

(20)  XP → Adv/PP[Limit] XP

My proposal is that, just as in (8), so, too, in (16a, e), *tot* is syntactically an adverb which acquires adjectival morphology by contamination with the truly adjectival use of the same element (for example, (16b)). We would have, then, a third pattern of 'misagreement' affecting a polyvalent lexical specifier. Apart from *tot*, the specifier expressions of (18), sisters of XP, are lexically distinct from the specifier words of (1), etc., which are sisters of X', a fact which is consistent with the structural and configurational difference between Adv/PP[Limit] and, for instance, Adv/PP[Q] that I am proposing.[7]

**8.** Of the items for which I am claiming Adjective status (1, 3d-f, 5), the great majority in Standard Catalan display the typical inflectional characteristics of adjectives — namely, number and gender agreement with NP heads/controllers. Those that do so include every one whose only, or rightmost, element is derived from a Latin inflected adjective. Also inflected are *gaire* (< Frankish *\*waigaro* 'with difficulty, hardly'), and *quin* (< Latin QUINAM, whose rightmost element was not a number/gender-bearing morpheme). The Adjectives which lack number inflection (or demonstrate 'underagreement') are those which derive from words of other categories in the source language: nouns or pronouns (*força, massa, que, cap*); adverbs (*menys, més, prou*); preposition (*cada*); and verb (*qualsevol*).[8] For an adjective in Catalan to lack number inflection is entirely anomalous, so it is not surprising that many varieties do indeed add plural marking (21a) to some of the items which lack it in the standard language.

(21)  a. *força : forces*
         *massa : masses*
         *prou : prous/proutes*
         *qualsevol : qualsevols*
      b. *bastant : bastanta*
         *prou : prouta*
         *gaire : gaira* (North-Western Catalan)
         *qualsevol : qualsevola* (Ibiza, Minorca).

Of the remainder of the Adjectives which lack number agreement in all dialects, *cap* and *cada* are inherently [–Plural];[9] *menys* and *més* already end in -*s* and thus, at least, are not in conflict with the plural 'schema' or word shape (Bybee & Slobin 1982); *que* is, perhaps, more potentially pluraliz-able, but differs from the remainder in being unstressed.

The polyvalent items lacking gender marking as Adjectives in Standard Catalan are again generally those which lacked it in the source language (*bastant, gaire, igual, tal, qual*). It is less anomalous for a Catalan adjec-tive to lack gender marking; there are many qualifier adjectives which do so. No polyvalent Adjective whose stem ends in -*a*, the typical feminine gender marker, (i.e., *cada, força, massa*), has developed a contrasted 'masculine' in -ø or -*e*. The attested innovative (non-standard) feminine forms are those in (21b). What the more recent inflectional adaptations of (21) suggest is that the core of the polyvalent set probably consists of those items — *molt, poc, quant*, and *tant* — which have been adverbs, pronouns, and inflected adjectives since Classical Latin times (see note 1). To these have gradually been assimilated, syntactically and morphologically, other words which were in the same semantic field and occurred in one or other of the syntactic contexts which *molt, poc, quant*, and *tant* occurred in. Possibly the trend is continuing and apparently recent, marginal, additions like *igual* may in due course become more fully integrated.

**9. Conclusion.** In dealing with sets of items like those in (1), conven-tional lexical accounts would, I think, have to take one of two lines: either that each A-Adv-N triplet consisted of three homonymous items which happened to share the same semantic representation; or that one of each triplet was categorially basic and that the others were derived from it by a process of conversion (or zero-derivation). In the latter case there would be five possible derivational analyses for each member of the triplet, as in (22), illustrating *molt*$_N$.

(22) *molt*$_N$:  [[*molt*]$_A$]$_N$;
  [[[*molt*]$_A$]$_{Adv}$]$_N$;
  [[*molt*]$_{Adv}$]$_N$;
  [[[*molt*]$_{Adv}$]$_A$]$_N$;
  [*molt*]$_N$.

Such a situation demands an implausible degree of ingenuity or insight, whether from the learner or from the linguist, in order to select one analysis as being synchronically well-founded in each case. I believe there is a third solution available to the question of the categorial status in the lexi-con of polyvalent items, which is to represent them as 'underspecified'

with respect to whichever features are not required so as to constrain their
presence in well-formed trees. Equivalently, one might take these items as
representative of 'archicategories' in contexts of categorial neutralization.
Making use of the standard category features [±N, ±V], then, the lexical
feature assignments of the polyvalent items would be as in (23), assuming
that none of the category gaps in (1) were semantically derivable.

> (23)   N + A   (e.g., *altre*):   [+N]
> N + Adv   (e.g., *quelcom*):   [−V]
> A + Adv/P   (e.g., *força*):   [$\alpha$N, $\alpha$V]
> N + A + Adv/P   (e.g., *molt*):   unspecified for [N] or [V]

Of these feature specifications (23), that of A + AdvP with Greek-letter
variables is unwelcome, and suggests that the association between Adjectives and Adverb/Prepositions needs to be expressed differently — by, for
example, a unary feature [A]. (We may not wish to force an unwanted
connection between nouns and verbs by incorporating a binary feature,
thereby permitting a [−A] classification.) Underspecified elements could
thus appear in any syntactic context their specified features did not exclude
and would inherit the feature specifications of the PS trees they were present in. Apparently the feature specifications of (23) would not prevent
most of the polyvalent items from surfacing as verbs. My provisional suggestion is that they do not do so because to be actualized as a verb a lexical
item requires a conjugation-class marker, which none of the polyvalent
items has. In Catalan, at any rate, whereas certain nouns and adjectives
may lack gender and/or number inflection, no verb can lack inflection.

The principle of categorial underspecification in the lexicon is not in
fact widely exploited by Catalan, nor, I suspect, by agglutinating or inflecting languages in general. But it may well be a particularly useful approach
for languages like English, in which a considerable proportion of the vo-
cabulary can serve underived in more than one category. In an inflecting
language, we may, perhaps, expect polyvalent items to display occasional
inflectional anomalies such as 'misagreement' or underagreement by contamination, particularly in those syntactic contexts where slightly different
configurations correspond to the same or similar functional roles, as is the
case with specifier phrases of N, A, and Adv/P head categories in Romance.

# Notes

*   I am very grateful to Joan Solà, Joan Veny, and Jordi Ginebra for their comments and suggestions in relation to an earlier version of this paper, and to Nigel Vincent, Adrian Battye, the participants in the Falmer Language Group seminar, and anonymous reviewers for all theirs in relation to a later one.

1.  The list in (1) contains items from standard Catalan. Some additional forms are included in Wheeler (1991). Latin and other Romance languages have comparable sets of polyvalent items, of which the following are some provisional lists, which could be expanded with synonyms in some cases.

    LATIN
    *aliquantus, -um, -o* 'some(what)'; *aliqui, aliquid* 'some'; *multus, -um, -o* 'much'; *nimius, -um* 'too (much)'; *paulus, -um, -o* 'little'; *plurimus, -um* 'very much'; *plus* 'more'; *satis* 'enough'; *quantus, -um, -o* 'how great'; *tantus, -um, -o* 'so great'

    SPANISH
    *algo* 'something, somewhat', *bastante* 'enough', *cuan(to)* 'how much', *demasiado* 'too (much)', *igual* 'same', *más* 'more', *medio* 'half', *menos* 'less', *mucho* 'much', *nada* 'no(thing)', *poco* 'little', *qué* 'what, how', *sólo* 'only', *tal* 'such', *tan(to)* 'so much', *todo* 'all, everything'

    OCCITAN
    *(ai)tant* 'so much', *assatz* 'quite, enough', *fòrça* 'a lot', *gaire* '(not) much', *gandré* 'a lot', *ge(n)s* 'no(thing)', *mai* 'more', *mens* 'less', *mièg* 'half', *pauc* 'little', *plan* 'much', *p(l)us* 'more', *pro* 'enough', *quant* 'how much', *que-non-sai* 'ever so (much)', *ren* 'nothing', *tal* 'such', *tot* 'all, everything', *tròp* 'too (much)'

    FRENCH
    (The adjectival role of the following items, where it can be justified at all, is somewhat marginal.)
    *assez* 'enough', *autant* 'so much', *beaucoup* 'much', *bien* 'much', *combien* 'how much', *davantage* 'more', *demi* 'half', *guère* '(not) much', *moins* 'less', *?moitié* 'half', *pas mal* 'quite a lot', *peu* 'little', *plein* 'a lot', *plus* 'more', *que* 'how', *tant* 'so much', *tout* 'all, everything', *trop* 'too (much)'

    ITALIAN
    *abbastanza* 'enough', *alquanto* 'some(what)', *altrettanto* 'as much again', *altro* 'other', *assai* 'a lot', *che* 'how', *meno* 'less', *mezzo* 'half', *molto* 'much', *parecchio* 'quite a lot', *più* 'more', *niente* 'no(thing)', *po(co)* 'little', *quanto* 'how much', *tanto* 'so much', *troppo* 'too (much)', *tutto* 'all, everything'

2.  Other Romance languages share this phenomenon. In Occitan, for example, *Es tota malauta* 'She is quite ill', *A lis aurelhas totis espelhadas* 'His ears are all scratched' (Ronjat 1930-1941:§528); in French, *Elle est toute pâle* 'She is quite pale', *Toutes raisonnables qu'elles sont* 'Wholly reasonable as they are'. (Grevisse 1964:§385 adduces as parallel *soupe bonne chaude, fenêtre grande ouverte*. Up to about 1660, *tout* before an adjective displayed both number and gender agreement (Togeby 1982-1985:§321). The modern French prescriptive rule has agreement before feminine consonant-initial adjectives only, but Wartburg & Zumthor (1958:§744) cite *vérité toute individuelle* from Proust.) In Italian we have *i tutti personali malanni* 'the quite personal misfortunes', *con le mani tutte screpolate* 'with his hands all chapped' (Macchi 1981; Brunet 1981). The phenomenon is absent from Spanish, where *todo* is not used as an Adv/P[Q].

3. The phenomenon is subject to different lexical restrictions in other Romance languages. For example, in Occitan, adverbial *mièg* 'half' is inflected (i); likewise, Italian *mezzo* (ii) (Brunet 1981:102). In Spanish, where the comparable construction with
   *todo* 'all' is not found, adverbial *cuanto* 'how much', *demasiado* 'too' and *mucho*
   'much' show adjectival inflection in certain contexts (Butt & Benjamin 1988:62, 63,
   85) (iii). In Spanish and Italian, pseudo-partitive *un poco* may, popularly, display
   gender agreement with a feminine head (iv) (Butt & Benjamin 1988:88; Real
   Academia Española 1973:224; Brunet 1981:188).

   (i)     *mièg is nuds* 'half naked'; *mièja fòla* 'half mad'
   (ii)    *mezza pazza* 'half mad'
   (iii)   a. *Más acentuado será el sabor del ajo cuanta mayor cantidad lleve.*
              'The greater the quantity of garlic it contains the stronger the flavour
              will be.'
           b. *Has traído demasiados pocos tornillos.*
              'you have brought too few screws'
           c. *Hay mucha mayor cantidad.*
              'There is a much bigger quantity.'
           But note:
           d. *La diferencia era mucho mayor.*
              'The difference was much greater.'
   (iv)    Spanish    *una poca de agua*
                      'a little water'
           Italian    *quella po' di luce*
                      'that small amount of light'.

4. Other non-personal pronouns (demonstrative or 'indefinite') are *això* 'this'; *algú*
   'someone'; *allò* 'that'; *alre* 'something else' (Majorca); *altri* 'someone else'; *cadascú*
   or *cada u* 'each', 'everyone'; *hom* 'one'; *ningú* 'no-one'; *qui* 'who'; *què* 'what'; *res* or
   *re* 'nothing'; *tothom* 'everyone'.

5. Perhaps *força* (N) is avoided because of the homonym *força* 'force', normally a mass
   noun; *massa* (N) 'too much' is acceptable because *massa* 'mass' is a count noun; *el
   mig* is 'middle' and the noun coresponding to 'half' is *meitat*.

6. Occitan examples (Alibert 1935; Ronjat 1930-1941; Mistral 1878-1886):
   [N *de* N']
   *mai de burre* 'more butter'
   *quant de fes* 'how many times'
   *pauc de pèças* 'few rooms'
   *tant de viures* 'so many groceries'
   *plan de pèiras* 'many stones'
   *tròp de carn* 'too much meat'
   *pro de mans* 'enough hands'
   [A N']
   *mai pena* 'more suffering'
   *quantis còps* 'how many times'
   *paucas gents* 'few people'
   *tantas gents* 'so many people'
   *plan pèiras/planas pèiras* 'a lot of stones'
   *tròpa paurieira* 'too much poverty'
   *pro tèrras/prossas tèrras* 'enough land'

[A *de* N']

*maisses de libres* 'more books'
*quantas de causas* 'how many things'
*pauquis de mestiers* 'few occupations'
*tantas de richessas* 'so much wealth'
*planas de gents* 'many people'
*tròpis d' ans* 'too many years'
*prossa d' aiga* 'enough water'

7. Note the contrast between *ben bé* Adv/P[Limit], *ben* Adv/P[Q], and *bé* Adv/P[Manner] 'well/quite'.

Although in Catalan *tot* is the only Adv/P[Limit] element affected by misagreement, there is a comparable phenomenon with *seul* 'only' in French (and with *sol* in Occitan). In French, it seems that *seul*$_{Adv/P}$ is used only for the limiting of subject phrases, *seulement* or *que* being used in other contexts:

(i)  *Seul le résultat compte.*
     'Only the result counts.'
(ii)  *Seuls les parents sont admis.*
     'Only parents are admitted.'
(iii)  *Seule l' imprudence peut être la cause de cet accident.*
     'Carelessness alone can be the cause of this accident.'
(iv)  Occ.  *Sola l' analisa sincronica es adeqüata.* (R. Teulat)
     'Only a synchronic analysis is adequate.'
(v)  *Ce n' est pas seulement sa maladie qui le déprime.*
     *\*Ce n' est pas seule sa maladie qui le déprime.*
     'It is not only his illness which makes him depressed.'
(vi)  *On ne leur permet de lire que le soir.*
     *\*On leur permet de lire seul le soir.*
     'They are allowed to read only in the evening.'

It may be relevant to point out that, in German, when *all* 'all' appears outside the determiner in a NP — that is, as an Adv/P — it is not inflected for gender or case: *wo kommt all das Wasser her?* 'what's all that water?'; *trotz all seines Reichtums* 'despite all his wealth'.

8. Plural *qualssevol* differs from singular *qualsevol* in orthography only.
9. The only 'plural' nouns before which *cap* is found seem to be *pluralia tantum*. Ruaix (1986:52) gives these examples:

(i)  *No tinc cap ganes de fer-ho.*
     'I am not at all keen to do it.' (*ganes* 'wish'; *gana* 'hunger')
(ii)  *Que tens cap estisores per deixar-me?*
     'Have you got any scissors to lend me?'

# References

Alibert, Loïs. 1935. *Gramatica occitana segón los parlars lengadocians.* Tolosa [Toulouse]: Societat d'Estudis Occitans.

Badía Margarit, Antonio M. 1962. *Gramática catalana.* 2 vols. Madrid: Gredos.

Battye, Adrian C. This volume. Aspects of quantification in French in its regional and diachronic varieties. 1-35.

Bonet, Sebastià & Joan Solà. 1986. *Sintaxi generativa catalana*. Barcelona: Enciclopèdia Catalana.

Brunet, Jacqueline. 1981. *Grammaire critique de l'italien*, Vol. 4. Paris: Université de Paris VIII-Vincennes.

Butt, John & Carmen Benjamin. 1988. *A New Reference Grammar of Spanish*. London: Arnold.

Bybee, Joan L. & Dan I. Slobin. 1982. Rules and schemas in the development and use of the English past tense. *Language* 58, 265-289.

Chomsky, Noam. 1970. Remarks on Nominalization. *Readings in English Transformational Grammar*, ed. R. Jacobs & P. Rosenbaum, 184-221. Waltham, Mass: Ginn.

————. 1986. *Barriers*. Cambridge, Mass.: MIT Press.

DCVB = A M Alcover & F de B Moll, *Diccionari Català-Valencià-Balear*. Palma de Mallorca: Moll, 1932-1960.

DE = *Diccionari de la Llengua Catalana*. Barcelona: Enciclopèdia Catalana, 1982.

DM = Pompeu Fabra, *Diccionari Manual de la Llengua Catalana*. Barcelona: EDHASA, 1983.

Emonds, Joseph. 1985. *A Unified Theory of Syntactic Categories*. Dordrecht: Foris.

Fabra, Pompeu. 1956. *Gramàtica catalana*. Barcelona: Teide.

Gazdar, Gerald, Ewan Klein, Geoffrey Pullum & Ivan Sag. 1985. *Generalized Phrase Structure Grammar*. Oxford: Blackwell.

Grevisse, Maurice. 1964. *Le Bon Usage*. 8ème édition. Gembloux: Duculot.

Jackendoff, Ray. 1977. *X-bar Syntax: A Study of Phrase Structure*. Cambridge, Mass.: MIT Press.

Jaeggli, Osvaldo. 1982. *Topics in Romance Syntax*. Dordrecht: Foris.

————. 1986. Three issues in the theory of clitics: Case, doubled NPs and extraction. *Syntax and Semantics 19. The Syntax of Pronominal Clitics*, ed. Hagit Borer, 15-42. Orlando: Academic Press.

Macchi, Vladimiro (ed.) 1981. *Sansoni Dictionary English-Italian Italian-English*. 2nd edition. Firenze: Sansoni.

McCawley, James D. 1988. *The Syntactic Phenomena of English*. 2 vols. Chicago: Chicago University Press.

Mistral, Frédéric. 1878-1886. *Lou Tresor dóu Felibrige, ou dictionnaire provençal-français*. Aix-en-Provence: Veuve-Remondet Aubin, etc.

Radford, Andrew. 1988. *Transformational Grammar. a first course*. Cambridge: Cambridge University Press.

Real Academia Española. 1973. *Esbozo de una nueva gramática de la lengua española*. Madrid: Espasa-Calpe.

Ronjat, Jules. 1930-1941. *Grammaire istorique des parlers provençaux modernes*. 4 vols. Montpellier: Société des Langues Romanes.

Ruaix i Vinyet, Josep. 1986. *El català/2. Morfologia i sintaxi*. 2nd edition. Moià: Ruaix.

Selkirk, Elisabeth O. 1977. Some remarks on Noun Phrase structure. *Formal Syntax*, ed. P. W. Culicover, T. Wasow & A. Akmajian, 285-316. New York: Academic Press.

Togeby, Knud. 1982-1985. *Grammaire française*. 5 vols. København: Akademisk Vorlag.

Wartburg, Walter von & Paul Zumthor. 1958. *Précis de syntaxe du français contemporain*. Berne: Francke.

Wheeler, Max W. 1991. Dels quantitatius i altres elements especificadors. *Els Marges* 43, 25-49.

# Index

A'-binding 18-19, 21-22
A'-position 19, 21
A-position 18, 19, 20, 23, 211
a-reduction 121, 122, 124, 126
Abney, S. P. 1, 29, 59, 60, 61
abstract Case 18, 21
accusative *a* 37ff
accusative Case 44-48, 71, 73, 78-79, 82,
    84-85, 109-110
accusative clitic 47, 52, 62, 65, 71
actualization 161, 174
adjectives 23, 124, 201ff
adjunct agent phrases 82
adjuncts 74
adnominal complement 10, 12
adverb-to-noun reanalysis 32
Affectedness Constraint 83
agent 84
agent, backgrounding of 87, 89, 90, 91,
    109, 112
agent demotion 91
agent, implicit 77, 79, 83, 97
agent θ-role 90, 92, 95
agent semantic role 108, 109, 110
agentive argument 84
Agnone 122, 123, 130
agreement 3, 5, 25, 60, 82, 150, 156,
    161ff, 206-207, 210, 215, 218, 222,
    225-226
agreement of the past participle 61-62,
    64, 65-68, 71-72, 74, 161ff
Alibert, L. 226
Aly-Belfadel, A. 154
ambiguity of government 16-17
anaphor 77
Anderson, J. M. 181, 182

aperture 184
apocope 118
arbitrary reference 99ff
archicategories 224
argument position, see A-position
Arquint, J. C. 163, 172
articulatory aperture 185, 187
articulatory component 184, 198
Ashby, W. 155
aspect 79, 156, see also name of aspect
aspect constraint 85-89, 91, 94-95, 99-
    100, 103
aspectual verbs 138, 140
Aspland, B. 24,-26
assimilation 117, 120, 196-197
atonic vowels 116
attributive adjectives 23
Autesserre, D. 184, 196
autosegmental phonology 174
Auvergnat 162
auxiliary 53
auxiliary selection 62, 68-69, 71-72, 74
Ayres-Bennett, W. 155
backgrounding 87, 89-91, 109, 112
Badía Margarit, A. M. 142, 144, 162,
    203, 212-214, 217
Badiot 172
Baker, M. C. 96
barriers 16, 17
Battye, A. C. 9, 10, 31-32, 149, 150-151,
    156, 215
Belletti, A. 30, 79, 81-82
benefactive 46
Benincà, P. 169
Benjamin, C. 226
Benucci, F. 154

In the CURRENT ISSUES IN LINGUISTIC THEORY (CILT) series (edited by: E.F. Konrad Koerner, University of Ottawa) the following volumes have been published thus far or are scheduled to appear in the course of 1995:

1.  KOERNER, Konrad (ed.): *The Transformational-Generative Paradigm and Modern Linguistic Theory.* 1975.
2.  WEIDERT, Alfons: *Componential Analysis of Lushai Phonology.* 1975.
3.  MAHER, J. Peter: *Papers on Language Theory and History I: Creation and Tradition in Language. Foreword by Raimo Anttila.* 1979.
4.  HOPPER, Paul J. (ed.): *Studies in Descriptive and Historical Linguistics. Festschrift for Winfred P. Lehmann.* 1977.
5.  ITKONEN, Esa: *Grammatical Theory and Metascience: A critical investigation into the methodological and philosophical foundations of 'autonomous' linguistics.* 1978.
6.  ANTTILA, Raimo: *Historical and Comparative Linguistics.* 1989.
7.  MEISEL, Jürgen M. & Martin D. PAM (eds): *Linear Order and Generative Theory.* 1979.
8.  WILBUR, Terence H.: *Prolegomena to a Grammar of Basque.* 1979.
9.  HOLLIEN, Harry & Patricia (eds): *Current Issues in the Phonetic Sciences. Proceedings of the IPS-77 Congress, Miami Beach, Florida, 17-19 December 1977.* 1979.
10. PRIDEAUX, Gary D. (ed.): *Perspectives in Experimental Linguistics. Papers from the University of Alberta Conference on Experimental Linguistics, Edmonton, 13-14 Oct. 1978.* 1979.
11. BROGYANYI, Bela (ed.): *Studies in Diachronic, Synchronic, and Typological Linguistics: Festschrift for Oswald Szemérenyi on the Occasion of his 65th Birthday.* 1979.
12. FISIAK, Jacek (ed.): *Theoretical Issues in Contrastive Linguistics.* 1981.     Out of print
13. MAHER, J. Peter, Allan R. BOMHARD & Konrad KOERNER (eds): *Papers from the Third International Conference on Historical Linguistics, Hamburg, August 22-26 1977.* 1982.
14. TRAUGOTT, Elizabeth C., Rebecca LaBRUM & Susan SHEPHERD (eds): *Papers from the Fourth International Conference on Historical Linguistics, Stanford, March 26-30 1979.* 1980.
15. ANDERSON, John (ed.): *Language Form and Linguistic Variation. Papers dedicated to Angus McIntosh.* 1982.
16. ARBEITMAN, Yoël L. & Allan R. BOMHARD (eds): *Bono Homini Donum: Essays in Historical Linguistics, in Memory of J.Alexander Kerns.* 1981.
17. LIEB, Hans-Heinrich: *Integrational Linguistics. 6 volumes. Vol. II-VI n.y.p.* 1984/93.
18. IZZO, Herbert J. (ed.): *Italic and Romance. Linguistic Studies in Honor of Ernst Pulgram.* 1980.
19. RAMAT, Paolo et al. (eds): *Linguistic Reconstruction and Indo-European Syntax. Proceedings of the Colloquium of the 'Indogermanischhe Gesellschaft'. University of Pavia, 6-7 September 1979.* 1980.
20. NORRICK, Neal R.: *Semiotic Principles in Semantic Theory.* 1981.
21. AHLQVIST, Anders (ed.): *Papers from the Fifth International Conference on Historical Linguistics, Galway, April 6-10 1981.* 1982.
22. UNTERMANN, Jürgen & Bela BROGYANYI (eds): *Das Germanische und die Rekonstruktion der Indogermanischen Grundsprache. Akten des Freiburger Kolloquiums der Indogermanischen Gesellschaft, Freiburg, 26-27 Februar 1981.* 1984.
23. DANIELSEN, Niels: *Papers in Theoretical Linguistics. Edited by Per Baerentzen.* 1992.
24. LEHMANN, Winfred P. & Yakov MALKIEL (eds): *Perspectives on Historical Linguistics. Papers from a conference held at the meeting of the Language Theory Division, Modern Language Assn., San Francisco, 27-30 December 1979.* 1982.
25. ANDERSEN, Paul Kent: *Word Order Typology and Comparative Constructions.* 1983.

26. BALDI, Philip (ed.): *Papers from the XIIth Linguistic Symposium on Romance Languages, Univ. Park, April 1-3, 1982.* 1984.

27. BOMHARD, Alan R.: *Toward Proto-Nostratic. A New Approach to the Comparison of Proto-Indo-European and Proto-Afroasiatic. Foreword by Paul J. Hopper.* 1984.

28. BYNON, James (ed.): *Current Progress in Afro-Asiatic Linguistics: Papers of the Third International Hamito-Semitic Congress, London, 1978.* 1984.

29. PAPROTTÉ, Wolf & René DIRVEN (eds): *The Ubiquity of Metaphor: Metaphor in language and thought.* 1985 (publ. 1986).

30. HALL, Robert A. Jr.: *Proto-Romance Morphology. = Comparative Romance Grammar, vol. III.* 1984.

31. GUILLAUME, Gustave: *Foundations for a Science of Language.*

32. COPELAND, James E. (ed.): *New Directions in Linguistics and Semiotics.* Co-edition with Rice University Press who hold exclusive rights for US and Canada. 1984.

33. VERSTEEGH, Kees: *Pidginization and Creolization. The Case of Arabic.* 1984.

34. FISIAK, Jacek (ed.): *Papers from the VIth International Conference on Historical Linguistics, Poznan, 22-26 August. 1983.* 1985.

35. COLLINGE, N.E.: *The Laws of Indo-European.* 1985.

36. KING, Larry D. & Catherine A. MALEY (eds): *Selected papers from the XIIIth Linguistic Symposium on Romance Languages, Chapel Hill, N.C., 24-26 March 1983.* 1985.

37. GRIFFEN, T.D.: *Aspects of Dynamic Phonology.* 1985.

38. BROGYANYI, Bela & Thomas KRÖMMELBEIN (eds): *Germanic Dialects:Linguistic and Philological Investigations.* 1986.

39. BENSON, James D., Michael J. CUMMINGS, & William S. GREAVES (eds): *Linguistics in a Systemic Perspective.* 1988.

40. FRIES, Peter Howard (ed.) in collaboration with Nancy M. Fries: *Toward an Understanding of Language: Charles C. Fries in Perspective.* 1985.

41. EATON, Roger, et al. (eds): *Papers from the 4th International Conference on English Historical Linguistics, April 10-13, 1985.* 1985.

42. MAKKAI, Adam & Alan K. MELBY (eds): *Linguistics and Philosophy. Festschrift for Rulon S. Wells.* 1985 (publ. 1986).

43. AKAMATSU, Tsutomu: *The Theory of Neutralization and the Archiphoneme in Functional Phonology.* 1988.

44. JUNGRAITHMAYR, Herrmann & Walter W. MUELLER (eds): *Proceedings of the Fourth International Hamito-Semitic Congress.* 1987.

45. KOOPMAN, W.F., F.C. Van der LEEK , O. FISCHER & R. EATON (eds): *Explanation and Linguistic Change.* 1986

46. PRIDEAUX, Gary D. & William J. BAKER: *Strategies and Structures: The processing of relative clauses.* 1987.

47. LEHMANN, Winfred P. (ed.): *Language Typology 1985. Papers from the Linguistic Typology Symposium, Moscow, 9-13 Dec. 1985.* 1986.

48. RAMAT, Anna G., Onofrio CARRUBA and Giuliano BERNINI (eds): *Papers from the 7th International Conference on Historical Linguistics.* 1987.

49. WAUGH, Linda R. and Stephen RUDY (eds): *New Vistas in Grammar: Invariance and Variation. Proceedings of the Second International Roman Jakobson Conference, New York University, Nov.5-8, 1985.* 1991.

50. RUDZKA-OSTYN, Brygida (ed.): *Topics in Cognitive Linguistics.* 1988.

51. CHATTERJEE, Ranjit: *Aspect and Meaning in Slavic and Indic. With a foreword by Paul Friedrich.* 1989.

52. FASOLD, Ralph W. & Deborah SCHIFFRIN (eds): *Language Change and Variation.* 1989.

53. SANKOFF, David: *Diversity and Diachrony.* 1986.

54. WEIDERT, Alfons: *Tibeto-Burman Tonology. A comparative analysis.* 1987
55. HALL, Robert A. Jr.: *Linguistics and Pseudo-Linguistics.* 1987.
56. HOCKETT, Charles F.: *Refurbishing our Foundations. Elementary linguistics from an advanced point of view.* 1987.
57. BUBENIK, Vít: *Hellenistic and Roman Greece as a Sociolinguistic Area.* 1989.
58. ARBEITMAN, Yoël. L. (ed.): *Fucus: A Semitic/Afrasian Gathering in Remembrance of Albert Ehrman.* 1988.
59. VAN VOORST, Jan: *Event Structure.* 1988.
60. KIRSCHNER, Carl & Janet DECESARIS (eds): *Studies in Romance Linguistics. Selected Proceedings from the XVII Linguistic Symposium on Romance Languages.* 1989.
61. CORRIGAN, Roberta L., Fred ECKMAN & Michael NOONAN (eds): *Linguistic Categorization. Proceedings of an International Symposium in Milwaukee, Wisconsin, April 10-11, 1987.* 1989.
62. FRAJZYNGIER, Zygmunt (ed.): *Current Progress in Chadic Linguistics. Proceedings of the International Symposium on Chadic Linguistics, Boulder, Colorado, 1-2 May 1987.* 1989.
63. EID, Mushira (ed.): *Perspectives on Arabic Linguistics I. Papers from the First Annual Symposium on Arabic Linguistics.* 1990.
64. BROGYANYI, Bela (ed.): *Prehistory, History and Historiography of Language, Speech, and Linguistic Theory. Papers in honor of Oswald Szemérenyi I.* 1992.
65. ADAMSON, Sylvia, Vivien A. LAW, Nigel VINCENT and Susan WRIGHT (eds): *Papers from the 5th International Conference on English Historical Linguistics.* 1990.
66. ANDERSEN, Henning and Konrad KOERNER (eds): *Historical Linguistics 1987.Papers from the 8th International Conference on Historical Linguistics,Lille, August 30-Sept., 1987.* 1990.
67. LEHMANN, Winfred P. (ed.): *Language Typology 1987. Systematic Balance in Language. Papers from the Linguistic Typology Symposium, Berkeley, 1-3 Dec 1987.* 1990.
68. BALL, Martin, James FIFE, Erich POPPE &Jenny ROWLAND (eds): *Celtic Linguistics/ Ieithyddiaeth Geltaidd. Readings in the Brythonic Languages. Festschrift for T. Arwyn Watkins.* 1990.
69. WANNER, Dieter and Douglas A. KIBBEE (eds): *New Analyses in Romance Linguistics. Selected papers from the Linguistic Symposium on Romance Languages XVIIII, Urbana-Champaign, April 7-9, 1988.* 1991.
70. JENSEN, John T.: *Morphology. Word structure in generative grammar.* 1990.
71. O'GRADY, William: *Categories and Case. The sentence structure of Korean.* 1991.
72. EID, Mushira and John MCCARTHY (eds): *Perspectives on Arabic Linguistics II. Papers from the Second Annual Symposium on Arabic Linguistics.* 1990.
73. STAMENOV, Maxim (ed.): *Current Advances in Semantic Theory.* 1991.
74. LAEUFER, Christiane and Terrell A. MORGAN (eds): *Theoretical Analyses in Romance Linguistics.* 1991.
75. DROSTE, Flip G. and John E. JOSEPH (eds): *Linguistic Theory and Grammatical Description. Nine Current Approaches.* 1991.
76. WICKENS, Mark A.: *Grammatical Number in English Nouns. An empirical and theoretical account.* 1992.
77. BOLTZ, William G. and Michael C. SHAPIRO (eds): *Studies in the Historical Phonology of Asian Languages.* 1991.
78. KAC, Michael: *Grammars and Grammaticality.* 1992.
79. ANTONSEN, Elmer H. and Hans Henrich HOCK (eds): *STAEF-CRAEFT: Studies in Germanic Linguistics. Select papers from the First and Second Symposium on Germanic Linguistics, University of Chicago, 24 April 1985, and Univ. of Illinois at Urbana-Champaign, 3-4 Oct. 1986.* 1991.

80. COMRIE, Bernard and Mushira EID (eds): *Perspectives on Arabic Linguistics III. Papers from the Third Annual Symposium on Arabic Linguistics.* 1991.

81. LEHMANN, Winfred P. and H.J. HEWITT (eds): *Language Typology 1988. Typological Models in the Service of Reconstruction.* 1991.

82. VAN VALIN, Robert D. (ed.): *Advances in Role and Reference Grammar.* 1992.

83. FIFE, James and Erich POPPE (eds): *Studies in Brythonic Word Order.* 1991.

84. DAVIS, Garry W. and Gregory K. IVERSON (eds): *Explanation in Historical Linguistics.* 1992.

85. BROSELOW, Ellen, Mushira EID and John McCARTHY (eds): *Perspectives on Arabic Linguistics IV. Papers from the Annual Symposium on Arabic Linguistics.* 1992.

86. KESS, Joseph F.: *Psycholinguistics. Psychology, linguistics, and the study of natural language.* 1992.

87. BROGYANYI, Bela and Reiner LIPP (eds): *Historical Philology: Greek, Latin, and Romance. Papers in honor of Oswald Szemerényi II.* 1992.

88. SHIELDS, Kenneth: *A History of Indo-European Verb Morphology.* 1992.

89. BURRIDGE, Kate: *Syntactic Change in Germanic. A study of some aspects of language change in Germanic with particular reference to Middle Dutch.* 1992.

90. KING, Larry D.: *The Semantic Structure of Spanish. Meaning and grammatical form.* 1992.

91. HIRSCHBÜHLER, Paul and Konrad KOERNER (eds): *Romance Languages and Modern Linguistic Theory. Selected papers from the XX Linguistic Symposium on Romance Languages, University of Ottawa, April 10-14, 1990.* 1992.

92. POYATOS, Fernando: *Paralanguage: A linguistic and interdisciplinary approach to interactive speech and sounds.* 1992.

93. LIPPI-GREEN, Rosina (ed.): *Recent Developments in Germanic Linguistics.* 1992.

94. HAGÈGE, Claude: *The Language Builder. An essay on the human signature in linguistic morphogenesis.* 1992.

95. MILLER, D. Gary: *Complex Verb Formation.* 1992.

96. LIEB, Hans-Heinrich (ed.): *Prospects for a New Structuralism.* 1992.

97. BROGYANYI, Bela & Reiner LIPP (eds): *Comparative-Historical Linguistics: Indo-European and Finno-Ugric. Papers in honor of Oswald Szemerényi III.* 1992.

98. EID, Mushira & Gregory K. IVERSON: *Principles and Prediction: The analysis of natural language.* 1993.

99. JENSEN, John T.: *English Phonology.* 1993.

100. MUFWENE, Salikoko S. and Lioba MOSHI (eds): *Topics in African Linguistics. Papers from the XXI Annual Conference on African Linguistics, University of Georgia, April 1990.* 1993.

101. EID, Mushira & Clive HOLES (eds): *Perspectives on Arabic Linguistics V. Papers from the Fifth Annual Symposium on Arabic Linguistics.* 1993.

102. GARGOV, Georg and Petko STAYNOV (eds) : *Explorations in Language and Cognition. Selcted Papers from the workshop : The notion of cognitive in linguistics, September 1989.* n.y.p.

103. ASHBY, William J., Marianne MITHUN, Giorgio PERISSINOTTO and Eduardo RAPOSO: *Linguistic Perspectives on Romance Languages. Selected papers from the XXI Linguistic Symposium on Romance Languages, Santa Barbara, February 21-24, 1991.* 1993.

104. KURZOVÁ, Helena: *From Indo-European to Latin. The evolution of a morphosyntactic type.* 1993.

105. HUALDE, José Ignacio and Jon ORTIZ DE URBANA (eds): *Generative Studies in Basque Linguistics.* 1993.

106. AERTSEN, Henk and Robert J. JEFFERS (eds): *Historical Linguistics 1989. Papers from the 9th International Conference on Historical Linguistics, New Brunswick, 14-18 August 1989.* 1993.

107. MARLE, Jaap van (ed.): *Historical Linguistics 1991. Papers from the 10th International Conference on Historical Linguistics, Amsterdam, August 12-16, 1991.* 1993.
108. LIEB, Hans-Heinrich: *Linguistic Variables. Towards a unified theory of linguistic variation.* 1993.
109. PAGLIUCA, William (ed.): *Perspectives on Grammaticalization.* 1994.
110. SIMONE, Raffaele (ed.): *Iconicity in Language.* 1995.
111. TOBIN, Yishai: *Invariance, Markedness and Distinctive Feature Analysis. A contrastive study of sign systems in English and Hebrew.* 1994.
112. CULIOLI, Antoine: *Cognition and Representation in Linguistic Theory. Translated, edited and introduced by Michel Liddle.* n.y.p.
113. FERNÁNDEZ, Francisco, Miguel FUSTER and Juan Jose CALVO (eds): *English Historical Linguistics 1992. Papers from the 7th International Conference on English Historical Linguistics, Valencia, 22-26 September 1992.* 1994.
114. EGLI, U., P. PAUSE, Chr. SCHWARZE, A. von STECHOW, G. WIENOLD (eds): *Lexical Knowledge in the Organisation of Language.* 1995.
115. EID, Mushira, Vincente CANTARINO and Keith WALTERS (eds): *Perspectives on Arabic Linguistics. Vol. VI. Papers from the Sixth Annual Symposium on Arabic Linguistics.* 1994.
116. MILLER, D. Gary: *Ancient Scripts and Phonological Knowledge.* 1994.
117. PHILIPPAKI-WARBURTON, I., K. NICOLAIDIS and M. SIFIANOU (eds): *Themes in Greek Linguistics. Papers from the first International Conference on Greek Linguistics, Reading, September 1993.* 1994.
118. HASAN, Ruqaiya and Peter H. FRIES (eds): *On Subject and Theme. A discourse functional perspective.* 1995.
119. LIPPI-GREEN, Rosina: *Language Ideology and Language Change in Early Modern German. A sociolinguistic study of the consonantal system of Nuremberg.* 1994.
120. STONHAM, John T.: *Combinatorial Morphology.* 1994.
121. HASAN, Ruqaiya, Carmel CLORAN and David BUTT (eds): *Functional Descriptions. Transitivity and the construction of experience.* 1995.
122. SMITH, John Charles and Martin MAIDEN (eds): *Linguistic Theory and the Romance Languages.* 1995.
123. AMASTAE, Jon, Grant GOODALL, Mario MONTALBETTI and Marianne PHINNEY: *Contemporary Research in Romance Linguistics. Papers from the XXII Linguistic Symposium on Romance Languages, El Paso//Juárez, February 22-24, 1994.* 1995.
124. ANDERSEN, Henning: *Historical Linguistics 1993. Selected papers from the 11th International Conference on Historical Linguistics, Los Angeles, 16-20 August 1993.* 1995.
125. SINGH, Rajendra (ed.): *Towards a Critical Sociolinguistics.* n.y.p.
126. MATRAS, Yaron (ed.): *Romani in Contact. The history, structure and sociology of a language.* 1995.
127. GUY, Gregory R., John BAUGH, Deborah SCHIFFRIN and Crawford FEAGIN (eds): *Towards a Social Science of Language. Papers in honor of William Labov. Volume 1: Variation and change in language and society.* n.y.p.
128. GUY, Gregory R., John BAUGH, Deborah SCHIFFRIN and Crawford FEAGIN (eds): *Towards a Social Science of Language. Papers in honor of William Labov. Volume 2: Social interaction and discourse structures.* n.y.p.
129. LEVIN, Saul: *Semitic and Indo-European: The Principal Etymologies. With observations on Afro-Asiatic.* n.y.p.
130. EID, Mushira (ed.) *Perspectives on Arabic Linguistics. Vol. VII. Papers from the Seventh Annual Symposium on Arabic Linguistics.* 1995.